MORE HYMNS *and their* WRITERS

by
Jack Strahan

Jack Strahan.

OCTOBER 2002
Published by:
GOSPEL TRACT PUBLICATIONS
7 Beech Avenue, Glasgow G41 5BY, Scotland

ISBN 0 948417 82 X

Copyright © 2002
GOSPEL TRACT PUBLICATIONS

Typeset and Printed by:
GOSPEL TRACT PUBLICATIONS

...I submit this my tribute of love;
And if others should censure, may Jesus approve.
His blessing and favour I humbly implore;
And if these should attend it, I ask for no more.

And if ought should be found that may profit or please,
May the God of all mercy and grace have the praise.

(John Kent)

Foreword
to
"Hymns and their Writers"

At the dawn of Creation, the book of Job declares, "the morning stars sang together and all the sons of God shouted for joy" (Job 38:7), and when the sun is about to set on man's civilization a great multitude in Heaven, as the voice of many waters and as the voice of mighty thunders, bursts with triumphant praise, "Alleluia; for the Lord God omnipotent reigneth" (Revelation 19:6). In between these outstanding events the Word of God is marked by the voice of praise for "Great is the LORD, and greatly to be praised" (Psalm 48:1). The psalmists and other persons of note have had their expressions of adoration recorded in the book of God and these have been the "song book" of the redeemed of numerous generations. Early in the history of the Church individuals began to compose hymns containing fundamental New Testament Truths and some of these find their place in our New Testament, e.g.

> "Great is the mystery of godliness; God was manifest in the flesh, justified in the Spirit, seen of angels, preached unto the Gentiles, believed on in the world, received up into glory" (I Timothy 3:16).

The centuries that have followed have brought forth a constant stream of poetic verse, dealing with various themes, all giving praise, worship and honour to our Glorious Lord.

The present publication is a selection of well-known and many well-loved hymns and their writers and we have no doubt the readers will be intrigued with such interesting information. The articles were first of all contributed by brother Strahan to the magazine, *Assembly Testimony*—they quickly became the most popular in the magazine and we are delighted that our brother agreed to revise and enlarge them—they are now presented in book form and we are sure they will bring much joy and profit to many. I heartily commend the book and urge you to read it.

A. M. SALWAY GOODING
1989

Preface

The earlier volume, "Hymns and their Writers" was warmly received and, since its publication in 1989, there has been request for "More Hymns and their Writers". This book is in response to that request.

Again there are fifty short studies, arranged chronologically. Most hymns are by English writers, but a few have been selected from the great wealth of German hymnody. One has been taken from the Welsh and one from the French. There are a few studies that are entirely new, the product of original research.

Others have previously written on many of these hymns. Throughout, I have sought to acknowledge such sources of help, but if inadvertently this has been overlooked, I trust that my apology in this regard will be accepted.

I tender my sincere thanks to all who have helped, and especially
- those whom I encountered on my research travels who provided invaluable help,
- my beloved brother, Jim Flanigan, for correcting the proofs and
- the staff of Gospel Tract Publications, Glasgow for their co-operation and help in the publication.

In looking back I can trace the hand of God in guiding my path on my many expeditions and guiding my hand in the writing of this book. I now send it forth in His Name and with the sincere prayer that the reader will find pleasure and profit through perusal of its pages. Above all I desire that God will have the glory.

JACK STRAHAN
ENNISKILLEN
MAY 2002

Contents

FOREWORD (Hymns and their Writers) 4
PREFACE 5
"A mighty Fortress is our God" 10
    Martin Luther (1483-1546)
"Thou Life of my life, blessed Jesus" 17
    Ernst Christoph Homburg (1605-1681)
"Praise to the Lord, the Almighty, the King of creation" 22
    Joachim Neander (1650-1680)
"Now I have found the ground wherein" 28
    Johann Andreas Rothe (1688-1758)
"Thou hidden love of God" 34
    Gerhard Tersteegen (1697-1769)
"Lord Jesus, who didst once appear" 41
    John Berridge (1716-1793)
"And did the Holy and the Just?" 47
    Anne Steele (1717-1778)
"Brethren, let us join to bless" 53
    John Cennick (1718-1755)
"Great God of wonders!" 59
    Samuel Davies (1723-1761)
"The God of Abraham praise" 65
    Thomas Olivers (1725-1799)
"Majestic sweetness sits enthroned" 71
    Samuel Stennett (1727-1795)
"Behold the Lamb of God" 77
    Thomas Haweis (1734-1820)
"Blest be the tie that binds" 84
    John Fawcett (1739/40-1817)
"'Twas on that night, when doomed to know" 91
    John Morison (1746-1798)

CONTENTS

"O Lord, I would delight in Thee" 97
    John Ryland (1753-1825)

"O blessèd God! how kind" 103
    John Kent (1766-1843)

"Our blest Redeemer, ere He breathed" 109
    Harriet Auber (1773-1862)

"Standing there amidst the myrtle" 114
    Ann Griffiths (1776-1805)

"Faint not, Christian, though the road" 121
    James Harington Evans (1785-1849)

"How sweet, my Saviour, to repose" 127
    Henri Abraham César Malan (1787-1864)

"Eternal Light! Eternal Light!" 133
    Thomas Binney (1798-1874)

"Jesus is our Shepherd" 138
    Hugh Stowell (1799-1865)

"Nearer, my God, to Thee" 144
    Sarah Flower Adams (1805-1848)

"What raised the wondrous thought?" 150
    George Vicesimus Wigram (1805-1879)

"Holy Saviour! we adore Thee" 156
    Samuel Prideaux Tregelles (1813-1875)

"The wanderer no more will roam" 162
    Mary Jane Walker (1816-1878)

"Jesus loves me! This I know" 168
    Anna Bartlett Warner (1822-1915)

"It is a thing most wonderful" 174
    William Walsham How (1823-1897)

"Low in the grave He lay" 180
    Robert Lowry (1826-1899)

"There is a Name I love to hear" 186
    Frederick Whitfield (1827-1904)

"'Midst the darkness, storm and sorrow" 191
    Emma Frances Bevan (1827-1909)

"My chains are snapt" 197
    Margaret Ledlie Carson (1833-1920)
"Crowned with thorns upon the tree" 204
    Henry Grattan Guinness (1835-1910)
"The gospel of Thy grace" 210
    Arthur Tappan Pierson (1837-1911)
"Praise the Lord, and leave tomorrow" 216
    William Gibson Sloan (1838-1914)
"We praise Thee, O God, for the Son of Thy love" 222
    William Paton Mackay (1839-1885)
"He dies! He dies! The lowly Man of Sorrows" 228
    Charles Russell Hurditch (1839-1908)
"Let us sing of the love of the Lord" 233
    Daniel Webster Whittle (1840-1901)
"Before the throne of God above" 239
    Charitie Lees Smith (1841-1923)
"I'm waiting for Thee, Lord" 246
    Hannah Kilham Burlingham (1842-1901)
"Not now, but in the coming years" 252
    Maxwell Newton Cornelius (1842-1893)
"O Lamb of God, we lift our eyes" 257
    Alexander Stewart (1843-1923)
"We love to sing of the Lord who died" 263
    Thomas Donald William Muir (1855-1931)
"In loving kindness Jesus came" 269
    Charles Hutchinson Gabriel (1856-1932)
"Glory to Thee, Thou Son of God, most High" 275
    Edward Christian Quine (1857-1942)
"I cannot tell why He, whom angels worship" 281
    William Young Fullerton (1857-1932)
"There are loved ones in the glory" 288
    Ada Ruth Habershon (1861-1918)
"He giveth more grace when the burdens grow greater" 294
    Annie Johnson Flint (1866-1932)

"Jesus, Lord, I need Thy presence" 300
    George Goodman (1866-1942)

"There's a Shepherd who died for the sheep" 306
    Hawthorne Bailie (1884-1964)

SELECTED BIBLIOGRAPHY 312
INDEX OF AUTHORS 316
INDEX OF HYMNS 317

"A mighty Fortress is our God"

Martin Luther (1483-1546)

Martin Luther

As the sixteenth century dawned the continent of Europe lay shrouded in spiritual night. Darkness covered the land and gross darkness the people. Men and women were enslaved by superstition and fear which held them in bondage to a system in which human primacy and men's fallacious traditions had displaced and dethroned Almighty God and the truth of His Word. Then out of the darkness there rose a great light, and the human hand that bore that heavenly torch was the hand of Martin Luther.

Martin Luther was born of humble parentage on 10th November 1483 in the little town of Eisleben in Saxony. His parents, Hans and

Gretha Luther, were honest and pious peasants and, as the day following his birth was St. Martin's day, they named their boy Martin. Though Hans and Gretha Luther raised their family amid circumstances of hardship and want, they appreciated the value of education and at great cost to themselves sent the family to school. Martin attended school, first at Mansfield, then at Magdeburg and Eisenach, and at the age of eighteen entered the University of Erfurt. There the whole university admired his genius. He thirsted for knowledge, but deep within his heart there was a greater thirst, a thirst for God. Martin's heart was directed heavenward.

In the library at Erfurt Martin discovered a book, a book different from any other book he had ever seen. He treasured it and read it assiduously. It was a Bible. He longed and prayed that one day he might have a copy of his own. Incidents of illness, accident and thunderstorm brought Martin nigh to death on several occasions. In these experiences a sense of eternity and judgement filled his heart and in one of these crises he vowed to dedicate his life to God. He kept his vow and at the age of twenty-two entered the Augustinian Monastery at Erfurt.

In the monastery Martin adopted the name of Augustine. He had resolved, "if ever a monk got to heaven by monkery, I was determined to get there". He obeyed the monastic rules scrupulously but soon discovered that severe disciplines didn't lead to holiness of life nor ease the pain of a troubled conscience. He fasted, he kept long night vigils till on occasions he collapsed and was taken up for dead. His body wasted to a skeleton. Yet withal, he despaired of salvation and heaven. Just then he met with John von Staupitz, Professor of Theology at the Wittenberg University, and Vicar General of the Augustinian monasteries in Germany. Staupitz showed to Martin the futility of trusting in human endeavour for salvation and explained to him God's way of salvation. He gave the young monk a Bible and encouraged him to read it, and especially to study the Epistle to the Romans. Luther did so and gradually the light of God's truth illumined his darkness. The Saviour's words were a calm repose for his troubled heart, "Thy sins are forgiven thee".

In 1507, Luther was ordained a priest. His old friend, Staupitz, spoke of him to Frederick, the Elector of Saxony, and Luther was invited to become Professor of Divinity at the University of Wittenberg. He was then only twenty-five years of age. In the University he studied the Bible in its original Hebrew and Greek texts and gave daily lectures on its teachings. The common people heard him gladly. His words were simple, yet spoken with authority. His message, though new, was clearly understood. He spoke from his heart. His great themes were of the Saviour's love and the forgiveness of sins.

Three years later Luther was commissioned to visit Rome. Hitherto he had regarded Rome as "the eternal city", "the supreme seat of holiness", "the very gate of heaven" and when he came within sight of the city he fell on his knees, "Holy Rome, I salute thee!" But when he arrived there he was shocked by what he found. Nevertheless he was loyal to Rome and in order to obtain a special indulgence from the Pope, he assayed to climb the steps of Pilate's staircase on his bare knees. Suddenly a "voice" spoke to him the words of Habakkuk the prophet. "The just shall live by his faith". He rose from his knees and shuddered at seeing to what depths superstition had plunged him. D' Aubigné, the historian, states, "It was in those words that God said, 'Let there be light!' and there was light".

Luther returned to Wittenberg with a new resolve to preach only the truths of the Bible and in his preaching was forthright and fearless. He urged his fellow monks to be done with tradition, superstition and philosophy and study only the Word of God. But in all those resolutions he was opposed and persecuted.

In 1517, a German Dominican friar, named Tetzel, was commissioned by the Pope to raise money for the building of St. Peter's Cathedral in Rome. He came to a village near to Wittenberg and there pressed upon the common people to purchase special indulgences from the Pope and thereby not miss their opportunity of securing heaven. Luther knew the falsehood of such indulgences, that they could in no way grant Divine pardon for sin. He opposed their sale and on Saturday, 31st October he nailed to the Castle Church door in Wittenberg his ninety-five simple doctrinal statements opposing the whole doctrine of indulgences. The advent of the printing press made possible their rapid transcript and "Luther's theses flew over Germany as if the angels of God had been his messengers".

Luther was branded a heretic and summoned to Rome but the Elector of Saxony refused to let him go. He was then summoned to Augsburg in Germany to be tried before the Italian Cardinal Cajetan. He attended and there stood firm in his defence, "Whosoever shall confess me before men him will I confess before my Father which is in heaven". He was then thirty-five years of age. The truth of God soon spread rapidly throughout Europe and Luther's publications were read with avidity in cottage, convent and castle.

In 1521 Luther was summoned to appear before the Diet of Worms to be tried in the presence of the Emperor. Though advised not to go, he insisted on appearing, taking for his encouragement the text. "The Lord of hosts is with us, the God of Jacob is our refuge" (Psa. 46:7,11). There at Worms, in the presence of over two hundred dignitaries and prelates, he was asked to retract his doctrine of justification by faith. He refused, but asked for time to reflect. After a night of prayer he presented himself again the following day before the same august assembly. He had resolved that the truth of God's Word must stand. He could not retract. "Here I stand, I can do no other, so help me, God! Amen!"

Luther was commanded to depart and not again disturb the peace with his preaching or writings. On leaving Worms he was secreted away by friends to the ancient Castle of Wartburg and there he commenced his greatest life work, the translation of the Holy Scriptures into the German language. In this great task his close friend, Philip Melanchthon, a man of remarkable talent and profound scholarship, assisted him. The German New Testament was quickly completed, printed and circulated among the people. After ten months Luther returned to Wittenberg and there continued his translation work. The printed New Testaments were condemned by the authorities and many copies were publicly burned. But the progress of truth could not be stayed. Many monks left their cells to proclaim the gospel and many martyrs laid down their lives in the cause of truth.

At the age of forty-two, Luther married Katherina von Bora, an ex-nun, and together they set up home in Wittenberg. Six children were born to their marriage and theirs was a happy home. In the comparative tranquillity of the years that followed Luther completed his translation of the whole Bible. Luther was a master of the German language and his translation was simple but vigorous. With the help of the printing press the Scriptures were soon in the hands of the common people.

Towards the close of life Luther returned to Eisleben where he had been born sixty-three years previously and there he died on 18th February 1546. His body was brought to Wittenberg and buried in the Castle Church. Dukes and nobles followed him to his grave and his dear friend, Philip Melanchthon, preached his funeral service.

Martin Luther was a spiritual giant. "I call this Luther a truly great man", says Thomas Carlyle, the eminent Victorian historian, "he is great in intellect, great in courage, great in affection and integrity; one of our most lovable and gracious men. He is great, not as a hewn obelisk is great, but as an Alpine mountain is great; so simple, honest, spontaneous; not setting himself up to be great, but there for quite another purpose than the purpose of being great!" But what was it that lay at the heart of Martin Luther's greatness? In this world he had no standing; his family was poor and without influence. The secret of Martin Luther's greatness lay in this. He knew God and he took his stand with God.

The Word of God was Martin Luther's one foundation and stay through life. Its light had illumined his own darkness and he shared that same light with his fellow men. He proclaimed fearlessly its great doctrines. He translated its text into the language of the common people. He expounded in his written commentaries the great themes of the Gospels and the Epistles. Luther's writings have indeed been vast and those translated into the English language have been collected into some fifty-five volumes.

But Luther, besides, was a gifted poet. The writing and distrubution of hymns he found to be a most effective way of propagating the reformed faith. "It is my intention to make German psalms for the people: that is spiritual songs, whereby the Word of God may be kept alive among them by singing". And in his lifetime "there burst forth in the lands of the Reformation a great burst of hymns, with the clear notes of the gospel, in the common tongue". In 1524 he saw *The German Hymn Book* published and placed into the hands of the people. Indeed, his enemies said of him, "he had done more harm by his songs than by his sermons".

Luther personally wrote at least thirty-seven hymns; some of these were translations from the Latin but most were his own compositions. His hymn, **"Ein' feste Burg ist unser Gott"** is the best known of all his verse. The occasion of its writing is not known with certainty but it was sung extensively during his lifetime and its first line is to be found inscribed upon his tombstone in Wittenberg. There have been over sixty translations of this hymn into English; the rendering here given is that by Dr. Frederick H. Hedge of America.

A mighty fortress is our God,
A bulwark never failing;
Our helper He, amid the flood
Of mortal ills prevailing;

*For still our ancient foe
Doth seek to work us woe;
His craft and power are great,
And, armed with cruel hate,
On earth is not his equal.*

*Did we in our strength confide,
Our striving would be losing;
Were not the right Man on our side,
The Man of God's own choosing;
Dost ask who that may be?
Christ Jesus, it is He,
Lord Sabaoth, His name,
From age to age the same,
And He must win the battle.*

*And though this world, with devils filled
Should threaten to undo us,
We will not fear, for God hath willed
His truth to triumph through us;
The Prince of Darkness grim—
We tremble not for him;
His rage we can endure,
For lo, his doom is sure,
One little word shall fell him.*

*That word above all earthly powers,
No thanks to them, abideth;
The Spirit and the gifts are ours
Thro' Him who with us sideth:
Let goods and kindred go,
This mortal life also;
The body they may kill:
God's truth abideth still,
His kingdom is for ever.*

Luther based his hymn on Psalm 46,

"God is our refuge and strength, a very present help in trouble". There, in the psalm, amid earth's ever-changing scene, God stands unchanged. And amid all the upheaval, devastation and noise of change, we hear Him say, **Be still and know that I am God"**.

"The LORD of hosts (the God of the multitude) **is with us; the God of Jacob** (the God of the individual) **is our refuge. Selah."** On such immutable and unshakable pledges Martin Luther placed his implicit trust. They became the bulwark and epitome of his life, the great theme of his immortal hymn.

"Thou Life of my life, blessed Jesus"

Ernst Christoph Homburg (1605-1681)

Ernst Christoph Homburg

Ernst Christoph Homburg was recognized in his generation as "a poet of first rank". In his early life he was a sensuous poet, given over to the writing of lewd permissive love-songs and robust drinking-songs. Then, following God's intervention in his life through suffering, his autumn years were spent in the composition of spiritual songs of exceptional depth and beauty.

Ernst Christoph Homburg belonged to the seventeenth century. He was born in 1605 in the German village of Mihla near to Eisenach. Of his early life not much has been left on record, but we know that in his youth he had unusual talent and gave early promise in the field of literature, manifesting a propensity for writing verse.

Homburg studied and practised law. His profession took him to Dresden, to Jena and then finally to Naumburg in Saxony, where he spent the greater part of his life. In that town he was highly esteemed in his profession as Clerk of the Assizes and as Legal-adviser. But, despite his high professional standing, he freely associated with companions of loose and base habits. Among them he was renowned for both his poetical talent and his licentious ways. The composition of lustful songs was his chief delight.

Homburg wrote his early worldly songs under the title, "Clio" and these appeared in two collections, in 1638 and 1642. In the year 1648 he received the high honour of being admitted as a member of the "Fruchtbringende Gesellschaft" ("The Fruitbearing Society") and there, in ironical allusion to his erotic songs, they called him "The Chaste". His "Tragico-cornoedia of the amorous shepherdess" was published in 1645 and his "When a turtle-dove sits sadly in the meadow" in 1658. He won high distinction in literature and became a member of the Elbe Swan Order.

Then a mighty transformation took place. Homburg was drawn out of the stream of worldly pleasure. He fell ill, severely plagued day and night with a painful skin complaint. His wife, Justine, at the same time suffered from a painful "stone" condition and together they had scarcely a pain-free hour. God spoke very clearly to Homburg's heart and in his agony he sought the Lord. He turned his back on his old ways and his old rhymes. Like the prodigal, with a heart bowed low in repentance, he came to the Lord and found in Him a welcoming loving Father. His whole life was changed.

Homburg knew that his former friends would not understand him It was no surprise when they mockingly asked in derision, "Is Saul also among the prophets?" (1 Sam. 10:11). He anticipated and accepted reproach for the reason that he had offered the best of his years to the world and gave God but the residue. But what were the reproaches of men! Homburg had found the Lord.

Homburg lived a life of practical godliness. He found in the Word of God daily strength to uphold him in times of persecution and adversity. He judged "the Christian without a cross and adversity to be nothing other than a pupil without books or a bride without flowers". He regarded the pathway of suffering as a blessed path and found his heavenly Father was a great comforter and sustainer in times of distress. Besides, he found God to be a great teacher, disclosing His greatest secrets to those in sorrow.

Homburg continued to exercise his poetical talent. But now, the theme of his song was changed. His compositions were now in praise of his Saviour and Lord. Some one hundred and fifty of his beautiful hymns and poems from this period in his life have survived. These were published in collected form in 1659, in two parts, Part 1, *Geistlicher Lieder, Erster Theil*, with one hundred hymns and Part 2, *Ander Theil*, with fifty hymns. In the preface Homburg speaks of how they came to be written, "I was specially induced and compelled by the anxious and sore domestic afflictions by which God...has for some time laid me aside".

Two of Homburg's hymns have been set to music by Johann Sebastian Bach, his "Der Herr ist mein getreuer Hirt," ("The Lord is my faithful Shepherd"), and his triumphant Easter hymn, "Jesus, unser Trost und Leben" ("Jesus, our Comfort and Life"), written towards the close of life. But, of all his compositions, the best known and the most popular is his **"Jesu meines Lebens Leben"**. It is entitled "Passiontide" and originally was headed "A Hymn of Thanksgiving to his Redeemer and Saviour for His bitter Sufferings".

This hymn first appeared just after the mighty transformation in Homburg's life. In its German original there were eight stanzas of eight lines each. Two of our well-known and particularly beautiful English hymns have been taken from Homburg's original, namely **"Jesus! Source of life eternal"**, a translation by Hannah K. Burlingham,

> *Jesus! Source of life eternal,*
> *Jesus! Author of our breath,*
> *Victor o'er the hosts infernal*
> *By defeat, and shame and death.*
> *Thou through deepest tribulation*
> *Deigned to pass for our salvation:*
> *Thousand, thousand praises be,*
> *Lord of Glory, unto Thee.*
>
> *Thou, O Son of God, wast bearing*
> *Cruel mockings, hatred, scorn;*
> *Thou, the King of Glory, wearing,*
> *For our sake, the crown of thorn:*
> *Dying, Thou didst us deliver*
> *From the chains of sin for ever;*
> *Thousand, thousand praises be,*
> *Precious Saviour, unto Thee.*

All the shame men heaped upon Thee
Thou didst patiently endure;
Not the pains of death too bitter,
Our redemption to procure.
Wondrous Thy humiliation
To accomplish our salvation:
Thousand, thousand praises be,
Precious Saviour, unto Thee.

Heartfelt praise and adoration,
Saviour, thus to Thee we give;
For Thy life humiliation,
For Thy death, whereby we live.
All the grief Thou wast enduring,
All the bliss Thou wast securing:
Evermore the theme shall be
Of thanksgivings, Lord to Thee.

Hannah K. Burlingham (1842 -1901)

and **"Thou Life of my life, blessed Jesus"**, a translation by Emma Frances Bevan.

Thou Life of my life, blessed Jesus,
Thy death was the death that was mine, *
For me was Thy Cross and Thine anguish,
Thy love and Thy sorrow divine;
Thou hast suffered the Cross and the anguish,
That I might forever go free.
A thousand, a thousand thanksgivings,
*I bring, my Lord Jesus, to Thee!***

* In some publications this second line is rendered, *Thou death was the death that was mine.*

**In some publications this last line is rendered, *I bring, blessèd Saviour, to Thee.*

For me Thou hast borne the reproaches,
The mockery, hate and disdain,
The blows and the spittings of sinners,
The scourgings, the shame and the pain,
To save me from bondage and judgement,
Thou gladly hast suffered for me.
A thousand, a thousand thanksgivings,
I bring, my Lord Jesus, to Thee!

O Lord, from my heart I do thank Thee,
For all Thou hast borne in my room,
Thine agony, dying, unsolaced,
Alone in the darkness and gloom,
That I, in the glory of heaven,
Forever and ever might be.
A thousand, a thousand thanksgivings,
I bring, my Lord Jesus, to Thee!

Emma Frances Bevan (1827-1909)

Miss Burlingham's rendering is in the plural and was designed for congregational singing. Mrs. Bevan's is in the singular and is very personal. Both express the deep gratitude of a forgiven and overflowing heart.

When the woman "which was a sinner" entered into the house of Simon the Pharisee she was not welcomed there by the host. Nevertheless, she knew that her Lord was there. She had been forgiven much and in return, she "loved much". She brought with her a box of ointment. Her heart was full. She made her way to His feet and there, midst tears and kisses, she poured forth her alabaster box and her overflowing heart (Luke 7:36-50).

And the Lord still appreciates the appreciation of a forgiven and overflowing heart!

O Lord, from my heart I do thank Thee,
For all Thou hast borne in my room,
Thine agony, dying, unsolaced,
Alone in the darkness and gloom,
That I, in the glory of heaven,
Forever and ever might be.
A thousand, a thousand thanksgivings,
I bring, my Lord Jesus to Thee!

"Praise to the Lord, the Almighty, the King of creation"

Joachim Neander (1650-1680)

Joachim Neander

The tranquillity of a beautiful little glen in West Germany provided the inspiration for this great song of praise. The glen or gorge is where limestone cliffs on each side hem in the valley and in its depths the little river Düssel makes its way to join the Rhine. This glen was originally known as "Hundsklipp" ("Dog's Cliff") or "das Gestein" ("The Rocks") but is now called Neanderthal (Neander valley). There, over three hundred years ago, Joachim Neander, then a young man in his twenties, often made recourse. There, it is reputed, he lived for a time in one of its limestone caves and it was there, from a heart in touch with God and in harmony with the beautiful creation around him, that he wrote some of his richest verse of praise to God, both words and music.

Neander had been born in Bremen in 1650, the eldest child of Johann Joachim Neander and Catharina Knipping. His father was a school teacher in Bremen, his maternal grandfather was a musician. His family name, Neander, had originally been that of Neumann ("New Man" or "Newman") but, as was popular at the time, his grandfather changed it to its Greek equivalent, Neander.

Neander, as a youth, went to his father's school and then proceeded to the Academic Gymnasium in Bremen to study theology. German student life at that time was anything but refined and Neander, like his fellows, entered its social round and questionable pleasures without reserve.

In the year 1670 Theodore Undereyk came to Bremen as pastor to St. Martin's Church. Undereyk was regarded in his time as a Pietist and a holder of conventicles. He was a preacher of repentance and most people scoffed at his preaching. One Sunday, Neander with two of his friends went to hear him. Their objective was to make a jest of his preaching but "the fools who came to scoff remained to pray". The preaching touched Neander's heart and he couldn't hold back the tears. On his way home he said to his friend, "I must go to that man and hear him speak further about the condition of my heart". Afterwards he sought out Undereyk in private and with a broken heart and in true repentance he sought and found the Saviour. This experience was the turning point in Neander's life and thereafter he desired only "to follow Jesus Christ with zeal and to study the book of the Scriptures".

In 1671 Neander became tutor to a group of well-to-do young men, sons of merchants from Frankfurt, and accompanied them to the University of Heidelberg. Some two years later he returned with the students to Frankfurt and there he made the acquaintance of two godly Christian leaders, Philipp Jakob Spener and his lawyer companion, Johann Jakob Schütz. Neander frequently attended Spener's Bible class and a warm friendship sprang up between them, which lasted throughout life.

At the early age of twenty-four Neander was appointed principal of the Reformed Grammar School at Düsseldorf. The school at that time was an institution of only two classes, controlled by the "Reformed" or Calvinistic branch of the Lutheran Church. His paltry stipend was seventy-eight thalers per annum, and he lived near the breadline. Nevertheless, he was happy. He preached frequently in the Reformed Church and under his control the school flourished. However, when he started to conduct private religious meetings the Church authorities became apprehensive. His links with Spener were regarded with suspicion and judged as a concerted rebellion against Church authority. The outcome of the conflict was that Neander was accused of heresy, deposed from his mastership and forbidden to preach.

Thus treated by his persecutors and feeling dejected and friendless, Neander resorted to the beautiful valley of the Düssel and there lived for some time in a cave. In that quiet retreat he found consolation in communion with God and in meeting with other like-minded believers for times of fellowship. It was there, amid the solitude of the rocks, caves, grottos and waterfalls, and during his period of enforced absence from the school, that Neander composed some of his choicest verse. His heart was not occupied in recrimination for the injustices he had received at the hands of men but in extolling the greatness and goodness of God. And as to whether or not he was ever reinstated to his post as teacher is difficult to ascertain with certainty.

In the year 1679 Neander was invited to become Undereyk's assistant at St. Martin's Church in Bremen, the very church that he had once entered in mockery. There he was granted a free house and a meagre salary of forty thalers a year. His ministry was severely restricted, indeed, his only preaching assignment was a 5.00 a.m. Sunday service which no one, bar a few market women, could possibly attend. The early hours on cold winter days in an unheated church had a telling effect on his health, and after a few months Neander fell ill. His condition, thought to have been due to the plague, gradually deteriorated and he died on Whit Monday, 31st May 1680. Ere he passed away he testified to a friend, "I would rather face death than live lost in unbelief". Thus there came to a close, at scarcely thirty years of age, one of the noblest lives of the seventeenth century.

Today, not even a grave remains to mark his resting-place. Nevertheless Neander lives on. Around the city of Düsseldorf his name was so greatly beloved and highly honoured that as a tribute to his memory the beautiful glen where he once lived and walked with God was renamed Neanderthal (Neander Valley). Besides, his hymns live on, for his are compositions that will never die.

The hymns of Joachim Neander are monumental. They marked a new beginning, a new development in song within the German Reformed Church where very few hymns were sung. His compositions, when written, were first circulated in manuscript form among friends at Düsseldorf and then in the year of his death (1680), the first collection of fifty-eight of his hymns appeared as *Alpha und Omega. Joachimi Neandri Glaub- und Liebesübung*. Some nineteen of these hymns were set to his own choral tunes. Further editions of his compositions followed and some seventy-two of his hymns remain today.

Joachim Neander's hymns are of the highest quality. Catherine Winkworth says of them, "Neander's style is unequal; occasional harshnesses contrast with very musical lines, but there is a glow, a sweetness, and a depth about his hymns which have made many of them justly and lastingly popular among the German people". Millar Patrick has judged them "of superlative quality, lyrical in a high degree, scriptural and evangelical". And James Mearns in Julian's Dictionary of Hymnology has added this, "The glow and sweetness of his better hymns, their firm faith, originality, Scripturalness, variety and mastery of rhythmical forms, and genuine lyric character fully entitle them to the high place that they hold".

Many translators have rendered Neander's hymns into English but perhaps one of the finest translators has been Catherine Winkworth (1829-1878). "The Winkworths were representative of a scholarly and consciously literary and musical world of middle-class piety" states Tyler Whittle. Catherine was one of four sisters. In her translation of Neander's verse from the German she was greatly encouraged by Christian Bunsen, the Prussian ambassador to the court of St. James. Her translations were published in two collections, *Lyra Germanica* in 1855 and a *Second Series* in 1858. Bunsen then persuaded Catherine to introduce German tunes to accompany the hymns and this resulted in *The Chorale Book for England* in 1863.

Of all Neander's compositions the best known and perhaps the finest is his **"Lobe den Herren den mächtigen König der Ehren"**. It is a great hymn of praise and Catherine Winkworth's translation of it into the English, **"Praise to the Lord, the Almighty, the King of creation"** is a worthy work.

> *Praise to the Lord, the Almighty, the King of creation!*
> *O my soul, praise Him, for He is thy health and salvation!*
> *All ye who hear, now to His temple draw near;*
> *Praise Him in glad adoration.*

Praise to the Lord, Who over all things so wondrously reigneth,
Shelters thee under His wings, yea, so gently sustaineth!
Hast thou not seen how thy desires ever have been
Granted in what He ordaineth?

Praise to the Lord, Who hath, fearfully, wondrously, made thee;
Health hath vouchsafed and, when heedlessly falling, hath stayed thee.
What need or grief ever hath failed of relief?
Wings of His mercy did shade thee.

Praise to the Lord, Who doth prosper thy work and defend thee;
Surely His goodness and mercy here daily attend thee.
Ponder anew what the Almighty can do,
If with His love He befriend thee.

Praise to the Lord, Who, when tempests their warfare are waging,
Who, when the elements madly around thee are raging,
Biddeth them cease, turneth their fury to peace,
Whirlwinds and waters assuaging.

Praise to the Lord, Who, when darkness of sin is abounding,
Who, when the godless do triumph, all virtue confounding.
Sheddeth His light, chaseth the horrors of night,
Saints with His mercy surrounding.

Praise to the Lord! O let all that is in me adore Him!
All that hath life and breath, come now with praises before Him!
Let the Amen sound from His people again,
Gladly for aye we adore Him.

(Verses 5&6 are probably by Percy Dearmer)

This is a magnificent hymn of praise to God. It is based on Psalm 103 and Psalm 150. Neander wrote both its text and its melody. The melody title, "Lobe den Heren", is taken from the first words of his German text.

This hymn is like to the psalms of David. It is a hymn devoted entirely to praise of the Lord. Like the psalmist, Neander's appreciation of the Lord was great and this may be traced in the verses of his hymn where the Lord is praised, as Creator, as Sovereign, as Defender, as a

Refuge and as Protector.

When its sweet strains first arose to God from the glen in the Düssel valley outside Düsseldorf, the valley itself was somehow hallowed by its music. Notwithstanding, in the years that have followed the valley has been desecrated. Mercenary men robbed it of its original beauty and tranquillity when for over a century its limestone walls were blasted and chipped away in pursuit of the cement industry, leaving in its wake a barren wilderness. Thankfully these pursuits have now ceased and the valley has been restored in part by the creation of natural wildlife reserves.

Then again, in the summer of 1856, puny men, in their vain pursuit to disprove God, heralded the find of a human skeleton in the Neander Valley ("Neanderthal man"), as one of the missing links in the evolutionary chain of modern man. God mercifully brought to naught their folly. The unusual skeleton that they applauded as one of man's ancestors, and some forty thousand years old, proved to be nothing other than that of a modern man whose skeleton had been deformed by severe arthritis.

Though men's attempts to disprove God and deface His creation have come to naught, God remains.

And the sweet strains of Joachim Neander's hymn still go up to God.

Praise to the Lord, O let all that is in me adore Him!
All that hath life and breath, come now with praises before Him!
Let the Amen sound from His people again,
Gladly for aye we adore Him.

"Let the people praise Thee, O God: let all the people praise Thee"(Psalm 67: 3).

"Let the people praise Thee, O God: let all the people praise Thee" (Psalm 67: 5).

"Now I have found the ground wherein"

Johann Andreas Rothe (1688-1758)

Johann Andreas Rothe

John Wesley thought John W. Fletcher, vicar of Madeley in Shropshire, the holiest man then living. "I have known him intimately for thirty years", says Mr. Wesley, "In my eighty years I have met many eloquent men, but I have never met his equal, nor do I expect to find such another on this side of eternity". "Never, since the birth of Christianity, was the life of Jesus more faithfully reproduced than in the pilgrimage of Fletcher". "His transparent sincerity, his essential humanness and his unflagging zeal for the good of others won all hearts". Many flocked to Madeley to hear him, many came just to see him. "We go to look at him", they said, "for heaven seems to beam from his countenance". "His thin wan countenance shone as with the light of heaven".

John Wesley had nominated Fletcher to succeed him as leader of the Methodist movement. But Fletcher died before Wesley, at the early age of fifty-six. He was stricken by "a putrid fever" which swept through Madeley and in his last illness experienced the tender ministrations, temporal and spiritual, of his devoted wife. Many of his parishioners filed past his bedroom door that they might catch but a glimpse of his face. But Fletcher, all the time, was otherwise occupied. He was engaged with another world. His heart was filled with ecstasy at the vastness and splendour of the love of God. Just before the close Mrs. Fletcher repeated to him some lines,

> *While Jesu's blood, through earth and skies,*
> *Mercy, free, boundless mercy, cries!*

These lines enraptured Fletcher's heart and, in his closing moments and with all the energy he could muster, he cried,

> "*Boundless! Boundless! Boundless!*"

And added,

> *Mercy's full power I soon shall prove,*
> *Loved with an everlasting love.*

Thus John W. Fletcher passed away to be with Christ.

The lines that so thrilled and sustained the heart of this notable saint of God in his greatest and most solemn hour, were taken from John Wesley's translation of Johann Andreas Rothe's eminent German hymn, **"Ich habe nun den Grund gefunden"**.

> *Now I have found the ground wherein*
>   *Sure my soul's anchor may remain –*
> *The wounds of Jesus, for my sin*
>   *Before the world's foundation slain;*
> *Whose mercy shall unshaken stay,*
> *When heaven and earth are fled away.*

Father, Thine everlasting grace
  Our scanty thought surpasses far,
Thy heart still melts with tenderness,
  Thy arms of love still open are
Returning sinners to receive,
That mercy they may taste, and live.

O Love, Thou bottomless abyss,
  My sins are swallow'd up in Thee!
Covered is my unrighteousness,
  Nor spot of guilt remains on me,
While Jesu's blood through earth and skies,
Mercy, free, boundless mercy cries!

With faith I plunge me in this sea,
  Here is my hope, my joy, my rest;
Hither, when hell assails, I flee,
  I look into my Saviour's breast:
Away, sad doubt and anxious fear!
Mercy is all that's written there.

Though waves and storms go o'er my head,
  Though strength, and health, and friends be gone,
Though joys be wither'd all and dead,
  Though every comfort be withdrawn,
On this my steadfast soul relies—
Father, Thy mercy never dies.

Fix'd on this ground will I remain,
  Though my heart fail and flesh decay;
This anchor shall my soul sustain,
  When earth's foundations melt away;
Mercy's full power I then shall prove,
Loved with an everlasting love.

The original German hymn was written by Johann Andreas Rothe, a Lutheran pastor in Germany in the early eighteenth century. The occasion of its writing was the birthday of Count Nicolaus L. von Zinzendorf on the 26th May and probably in the year 1725. Rothe and Zinzendorf, at that time, were very close friends and it was not uncommon for each of them to compose some verse for the other on such occasions. The composition, in its German original, contained ten stanzas of six lines each.

Johann Andreas Rothe was the son of Aegidius Rothe, pastor of the Lutheran church in Lissa near Görlitz in Silesia. Johann was born at Lissa on 12th May 1688.

After studying theology at the University of Leipzig he was licensed at Görlitz as a general preacher at the age of twenty-four. In 1718 he became tutor to the family of Herr von Schweinitz at Leube and while there he frequently preached in neighbouring churches. Count Zinzendorf heard him preach at Gross-Hennersdorf and was greatly impressed, and when the pastorate of Berthelsdorf fell vacant in 1722, Rothe was invited by Zinzendorf to fill the post. In the letter of invitation (19th May 1722), the Count said, "You will find in me a faithful helper and an affectionate brother, rather than a patron". And so it proved to be. They became affectionate brothers and Rothe cooperated with the Count in various enterprises. He began his duties at Berthelsdorf on 30th August 1722 and when a Moravian community was established at Herrnhut soon afterwards, he undertook a pastor's work there. Rothe took a deep interest in the Moravian community at Herrnhut. And on one occasion, Sunday 6th August 1738, when John Wesley paid a visit to Berthelsdorf and Herrnhut, he heard Rothe preach. Wesley was greatly impressed by the preaching and especially by the singing.

Rothe and Zinzendorf, however, did not always see eye to eye and eventually an estrangement crept in, when Rothe was glad to accept a call to the Lutheran church at Hermsdorf near Görlitz. Nevertheless, Zinzendorf always held Rothe in high regard, speaking of him in very generous terms, "Rothe was profoundly learned, and possessed in a high degree the talent of teaching; he so clearly comprehended everything which he discussed, that he preached without the slightest hesitation, and in the most systematic manner...he was never dry, nor did he ever appear long and tedious. ...The lowliest peasant understood him, and the greatest philosopher heard him with attention and respect. He was admired even by his enemies, and the brethren acknowledged, that of all the apostolic discourses which were ever delivered among them at that time, none were to be compared for solidity of thought, spiritual unction, or wise admonition with those of Rothe".

In 1739 Count von Promnitz appointed Rothe as assistant pastor at Thommendorf, near Bunzlau. He became chief pastor in 1742 and there he ministered, fearlessly and faithfully, up until his death on 6th July 1758.

Rothe wrote some forty to fifty hymns, all "characterized by glow and tenderness of feeling and depth of Christian experience". Many of his compositions were published in Zinzendorf's hymnbooks. "Ich habe nun den Grund gefunden" first appeared in print in Zinzendorf's hymnbook of 1727. It is a powerful and beautiful hymn and is still found in many German collections. It has received many translations into English, but probably none more beautiful than that by John Wesley. "Now I have found the ground wherein".

This hymn was one of thirty-three German hymns translated by John Wesley in the early years of his life. These translations of Wesley from the German have made a rich contribution to both Methodist and English hymnology. Garrett Horder says that, "Wesley's translations have indeed never been surpassed" and contends that in the great Methodist movement of the eighteenth century, John's translations were as important as Charles' poems. And Robert Southey, the Poet Laureate, adds, "Perhaps no poems have been so devoutly committed to memory as these, nor quoted so often upon a deathbed".

John Wesley first heard these German hymns when on board ship to Georgia in North America. On that outward voyage a group of twenty-six Moravian missionaries sang them to sweet German melodies. They sang them daily and in all weathers, but never more lustily than in the face of a storm. And it pleased God to use the singing of those German hymns to convict Wesley's own heart. On that outward journey John Wesley started to learn the German language, using as his textbook the Moravian hymnal, "Herrnhuter Gesang-Buch". He then set himself to translate some of the German hymns into English.

John Wesley's first translation of Rothe's great hymn, "Ich habe nun den Grund gefunden", appeared in 1740, in his *Hymns and Sacred Poems*. Initially it was something of a very free translation. But John Wesley was no mean scholar and thoroughly revised his work and many scholars now admit that Wesley's translation, "Now I have found the ground wherein" surpasses that of the German original. Of the ten stanzas in the German original, Wesley translated six; stanzas Nos. 3, 7, 8 and 9 have been omitted.

This hymn has had a wide influence and has been a great stay to many hearts in life's direst experiences. G. J. Stevenson says of it, "Perhaps there is not in the whole collection (i.e. of Wesley's translations) a hymn that is so full of Scripture truth in Scripture phraseology". Indeed, someone has traced in its lines no fewer than thirty-six texts of Scripture. And truly it has been a companion and comfort to many in the vicissitudes of life.

This is a hymn of assurance for the trembling soul. The truths therein are a firm foundation when all else is tottering, an "anchor of the soul, both sure and steadfast" when all else is drifting.

> *Fix'd on this ground will I remain,*
> *Though my heart fail, and flesh decay:*
> *This anchor shall my soul sustain,*
> *When earth's foundations melt away;*
> *Mercy's full power I then shall prove,*
> *Loved with an everlasting love.*

"Thou hidden love of God"

Gerhard Tersteegen (1697-1769)

Gerhard Tersteegen

Gerhard Tersteegen ranks as one of Germany's foremost hymnists. On the threshold of life he set out on a search after God and pursued that quest with all his heart until he found Him. Thereafter he lived on earth a life of frugal simplicity while in spirit he lived in the luxury of a deep communion with God. Throughout life his spirit sang and the overflow of that full heart (in verse) has greatly enriched the centuries that have followed.

Gerhard was born on the 25th November 1697 at Mörs, near to Düsseldorf in Germany. He was the youngest in the family of eight children of Heinrich and Cornelia Tersteegen. His father was a devout tradesman of Mörs but died when Gerhard was only six; thereafter the guidance of his youth rested with his mother. The family had early hopes that one day Gerhard would become a minister in the Reformed Church in Germany, but such aspirations had to be set aside because of poor circumstances. Instead, Gerhard was sent to the Latin School at Mörs and there he excelled in his studies. He had mental ability far beyond others and was very proficient in Latin besides obtaining a good grasp of Greek, Hebrew and French. Indeed, he once so brilliantly delivered an oration in Latin at a public celebration that he was hailed with universal applause and one of the chief magistrates there present urged upon his mother to allow her son to devote himself to learning. But there were no means.

When school days finished, Gerhard, at the age of fifteen, went to Mülheim-on-the-Ruhr as an apprentice to his brother-in-law who was a trader in the town and there he spent four years. However, all the while Gerhard was searching for something higher. He was searching for God. Just about that time a spiritual awakening had come to Mülheim and many people experienced conversion. Gerhard came under its influence and for some time sought deliverance from sin and peace with God. He tried prayer, he tried Bible study, he attended the conventicles, but all was in vain. Then William Hoffmann, the leader of the spiritual movement at that time, took a special interest in him and sought to direct his burdened soul to the Saviour. At length Gerhard came to appreciate the blessedness of "peace with God through the Lord Jesus Christ" and through faith entered into that peace.

Gerhard thereupon, terminated his apprenticeship with his brother-in-law and spent the next two years in his own trading business. He desired time for Bible study and meditation, but found that business conditions were not conducive to this. He then learned the weaving trade, moved to a simple cottage outside Mülheim, and there engaged in weaving silk ribbons. He found he could now follow a prayerful life, hold communion with God and devote time to study. His only human companion in those days was a little girl who came each day to wind his silk.

In the cottage Gerhard worked long hours. He cooked his own meals; these were very frugal, generally milk and water and meal. His earnings were scanty, yet whatever he acquired he shared with the poor, the sick and the needy. He was looked down upon by his own family but was extremely happy in his solitude and with his lot.

Then followed a period of deep spiritual darkness, and this lasted for five years. God subjected his child to a severe testing. Gerhard's extreme seclusion, his austere manner of life and his intense study of Behmen's works all had a depressing effect, as he confessed, "I read till I was filled with strange fears and bewilderment". Within there was a battle; he wrestled with deep problems — the prosperity of the wicked, divisions among Christians, the apostasy of some who once professed faith in Christ. Indeed there were times when he staggered on the brink of unbelief as to the very existence of God and no one could help him. In his extremity he cried alone to God.

Then one spring morning in 1724, as he journeyed to the city of Duisburg, he stopped by the roadside. He was so utterly cast down that he cast himself once more upon God's grace and there came to him "such an internal manifestation of the goodness of God and the sufficiency of the Saviour that all his doubts and troubles vanished in a moment". He returned from his journey, retired to the quiet of his room and in his own blood wrote a "love letter" to his "Best Beloved". This "love letter" was, in effect, a life pledge, henceforward to live only for his Lord and his Redeemer. For Gerhard, this marked a new beginning.

Gerhard settled again into his cottage routine, but this time with a difference. He knew not only fellowship again with God but enjoyed besides the companionship of a devout Christian lad of kindred spirit, Heinrich Sommer. Gerhard taught Heinrich the art of ribbon making and together they shared life in the cottage. Their day started with a hymn, then a light breakfast and a time of prayer. Five hours were spent at the loom, followed by one hour of private prayer. Then together they shared a frugal mid-day meal. Then followed five more hours at the loom and a further hour of private prayer. The evenings were reserved for literary work and visitation. Thus three years went by.

In the year 1727, Mülheim was again visited by a spiritual awakening. Gerhard was urged upon to take part in the services. His spiritual insight and discernment were such that the Lord used him greatly, both in the conversion of unbelievers and in the restoration of believers. Besides the work at Mülheim, there came calls for spiritual help from wider fields and in the following year Gerhard relinquished his secular employment to give all his time to the work of God.

Gerhard's days of solitude were past. Demands made upon him were heavy. Oftimes there would be as many as twenty to thirty troubled souls waiting to see him. He spake with them individually and collectively, the rooms of his simple home accommodating up to four hundred people. Some travelled from as far as England, Holland, Sweden and Switzerland to see him. In dealing with their spiritual needs he was strict, very thorough and penetrating. He always regarded soul work as the realm of the Spirit of God and conversion to be based only upon the Atonement and to be the starting point of a holy life. He was a wise guide to souls.

Besides caring for souls, Gerhard was not negligent of people's physical needs. He personally compounded simple medicines and used his home as a small dispensary. For these ministrations he never accepted any payment, but supported himself from sale of his books and gifts from kind friends.

Thus Gerhard spent thirty years, from the age of thirty to the age of sixty, and through those years he was no stranger to opposition and persecution. But all the enmity, bitterness, defamation, slander, scorning and blasphemy Gerhard bore with meekness, yet when it came to God's honour and God's truth he never swerved a hair's breadth. State laws had been designed and passed against conventicles; all irregular meetings were prohibited. When Gerhard spoke to an assembled company of enquirers in his cottage the official clergymen reported him to the magistrates. But generally they took no action. Indeed, the chief magistrate, on attending his sermon one Christmas day, said to Gerhard at the close, "Not a single word has escaped me, I shall attend you tomorrow". And, addressing the others, the magistrate added, "Those who now revile must only do as I do, and come and hear".

By the year 1756 Gerhard's health started to fail and his activities had to be curtailed. Distant travel was suspended and he spoke only to small gatherings. However, he continued to visit his close friends and together they would retire to the woods for times of communion. But right to the close his pen remained active and his intercession for souls continued unabated. Oftimes he would spend whole nights in intercession and with many tears. But he was happy, ever encouraging his fellows in the faith, "the sweet eternity is our home and Jesus our companion on the road".

The close came in the spring of 1769. He became a victim to dropsy, much pain and shortness of breath. These afflictions increased up until the early hours of 3rd April, when he passed from "the forecourt of eternity" into the presence of the King, and his chronicler adds, "Those standing around thought there were many angels about them who took his soul away with joy".

But the sweet fragrance of Gerhard Tersteegen's life remains, that unique life of close communion with God and total commitment to the will and the work of God. And there remain, besides, all his writings and these are a rich legacy. His collected writings, published in 1846, ran into eight volumes. These included *The Way of Truth*, his translations of the early mystics and his *Lives of the Saints*, which latter work manifested much arduous labour and research. *The Spiritual Lottery* was a volume of some two hundred of his aphorisms translated by Lady Durand. His sermons were published in various editions from 1769 to 1773 and subsequently collectively under the title *Spiritual Crumbs fallen from the Master's Table, gathered by Good Friends and given to Hungry Hearts*". A collection of his tracts was published in 1750.

Notwithstanding, Gerhard Tersteegen is best remembered for his hymns. In all, he wrote some one hundred and eleven. It was not his initial intention that they should be published but in 1729 they were collected together into his outstanding hymnological work, *Geistliches Blumen-Gärtlein (The Spiritual Flower Garden)*, which work ran into many editions. For almost a century the hymns of Tersteegen lay in obscurity. Then in 1833 Chevalier Bunsen retrieved them and gave them to a wider world. He termed their author, "the foremost master of spiritual song". H.E. Govan, in speaking of Tersteegen's compositions, said, "the simplicity and peacefulness of his spirit, serene in the constant presence of God, breathes in his verses".

Tersteegen's hymns have now been received into almost all the German hymnbooks. Many have been translated into the English language, indeed, some have been beautifully rendered. There are translations by John Wesley who first heard them sung by Moravian missionaries when on board ship to Georgia; there are translations by Catherine Winkworth, *Lyra Germanica*; there are translations by Jane Borthwick, *Hymns from the Land of Luther* and there are translations by Emma Frances Bevan, *Hymns of Ter Steegen and Others*.

Two of Tersteegen's hymns, translated by John Wesley, have received acceptance and acclaim beyond all the others, namely, "God is here! Let us adore", termed by Lauxmann "a hymn of deepest adoration of the All Holy God" and **"Thou hidden love of God"**. The latter, in its German original, **"Verborgne Gottesliebe du"**, was written by Tersteegen in his early Christian experience and appeared in his first edition of *Geistliches Blumen-Gärtlein* in 1729. He entitled it, "The longing of the soul quietly to maintain the secret drawings of the love of God". In its original there were ten stanzas of seven lines each.

Wesley's translation is in six line stanzas.

> *Thou hidden love of God, whose height,*
> *Whose depth unfathomed, no man knows,*
> *I see from far Thy beauteous light,*
> *Inly I sigh for Thy repose:*
> *My heart is pained, nor can it be*
> *At rest, till it find rest in Thee.*
>
> *Is there a thing beneath the sun*
> *That strives with Thee my heart to share?*
> *Ah, tear it thence, and reign alone,*
> *The Lord of every motion there!*
> *Then shall my heart from earth be free,*
> *When it has found repose in Thee.*
>
> *O hide this self from me, that I*
> *No more, but Christ in me, may live!*
> *My vile affections crucify,*
> *Nor let one darling lust survive!*
> *In all things nothing may I see,*
> *Nothing desire or seek, but Thee!*
>
> *Each moment draw from earth away*
> *My heart, which lowly waits Thy call;*
> *Speak to my inmost soul, and say,*
> *"I am thy Love, thy God, thy All!"*
> *To know Thy power, to hear Thy voice,*
> *To taste Thy love, be all my choice.*

God has intended the citadel of the human heart to be a solitary throne, not to be shared with another. There is but one rightful ruler there, the Lord Himself. All other interceptors are but usurpers, idols. "Little children, keep yourselves from idols" is the clarion call of one who had enthroned Christ there (1 John 5:21). And Gerhard Tersteegen, of kindred spirit, exhorts us likewise lest any usurper steal that solitary throne.

> *Is there a thing beneath the sun*
> *That strives with Thee my heart to share?*

Ah, tear it thence, and reign alone,
The Lord of every motion there!
Then shall my heart from earth be free,
When it hath found repose in Thee.

"Lord Jesus, who didst once appear"

John Berridge (1716-1793)

John Berridge

    John Berridge, "the Apostle of Cam and Fen", never married, yet he has given to us a beautiful marriage hymn. It was told of him that a lady once visited him in the vicarage at Everton in Bedfordshire. She had travelled all the way from London in her carriage "to solicit his hand in marriage", assuring him that the Lord had revealed to her that she was to become his wife. Somewhat surprised, he replied, "Madam, if the Lord had revealed to you that you are to become my wife, surely He would have revealed to me that I was designed to be your husband; but as no such revelation has been made to me, I cannot comply with your wishes". He remained a bachelor till the close of life and died without natural issue. On the other hand he was greatly used of the Lord and became the father of innumerable spiritual children.

John Berridge was born at Kingston in Nottinghamshire on lst March 1716, the first of four sons of John Berridge and Sarah Hathwaite. John (Sen.) was a wealthy farmer and intended that his son John should stay on the farm. John, however, spent his early years with a favourite aunt who lived in Nottingham City and there he went to school. During those years he had little spiritual contact and no spiritual instruction of any kind, either in the home or at school. Nevertheless he could recall occasions, when returning home from school, that another youth invited him into his home and read to him from the Bible. And on one occasion, as he was returning from a fair, that same friend invited him in again and after Scripture reading, they both prayed together.

At the age of fourteen John returned home to his parents but showed no aptitude for farming. In fact, he behaved so stupidly that his father was constrained to say to him one day, "John, I find you are unable to form any practical idea of the price of cattle and therefore I shall send you to college, to be a light to the Gentiles". However, John continued to struggle on for a few more years at the farming and then, in October 1734, at the age of eighteen, he entered Clare College in Cambridge.

At college John shone brilliantly, but sank spiritually. He studied classics, mathematics, philosophy, logic, and metaphysics, and read the works of the eminent divines. He was most diligent in his application, often studying for fifteen hours in the day. He attained high academic distinction and progressed to graduate M.A. and become a Fellow of Clare College. In College society John was a great favourite, widely famed for his unique wit and quaint charm. But during those years any faith that he ever had in God became almost totally eroded. He turned completely from the Scriptures and for a period of ten years never once bowed his knee in private prayer.

In 1749 John was ordained as curate to the parish of Stapleford, near to Cambridge. There he laboured for six years, but with little success. In 1755 he moved to Everton in Bedfordshire, and with similar outcome. There was something vitally lacking in his ministry. It was, as he said, "a solar system without the sun". And no wonder his congregation remained unblessed!

John finally drew rein and searched his own heart. Driven to his knees, he cried out to God, "Lord, if I am right, keep me so; if I am not right, make me so. Lead me to the knowledge of the truth as it is in

Jesus". Deep soul trouble followed and continued for ten days but God had heard his cry. At length the light of salvation shone into his darkened soul. But let John recount what happened in his own words. "As I was sitting in my house one morning and musing upon a text of Scripture, the following words were darted into my mind with wonderful power, and seemed indeed like a voice from heaven, 'Cease from thine own works, only believe'—The scales fell from my eyes immediately and I now clearly saw the rock I had been splitting on for nearly thirty years". "The rock" had been of his own making, "the mixed covenant of man's own invention", "consisting partly of works and partly of grace". He appreciated that the means of salvation was not Christ's righteousness and his own, rather "Christ will either be a whole Saviour or none at all". Light dawned at last. "Salvation was by faith in Christ alone" and in simple trust John Berridge stepped onto that one sure foundation, the Rock, Christ Jesus. He was then forty years of age.

Salvation wrought a mighty transformation in the life and ministry of John Berridge. From being a preacher of morality, he became a preacher of the glorious gospel. John described the change in his own quaint way, "Once I used Jesus as a healthy man will use a walking-staff—lean an ounce upon it or vapour with it in the air. But now He is my whole crutch; no foot can stir a step without Him". He often reproached himself for having preached error for years. Indeed, he burned all his old sermons, even shedding tears of joy over their conflagration.

Few ministers in the Church of England knew better how to get in touch with the common people than John Berridge. His messages were couched in homely terms which country folk could understand. People flocked from near and far to hear him; the church was crowded. John threw himself wholeheartedly into the work. He preached within the parish church and he preached without. His going outside incurred the wrath of the bishops, yet in homes, barns and in the open air throughout Bedfordshire John made known the everlasting gospel, often preaching up to twelve times in the week. By his turn of phrase he could attract, gather and hold a crowd and though opposition waxed strong, he continued faithfully and God was with him. Once a man, who came to Everton with intent of confusing him, left convinced that he was a lost sinner, and those armed with stones to stone him dropped their ammunition and asked him to pray for them.

During the first twelve months of John's transformed ministry at

Everton, some one thousand people in soul trouble visited him at the vicarage, inquiring the way of salvation. But greater things were still to come. A mighty revival, under John's ministry, commenced in all its fervour on Sunday, 20th May 1759. Audiences of ten to fifteen thousand gathered to hear him. No church could hold the crowds that came, so "he took to the fields". Troubled souls were stricken down in prostration and many cried out to God under conviction of sin. The movement was of the Spirit of God. John was but the human instrument. Naturally speaking he was not eloquent, but God used him. Within his heart there was but one desire, "I wish to be nothing, that Christ may be all".

The revival at Everton opened up the way for John Berridge's itinerant ministry in the years that followed and this form of ministry occupied him for the remainder of his life. He covered in his circuit the counties of Bedford, Cambridge, Essex, Hertford and Huntington and the blessing experienced was incalculable. In his latter years he was almost completely blind and deaf but continued preaching up until a few months before he died.

John passed away on 22nd January 1793, in his seventy-seventh year, in his home at Everton and is buried in Everton churchyard. A somewhat unique epitaph marks his tombstone. John himself wrote it, in his own characteristic manner, (exempting the date of death).

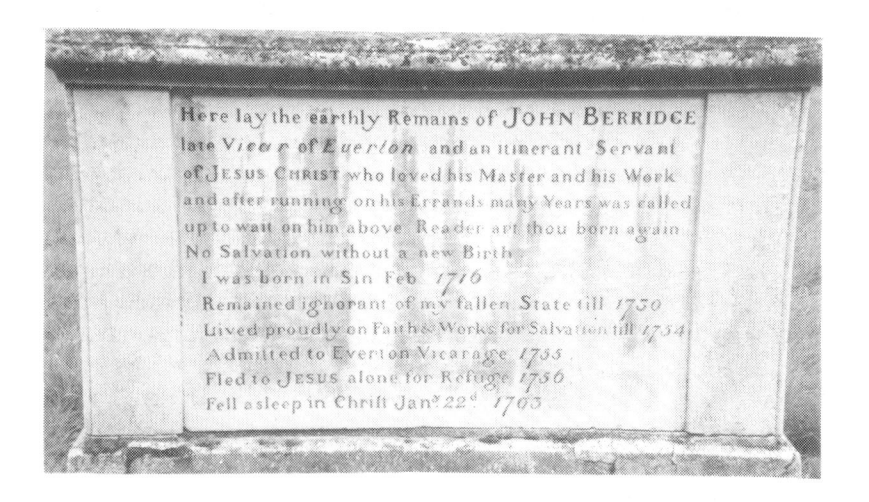

> Here lay the earthly Remains of JOHN BERRIDGE late Vicar of Everton and an itinerant Servant of JESUS CHRIST who loved his Master and his Work and after running on his Errands many Years was called up to wait on him above Reader art thou born again No Salvation without a new Birth
> I was born in Sin Feb 1716
> Remained ignorant of my fallen State till 1730
> Lived proudly on Faith & Works for Salvation till 1754
> Admitted to Everton Vicarage 1755
> Fled to JESUS alone for Refuge 1756
> Fell asleep in Chrift Jan 22ᵈ 1793

John Berridge, like John the forerunner of the Lord Jesus, was "a burning and a shining light". In life he was greatly beloved, and in death greatly lamented. There were few men greater, more holy, or more used of God in the eighteenth century than he, a man of rare gifts and deeply taught in the Scriptures. In his personality he was quaint, indeed, quite eccentric. Bishop Ryle said of him, "the habit of quaintness was bone of his bones and flesh of his flesh. It stuck to him as closely as his skin, and never left him until he was laid in the grave. Quaintly he thought and quaintly he spoke, quaintly he preached and quaintly he wrote, quaint he lived and quaint he died".

John's writings were as quaint as his preaching, but most wholesome. *The Christian World Unmasked* was a volume flavoured with his wit, yet full of proofs of his spiritual wisdom. It was a pithy account in dialogue form of the difference between "common sense religion" and the gospel of Jesus Christ.

John also wrote hymns. His first compilation, *A Collection of Divine Songs (1760)*, contained some hymns of Watts and Wesley (greatly altered) and some originals. This volume he later suppressed, indeed, he used to burn it wherever he met with it. Then in 1785 he published a completely original work of three hundred and forty two hymns and entitled it *Zion's Songs*. Of its origin he said. "Ill health, some years past, having kept me from travelling and preaching, I took up the trade of hymn making, a handicraft much followed of late, but a business I was not born or bred to, and undertaken chiefly to keep a long sickness from preying on my spirits, and to make tedious nights pass over more smoothly. The doctrine of these hymns was sound, but the poetry was extremely poor. Indeed, most were quaint and have not survived.

However, one of John Berridge's compositions remains, his lovely wedding hymn, **"Lord Jesus, who didst once appear"**. It has stood the test of time and is still a great favourite at weddings. It appeared first in "The Gospel Magazine" in August 1775 as, "Since Jesus freely did appear" and consisted of six stanzas of four lines each. It was headed with the text, John 2, 1,2, followed by the title "A Wedding Hymn" and signed "Old Everton". In his publication, *Zion's Songs*, it appeared as, "Our Jesus freely did appear". As the hymn stands today it has been greatly modified from its original and in most of today's hymnals it is given as, "Lord Jesus, who didst once appear".

Lord Jesus, who didst once appear
   To grace a marriage feast,
We now beseech Thy presence here,
   To make this wedding blest.

With grace the bride and bridegroom speed;
   Thy love their pattern be;
May heart with heart be true indeed,
   As knit, O Lord, in Thee.

With gifts of grace their hearts endow,
   Of all rich dowries blest;
Their substance bless, and peace bestow,
   To sweeeten all the rest.

In purest love their souls unite,
   That they with Christ-like care
May make each other's burden light,
   By taking mutual share.

And looking to their heavenly home,
   O may they dwell each day
As heirs of life till Thou shalt come
   To take Thy bride away.

In this hymn, John Berridge points to **the chief things in any Christian marriage,**

In verse 1 — the noblest guest, — the Lord Himself,
In verse 2 — the strongest bond, — the love of Christ,
In verse 3 — the richest dowry, — the gifts of grace,
In verse 4 — the surest recipe for future happiness, — mutual love and care,
In verse 5 — the greatest expectation, — the prospect of eternal life.

How blest are the couples who start married life on such foundations!
Beside them, the wedding attire, venue and fare rank as exceeding small!

"And did the Holy and the Just?"
Anne Steele (1717-1778)

'Grandfathers'
(Birthplace of Anne Steele)

Within the bounds of Hampshire, close to its Wiltshire border, the attractive village of Broughton nestles in the valley of the Wallop Brook about halfway between the cathedral cities of Winchester and Salisbury. This delightful settlement still retains many features from its past, its many timbered and thatched cottages decked with all manner of spring and summer flowers, its well-wooded laneways, its quiet meadow paths, its bridleways and footbridges. Even today a quiet serenity pervades the village. In its centre St. Mary's ancient twelfth century Parish Church keeps vigil; at its north end stands a Baptist Church dated 1655 and from its south end winds its secluded Rookery

Lane. This quiet picturesque laneway leads past the rear entrance to a stately home named 'Broughton House', then past two beautiful thatched cottages till a third is reached with the name 'Grandfathers' inscribed on its entrance gateway. 'Grandfathers' was the birthplace of Anne Steele.

The Steeles of Broughton were a notable family in the seventeenth and eighteenth centuries, well-to-do farmers and timber merchants who supplied timber for the ships of the Royal Navy at Portsmouth dockyard.

The Steeles were, besides, devoted members of the Baptist Church. The date, 1655, on the present Baptist Church refers to the beginnings of the Baptist movement in that part of Hampshire and Wiltshire. In those early days the Baptists met in houses or cottages often with a 'watcher' on duty at the door because of religious intolerance. Fines were imposed for non-attendance at parish churches and 'The Conventicle Act' of 1644 banned all meetings of five or more persons for religious worship not according to the State Church. Then in the year 1672 'The Declaration of Indulgence' granted again liberty of conscience to nonconformists and soon afterwards the Steele family donated two cottages at the north end of Broughton village to be converted into a Baptist meeting house.

In 1699 Henry Steele was appointed pastor of Broughton Chapel and the duties there were shared with his nephew, William. William Steele gave voluntary, unstinted and unbroken service to the Baptist Church for some sixty years, first as a preacher, then as co-pastor and finally as pastor. This William Steele was the father of Anne, our hymn writer and poet.

Anne Steele was the only daughter of William Steele and Anne Frowde and was born in April (or possibly May) 1717, two years after her brother, William. At a tender age Anne lost her mother, an event probably related to childbirth. This tragedy struck early in the children's lives, Anne being only three and her brother William five. Initially Anne and William were cared for by an aunt.

When Anne was six her father remarried and in the following year a daughter, Mary, was born. Anne, her brother William and half-sister Mary grew up together at 'Grandfathers'. Anne's father kept busy with his business and as co-pastor of the Baptist Church. Anne's stepmother (also Anne) was a deeply spiritual woman. Her first priority was the spiritual welfare of the family. Over the years she kept a detailed diary and, though entries therein were mainly about her personal spiritual condition, family happenings and illnesses also found mention.

From the stepmother's diaries we learn that 1732 was an important year in Anne's life. She was then almost fifteen years of age. In March of that year Mrs Steele had entered in her diary, "I have great hope that God has indeed begun to work upon the souls of our children". Three months later Anne related to 'Uncle Steele' and other members of the family her personal experience of Christ as Saviour and Lord, and was baptised by immersion on the 9th July 1732. These formative years of Anne's early Christian life were greatly influenced by the deep interest and prayers of her stepmother. At times, however, Mrs Steele had concerns for her family, "because our young people are much inclined to read books that I apprehend cannot promote their spiritual advantage". She desired the Lord, "to make them sensible of the ensnaring nature of these books which seem to them innocent, but by nature they are not spiritual but the reverse".

Anne, throughout life, never enjoyed good health. The nature of her ailment, however, was uncertain but much speculation has surrounded it. The suggestion that the tragic drowning of her friend, James Elcombe of Ringwood, just prior to their marriage had left a life-long scar on her sensitive personality appears to be without foundation. We know that such an accident did take place but there are no substantial grounds to believe that there was any fond relationship (or impending marriage) between these two young people. The more likely cause of Anne's ailment appears to have been chronic malaria, which at that time was endemic in that part of the south of England where the land was low-lying and marshy. Malaria, in the eighteenth century, was known as 'marsh fever' and it is to be noted that the Steele home, 'Grandfathers', was very near to the water meadows of Wallop Brook. Throughout life Anne was afflicted by various body pains, lassitude, recurring fevers and anaemia. Nevertheless, her spirit kept bright and she was ever thankful to God for the blessings she did enjoy.

> Lord of my life! To Thee I owe
> A thousand gifts enjoyed below
> Of providence and grace.
> While nature in her various forms
> My heart enlivens, raises, warms,
> Thy hand, O bid my heart with rapture trace.

Anne's stepmother died in June 1760 and this brought changes at 'Grandfathers'. Anne took over the care of her ageing father and the running of the home, besides acting as mother and governess to her niece, Polly. In 1769 Anne's father also died and then Anne went to live with her brother, William, at nearby 'Broughton House'. Ill health accompanied her for the remainder of life and she was confined to bed in her closing years. Throughout, she was devotedly cared for by her niece, Polly.

Anne died on 11th November 1778. The last text upon her lips was Job 19:25, "I know that my Redeemer liveth". Josiah Lewis who preached at her funeral service told his hearers, "She was an ornament to her holy profession... she had a distinguished talent... her publications were a proof of the goodness of her understanding and particularly of her substantial piety". He concluded "Now she has put off her sackcloth and is girded with gladness; and long before now, it has been echoed through the heavenly plains, 'here is one who is come out of great tribulation, who has washed her robes and made them white in the blood of the Lamb' ".

Anne's body was laid to rest in the family vault, a stone tomb chest, in St. Mary's parish churchyard close by the south door of the church and within sight of 'Broughton House'. Inscribed upon her tomb are lines that bear eloquent testimony to her talented and consecrated life.

Silent the lyre and dumb the tuneful tongue,
That sung on earth her great Redeemer's praise,
But now in heaven she joins the angelic song,
In more harmonious more exalted lays.

Anne Steele was one of the foremost of Baptist hymn writers. She wrote most of her hymns and poems at 'Grandfathers' prior to the death of her stepmother. Her brother, William, took a collection of them to London in 1760 and these were published in two leather bound volumes *Poems on Subjects chiefly Devotional, by Theodosia*. One of these volumes contained Anne's hymns, the other her verses on everyday subjects and the Psalms. In the year 1780, shortly after Anne's death, Dr. Caleb Evans of Bristol republished her works together with a third volume of miscellaneous poems and prose meditations. In all there were one hundred and forty-four hymns, thirty-four versified Psalms and about thirty short poems. These three volumes (excluding the prose meditations) were then collated by Daniel Sedgwick and published as one volume in 1863.

Dr. Hatfield has styled Anne, "the female poet of the sanctuary". She wrote on a wide variety of subjects but in the main her verse was the product of her experience of life, her pathway of affliction and sorrow, which were sanctified to her. Throughout, her hymns denote a grateful spirit. W.R. Stevenson, late editor of the Baptist Hymnal speaks of her verse as, "simple in language, natural and pleasing in imagery, and full of genuine Christian feeling".

Anne's hymns were widely used in the eighteenth and nineteenth centuries but in the past century have waned in popularity. However, two of her hymns are still in common usage and are great favourites.

One is her hymn entitled "The Excellency of the Holy Scriptures", which is one of the finest hymns existing today on the Word of God. In its original form there were twelve stanzas. The opening and concluding stanzas are,

> *Father of mercies, in Thy Word*
> *What endless glory shines!*
> *For ever be Thy Name adored*
> *For these celestial lines.*
>
> *Divine Instructor, gracious Lord,*
> *Be Thou for ever near,*
> *Teach me to love Thy sacred Word,*
> *And view my Saviour there.*

Her other was entitled "The Wonders of Redemption" and was headed, 1 Pet. 3:18. Five of its stanzas, somewhat modified, are widely used today, though there were six stanzas initially.

> *And did the Holy and the Just,*
> *The Sovereign of the skies,*
> *Stoop down to wretchedness and dust,*
> *That guilty worms might rise?*
>
> *Yes, The Redeemer left His throne,*
> *His radiant throne on high,*
> *(Surpassing mercy! Love unknown!)*
> *To suffer, bleed and die.*

He took the ruined sinner's place,
And suffered in his stead;
For man (O miracle of grace!)
For man the Saviour bled!

Jesus! my soul, adoring bends
To love, so full, so free;
Though vile I am, that love extends
It's sacred power to me.

What glad return can I impart
For favours so divine?
O take my all, my weary heart,
And make it only Thine.

Anne's title, **"The Wonders of Redemption"**, is most fitting.

First, the wonder of the down stooping of *the Sovereign of the skies* from the glory to the dust of death!
Then the wonder that *the Holy and the Just* should take the place of the unjust and the guilty!
But greater still, Anne felt, was the wonder that such love extended to her personally!
At this her heart was bowed, in adoration and in consecration.

"Brethren, let us join to bless"

John Cennick (1718-1755)

John Cennick

"The Eighteenth Century Revival produced no more beautiful and holy life than that of John Cennick" is the testimony of Arnold Dallimore in his biography of George Whitefield. Cennick's early ancestors were Moravian. His paternal grandparents became Quakers, his maternal grandparents Baptists. His parents were Anglican. Cennick was brought up an Anglican; for a short time he embraced Methodism but in the closing years of life he returned to the Moravian Church. Notwithstanding such diversity of church affiliations, John Cennick, in a short life span of thirty-six years, was a mighty instrument in God's hand in the eighteenth century.

John Cennick was born at Reading, Berkshire, on 12th December 1718, into a good home where piety and a strict adherence to religious principles were practised. He was the youngest child and only son of a family of seven children. His parents attended St. Lawrence Church and there young John, together with his sisters, was taken daily to prayers. Sundays were strictly observed. The family was not allowed to play but spent most of the day reading or reciting hymns. By nature John was a serious boy, but obstinate in his way and given to lying.

At the age of fifteen John rebelled against the rigorous discipline of home and against God and pursued a life of revelry and sin. He went to London. One day in 1735, while walking in Cheapside, the Lord spoke very definitely to him. He was convicted, as never before, of his sin and the path he was pursuing. He sought salvation but found the way thereto long and difficult. First he tried a life of abstinence, of prayer and of fasting, even in his desperation contemplating monastic life, but all this was in vain. His sins had become an unbearable burden.

Then one day, 7th September 1737, while sitting in St. Lawrence Church at prayers and feeling hopelessly destitute, he heard as it were the voice of the Lord saying to him, "I am thy salvation". What would he do? This he tells us in some lines written soon afterwards.

> *Lo! Glad I come; and Thou, blest Lamb,*
> *Shalt take me to Thee as I am!*
> *Nothing but sin have I to give,*
> *Nothing but love shall I receive.*

There and then he came to Christ and in coming found peace. He was then eighteen years of age.

In the following year someone loaned him a part of Mr. Whitefield's "Journal". On reading it he longed that he might meet this man and about a year afterwards, after walking all night from Reading to London, he met Whitefield. Their hearts were immediately knit and they spent several days together. Whitefield told Cennick that John Wesley purposed to build a school at Kingswood near Bristol for collier's children and asked if he would be willing to be one of the masters there. He consented and thereupon set out for the West Country.

On reaching Kingswood a crowd of some four to five hundred colliers were gathered under a sycamore tree awaiting the arrival of their preacher who had been delayed. Cennick was prevailed upon to speak to them. This was for him a new experience but after a brief time of earnest prayer he stepped forward. His message was delivered with soul conviction and with power. God was pleased to bless; many believed and on that day God confirmed to him his vocation as a preacher of the gospel.

Cennick spent some time around Kingswood and then in company with fellow evangelist, Howell Harris of Talgarth, preached in the towns and villages of N. Wiltshire. There again he proved the presence and power of God and continued fearlessly in the face of fierce mob opposition, goaded on by the aristocracy of the district. Thus began the "awakening of Wiltshire" which continued till 1745. During this time Cennick lived at Tytherton in Wiltshire while at the same time he kept in touch with Mr. Whitefield in London, oftimes visiting there and preaching in Moorfield's Tabernacle. On these London visits Cennick came under the influence of leading figures in the Moravian Church, as Count Zinzendorf and Peter Böhler. He felt drawn to them and in December 1744 dissociated from the Methodist movement and joined with the Moravian brethren.

Cennick, at that time, had an exercise to visit Ireland. He desired to fulfil a long-standing invitation from the Baptists there. After a visit to Germany, he went to Ireland in 1746 and his going heralded a new day in that needy land. He began his ministry in the Baptist church in Skinner's Alley in the city of Dublin. The church was soon filled to capacity, the windows were then removed to allow the crowds in the surrounding churchyard to hear the Word and, though Satan bitterly opposed, God was pleased to work. Cennick wrote of those days, "the Lamb was with me, and hundreds were swept into the Kingdom".

Joseph Deane, a merchant from Ballymena in the north of Ireland, was one who heard Cennick preach in Dublin and prevailed upon him to come north. Cennick consented but found the initial reception so hostile that he was compelled to flee back to Dublin. Two years later he returned and this time got a mixed reception. The clergy were prejudiced and jealous and complained to the Bishop that Cennick was emptying their churches. "Preach what Cennick preaches, preach Christ crucified, and the people will not have to go to Cennick to hear the gospel," replied the Bishop. Cennick made his headquarters at Crebilly, Co. Antrim and for the succeeding seven years spent most of his time in the towns and villages of Ulster. Cennick preached the gospel with power, sometimes to crowds of up to ten thousand people. Ulster experienced a great awakening and God blessed in the salvation of many souls. Among the early converts in the Ballymena district was a sixteen-year-old lad called John Montgomery, father of James Montgomery, the notable hymnwriter of the early nineteenth century. As the work continued, prejudices were broken down and John Cennick, the man treated initially with such hatred and hostility, became greatly loved and revered by all classes and creeds. Dallimore in "George Whitefield" (Vol.2) records that, "at Moneymore the Presbyterians asked him to stop and be their minister. At Ballynahone the Roman Catholics said if he would only settle there they would never go to mass again. He was so beloved that many of the innkeepers gave him board and lodgings free of charge. Cennick often addressed thousands, in the open air with rain coming down in torrents—He preached in old barns, in disused cloth mills and in village cock-pits.—He slept in the old ruined church at Portmore.—He sat on the roadside, cold and lonely, munching his meagre lunch of bread and cheese. If money was plentiful, he used a horse; if not, he would walk twenty miles to preach".

By the year 1755 Cennick was worn out by toil, persecution and privations. Ill health had overtaken him and he seemed to feel his work was done. He returned to England to die. His journey there entailed travelling to Dublin, crossing to Holyhead and then five days on horseback. He was ill with fever and when he reached London he was a dying man. His closing days were spent at Fetter Lane where he was tenderly cared for by his Moravian friends and on 4th July, at the early age of thirty-six, he went to be with Christ. His body was laid to rest in the Moravian Burial Ground, called Sharon's Garden, in Chelsea. After his death the following lines were found among his papers.

> But take it not amiss! O! Be not grieved!
> I want from pilgrimage to be relieved,
> I want to be dissolved and no more here
> A wanderer be, a banished foreigner.
> I would not Thee offend: Thou know'st my heart,
> Nor one short day before Thy time depart;
> But I am weary and dejected, too:
> O let me to eternal mansions go.

Thus concluded Cennick's brief pilgrimage of thirty-six years – eighteen years lived wholly without Christ, and eighteen years lived wholly for Christ.

John Cennick, throughout life, was a prolific hymnwriter, writing in all some seven hundred and fifty hymns. Most were written during his time at Kingswood and appeared in four separate publications - *Sacred Hymns for the Children of God in the days of their Pilgrimage* (1741/1742), *Sacred Hymns for the Use of Religious Societies* (1743/1744), *A Collection of Sacred Hymns* (1749) and *Hymns to the Honour of Jesus Christ composed for such Little Children as desire to be saved and go to heaven* (1754). Some additional hymns were published after his death.

Today, Cennick's hymns might be judged a little quaint, even somewhat jarring but this is due in part to some change in the use of the English language and the fact that Cennick was concerned more with heart worship than with fine flowing verse. His hymns, in the main, were born out of a deep devotion to his Lord and Saviour.

"Lo! He cometh, countless trumpets" was one of Cennick's early hymns. Its revised form by Charles Wesley, "Lo! He comes with clouds descending", is still widely used today.

Cennick's "Graces before and after meat" have had wide circulation and are great favourites in England.

"Before meat", *Be present at our table, Lord!*
Be here, and everywhere adored;
Thy creatures bless, and grant that we
May feast in Paradise with Thee.

(These lines so appealed to John Wesley that he had them engraved on his family teapot.)

"After meat", *We bless Thee, Lord, for this our food,*
But bless Thee more for Jesus' blood!
May Manna to our souls be given,
The Bread of Life sent down from heaven.

One of Cennick's best hymns is that commencing, **"Brethren, let us join to bless"**. It first appeared in his 1742 collection and is still a favourite among saints gathered at the Lord's supper.

Brethren, let us join to bless
Jesus Christ, our joy and peace;
Him, who bowed His head so low
Underneath our load of woe.

> *His the curse, the wounds, the gall,*
> *His the stripes – He bore them all;*
> *His the dying cry of pain*
> *When our sins He did sustain.*
>
> *He, the accepted Sacrifice,*
> *From the vanquished grave did rise;*
> *Free Himself, He set us free*
> *In His perfect liberty.*
>
> *Ransomed now, accepted, free,*
> *Safe from judgment, Lord, in Thee,*
> *We rejoice that God can bless*
> *All who do Thy name confess.*
>
> *Praise our God who willed it thus;*
> *Praise the Lamb who died for us;*
> *Praise the Father, through the Son,*
> *Who so vast a work hath done.*

This is a hymn of praise. Therein, "the blessed" join to bless "the Blesser". After Cennick recounts the unprecedented suffering of the Saviour and the blessings that thereby accrue, a worthy crescendo of praise is struck in the closing stanza.

> *Praise our God who willed it thus;*
> *Praise the Lamb who died for us;*
> *Praise the Father, through the Son,*
> *Who so vast a work hath done.*

"Great God of wonders!"
Samuel Davies (1723-1761)

Samuel Davies

Samuel Davies, son of David Davies and Martha Thomas, was born in humble circumstances on a small farm near Summit Ridge in Newcastle County, Delaware, U.S.A, on 3rd November 1723. Both his parents were of Welsh extraction and both were devout Christians. At the time of Samuel's birth, his mother, believing that God had given to her a son in answer to her prayers, named him Samuel, meaning "asked of God". Within her heart she secretly dedicated him back to God and her prayers followed him right through life.

For several generations none of the Davies family could read or write. Samuel became the first. His mother, however, was literate and she became his instructor for the first ten years of his life. Thereafter, for a period of two years, he came under the instruction of Abel Morgan, a Welsh Baptist. Samuel was an apt student, diligent in his studies and an avid reader.

At the age of twelve Samuel got to know the Lord, though he did not make open confession of faith in Christ until he was fifteen. His mother's prayers then appeared to have been answered, but she was not fully satisfied. She longed and prayed that Samuel would be greatly used of the Lord. He needed further education, but the family was poor. He commenced studies at the classical academy of Samuel Blair at Fagg's Manor, Chester County, Pennsylvania. But his continuation there was uncertain because of financial constraints. Then God answered the need in a most remarkable way.

In the year 1740 a movement of God had commenced in Hanover County, in the State of Virginia. A wealthy planter there had been converted through reading some pages of Thomas Boston's "Fourfold State of Man". Then a Mr. Morris also was converted through reading "Luther on Galatians". Mr. Morris built a meeting room for the preaching of the gospel and this room thereafter was known as "Morris' Reading Room". William Robinson, the family minister of the Davies in Delaware, paid a visit to that "Reading Room" and his labours in the gospel were so blessed of the Lord that on his departure the people presented him with a substantial sum of money as a token of their appreciation. He initially refused the gift but the people insisted, finally slipping it into his saddlebags. William Robinson then suggested to them, "There is a young man now studying divinity whose parents are very hard scuffed and finding great difficulty in supporting him at his studies. I will take the money and it shall be given to help him through. When he is licensed, he shall come and be your preacher". And so it transpired and Samuel Davies, after his training, gave the most of his years of service to that part of Hanover County in Virginia from whence the gift had come. Thus, through the pecuniary assistance of William Robinson, Samuel was enabled to have his necessary education.

In the year 1746 Samuel was licensed as a preacher of the gospel and in the same year he married Miss Sarah Kirkpatrick of Nottingham. In the following year he was ordained as an evangelist and after a brief period of service around his home county of Newcastle he moved to the county of Hanover in Virginia. Hanover County became Samuel's field of service and there, over the next twelve years, he laboured faithfully for God, with but one interruption, in 1753, when he visited England.

But Samuel Davies' labours for God in Virginia were not without difficulties. In September 1747 his wife, Sarah, died in childbirth. At the same time his own health was greatly impaired and consumption (pulmonary tuberculosis) was feared. However, by the spring of the following year his health had improved and he was installed as minister of Hanover Presbyterian Church. He found a suitable partner again in Joan, daughter of John Holt of Hanover. He remarried and settled into the work.

Further difficulties arose. In the State of Virginia the Episcopal Church was regarded as the Established Church and Davies was regarded as a dissenter. There were difficulties with the civil authorities regarding his license and liberty to preach. The problem concerned the "Act of Toleration" which had been passed in England. Did it, or did it not, extend to the Colony of Virginia in America? The matter was finally resolved and Davies was granted license and liberty to continue with his evangelical labours.

Davies' commitment to the work in Hanover was wholehearted. Against a background of ill health he laboured diligently and the work grew. New churches were established and soon he found himself with responsibility for seven preaching stations, scattered widely in five different counties. Davies was a popular and powerful preacher. "He could address his auditory, either with the most commanding authority, or with the most melting tenderness". He was accepted, appreciated and revered by all.

In his preaching there were times when his utterances were almost prophetic. On the occasion of the salvaging of General Braddock's defeated and beleaguered army in July 1755 through the skill and courage of a Colonel Washington, then only a youth of twenty three years, Davies stated, "That heroic youth, Colonel Washington, whom I cannot but hope Providence has hitherto preserved in so signal a manner, for some important service to his country". And so it came to pass, the young Colonel Washington going on to become the first President of the United States of America. But first of all Samuel Davies was a preacher of the gospel.

The year 1753 brought an interlude in his busy ministry. Together with Gilbert Tennent of New Jersey, he had been selected by the trustees of The Presbyterian College in New Jersey to visit the British Isles to solicit funds for the College. The mission occupied just over a year and throughout Davies was busily occupied preaching in the towns and cities of England. On that tour he met with universal acceptance and admiration wherever he went. When in London he met with George Whitefield and John and Charles Wesley and formed a close relationship with Dr. Thomas Gibbons. In early 1755 he returned home to Hanover County to resume his busy pastoral ministry.

In the year 1758, when Jonathan Edwards died as a consequence of a smallpox inoculation, the trustees of the New Jersey Presbyterian College in Princeton invited Samuel Davies to become his successor as President of the College. On the first invitation he declined, so closely was he devoted to his own people in Hanover. But when a repeat invitation came in the following May he felt it to be the will of God. He accepted, looking to the Lord for Divine enabling, and was duly elected in July 1759. He appeared admirably fitted for such responsibility. He had wisdom, piety and eloquence. A seemingly useful career stretched out before him and he was then only thirty-five years of age.

But Samuel Davies was not long spared to fill his position of trust and within nineteen months his promising career had come to a seemingly untimely close. In January 1761 he developed a severe cold. This was treated by venesection. Inflammation of his arm ensued. This led to septicaemia and within ten days Samuel Davies went to be with the Lord. He died on 4th February 1761 at the early age of thirty-seven, greatly lamented both at home and abroad. As his dear mother gazed upon his casket she was heard to say, "There is the son of my prayers, and my hopes – my only son – my only earthly support. But there is the will of God and I am satisfied".

The loss was deemed incalculable. Samuel Davies was one of the most gifted men of his time. Dr. John H. Livingston of New York City, the patriarch of the Reformed Dutch Church, judged him to be "without exception the first pulpit orator to whom he had ever listened. His voice, his attitudes, his gesture, everything pertaining to manner, come up to the most perfect ideal that he was able to form". Dr. Samuel Finlay, his close friend and successor, in a memorial sermon at Princeton, gave his appraisal, "As to his natural genius, he was strong and masculine. His understanding was clear, his memory retentive, his invention quick, his imagination lively and florid, his thoughts sublime, and his language elegant, strong and expressive.— He sought truth for its own sake. — I have never known one who appeared to lay himself more fully open to the reception of truth, from whatever quarter it came, than he". And Dr. Lloyd-Jones, writing at a later date, termed

GREAT GOD OF WONDERS!

him "the greatest preacher ever produced in America".

After Samuel Davies' death, all his manuscripts were entrusted to his close friend, Dr. Thomas Gibbons of London. From these files Gibbons published Davies' sermons in five volumes (1767 – 1771). These were regarded by many as the most able and eloquent sermons in the English language. But also included with the manuscripts were sixteen hymns of Davies' own composition. Dr. Gibbons published these, together with others, in 1769 as *Hymns Adapted to Divine Worship*.

Samuel Davies was one of America's earliest hymnwriters. His compositions have been judged as "weighty and lofty". Notwithstanding, only one of his hymns has survived the years of time and is widely used today. It is his majestic hymn, "Great God of wonders!" It was originally entitled "The Pardoning God". In Dr. Gibbons' collection of 1769 it was entitled, "The Glories of God in pardoning sinners".

"Great God of wonders!" is one of the great hymns of the eighteenth century. But like so many other great hymns of that period it has suffered much from alteration by hymnbook compilers. Indeed, it is difficult to know now with certainty the exact words written originally by Samuel Davies. The original hymn, however, did contain five stanzas of six lines each with the last two lines of each stanza used as a refrain. The hymn today is treasured by almost all denominations. In most collections three of its verses are commonly given.

Great God of wonders! all Thy ways
Are worthy of Thyself - Divine!
But the bright glories of Thy grace
Beyond Thine other wonders shine.

Who is a pardoning God like Thee?
Or who has grace so rich and free?

Such deep transgressions to forgive!
Such guilty, daring worms to spare!
This is Thy grand prerogative,
And in this honour none shall share.

Pardon from an offended God!
Pardon for sins of deepest dye!
Pardon, bestowed through Jesus' blood!
Pardon that brings the rebel nigh!

This hymn is a passionately majestic piece of writing. Its lines are sublime, its words massive and mighty, loaded with "brilliant metaphors" and "thundering epithets". Davies paints a dark picture of man's ruin. Transgressions are "deep", sinners are but "guilty, daring worms" with sins "of deepest dye". This is the dark, dark scene into which God moves in sovereign grace. It is God's prerogative to pardon the guilty and His pardoning grace is commensurate with the enormity of human guilt. Well might the prophet ask, "Who is a God like unto Thee, that pardoneth iniquity?" (Micah 7:18).

God is a God of wonders. There are wonders in God's works (Job 37:16). There are wonders in God's word (Psa. 119:18). There are wonders in God's ways (Romans 11:33). But like a mountain peak, rugged and majestic and towering above all other Divine wonders is the wonder of God's grace. It transforms human lives and brings guilty rebels to Himself.

This is God's greatest wonder. It is His brightest glory.

> *Who is a pardoning God like Thee?*
> *Or who has grace so rich and free?*

"The God of Abraham praise"

Thomas Olivers (1725-1799)

Thomas Olivers

"As the lark, ascending from the hidden depths of the grassy hollow, rises high and sings long and sweetly, so Olivers, coming of humble parentage, was at length known and honoured as a sweet singer of Israel". Thus writes Josiah Miller of Thomas Olivers in his "Singers and Songs of the Church". Olivers, like his contemporary, John Newton, was a trophy of the saving grace of God. Prior to his conversion he was a profligate; afterwards, he lived a life to the glory of God for almost sixty years. He was no mean writer and, besides, he was a poet and a musical composer. It is to Thomas Olivers that we owe the majestic hymn of adoration, "The God of Abraham praise".

Thomas Olivers was born at Tregynon, near to Newtown in Montgomeryshire (now Powys) in Wales in 1725. His father's death when he was four, followed by that of his mother soon afterwards, left him orphaned in this world ere he was five years of age. For a short time he was cared for by an uncle and thereafter by a distant relative and guardian, a Mr. Tudor of Forden, who was a farmer of the same county. There he attended the local school. "I received such learning as was thought necessary", recounts Olivers, and "as to religion I was taught to say my prayers morning and evening, to repeat my catechism, to sing psalms and to go to church twice on Sunday".

But Thomas soon fell into evil ways and, by the age of fifteen, he was reckoned to be the worst boy known in all that part of Wales in thirty years. At the age of eighteen, he was apprenticed to a shoemaker but did not apply himself. His life was one of rank ungodliness and wickedness, characterized by gambling, drunkenness, dancing, immorality and blasphemy. Olivers himself records that of sixteen consecutive days and nights at that time, "I was fifteen of them without ever being in bed". Indeed, so wild and dissolute were his ways that he was obliged to leave his native county.

For a time he lived a vagabond life. First, he went to Shrewsbury, then to Wrexham and then, in Divine providence, moved south to Bristol. There he was converted. One day he saw crowds of people making their way through the city, and on enquiry learned that George Whitefield was expected to preach. He had heard of Whitefield and resolved to attend his meeting, but not to listen. However, two evenings later Olivers was found listening attentively to Whitefield as he preached in the power of the Spirit of God from the text, "Is not this a brand plucked out of the fire?" (Zech. 3: 2). Let Olivers himself tell his story.

"When the sermon began" he says "I was certainly a dreadful enemy to God and to all that is good, and one of the most profligate and abandoned young men living; but, by the time it was ended, I was become a new creature. For, in the first place, I was deeply convinced of the goodness of God towards me in all my life; particularly in that He had given His Son to die for me. I had also a far clearer view of all my sins, particularly my base ingratitude towards Him. These discoveries quite broke my heart and caused showers of tears to trickle down my cheeks. I was likewise filled with an utter abhorrence of my evil ways, and was much ashamed that I had ever walked in them. And, as my heart was thus turned from all that is evil, so it was powerfully inclined to all that is good. It is not easy to express what strong desires I felt for God and His service; and what resolutions I made to seek Him and serve Him in the future. In consequence of this, I broke off all my evil practices, and forsook all my wicked and foolish companions without delay. I gave myself up to God and His service with my whole heart. Oh, what reason have I to say, 'Is not this a brand plucked from the burning?' "

Thomas Olivers had become a new creature in Christ Jesus. The transformation was remarkable. First, he settled all his debts, some seventy of them, at times travelling many miles to pay a very meagre sum. Then he gave himself to prayer and attended regularly to the preaching in the area, not missing a single sermon in the space of two years. His first compulsion was to follow George Whitefield, but was discouraged from this path. He then moved to Bradford-on-Avon in Wiltshire, there purposing to carry on his trade as a shoemaker, but when John Wesley heard of him, of his transforming experience and of his ability and zeal for the Lord, he appointed him as a travelling preacher.

Olivers' early labours for the Lord were in Cornwall, going there on 1st October 1753. Subsequently, he travelled widely throughout Britain and Ireland as an evangelist; indeed, he became one of the most noted of the first group of Methodist travelling preachers, perhaps second only to Mr. Wesley himself in his zeal and labours for the Lord. In Tiverton Olivers bought a horse for five pounds and over the next twenty-five years used it almost daily, covering in excess of one hundred thousand miles on horseback in the service of the gospel. In his witness he was fearless. He met with much opposition, hostility and violence, and on one occasion was put into the stocks by order of the magistrates. Yet withal he continued faithfully for forty-six years, almost without interruption, right up to the close of life.

Olivers passed away in London, suddenly and unexpectedly, in March 1799, at the age of seventy-four and was buried in the City Road Chapel burying ground in John Wesley's vault. At the time of his decease one commentator wrote, "Olivers died, advanced in years. In his younger life he was a zealous, able, and useful travelling preacher; but for a long period was employed by Mr. Wesley as a corrector of his press. His talents were very considerable; and his attachment to Mr. Wesley and Methodism was fully evidenced by several masterly publications".

Thomas Olivers was as able writer, both in prose and in poetry. For a time he was assistant editor of the "Arminian Magazine" but was deposed by Mr. Wesley because his lack of education unfitted him for the job; "the errata are insufferable", commented Mr. Wesley. At the time of Mr. Wesley's death (1791), Olivers wrote *A Descriptive and Plaintive Elegy on the death of the late Rev. John Wesley.*

Olivers was the writer of a number of hymns and tunes and is remembered today as the author of the majestic hymn, **"The God of Abraham praise".**

The God of Abraham praise,
Who reigns enthroned above;
Ancient of everlasting days,
And God of Love:
Jehovah, great I AM!
By earth and heaven confest;
I bow and bless the sacred Name,
For ever bless'd

The God of Abraham praise,
Whose all-sufficient grace
Shall guide me all my happy days,
In all my ways:
He calls a worm His friend!
He calls Himself my God!
And He shall save me to the end
Thro' Jesu's blood.

He by Himself hath sworn,
I on His oath depend,
I shall, on eagle's wings up-borne,
To heaven ascend;
I shall behold His face,
I shall His power adore,
And sing the wonders of His grace
For evermore.

The whole triumphant host,
Give thanks to God on high;
"Hail, Father, Son and Holy Ghost",
They ever cry:

THE GOD OF ABRAHAM PRAISE

Hail, Abraham's God – and mine!
(I join the heavenly lays),
All might and majesty are Thine
And endless praise.

This hymn was written by Olivers in London, probably in the year 1770. He was staying there with his friend and colleague, John Bakewell, and visited The Great Synagogue at Duke's Place, Aldgate. There he heard the Hebrew Yigdal (Doxology), sung to a Hebrew melody by the chorister, Signor Leoni (Meyer Lyon). Its melody, so noble and impressive, captivated and haunted him. He learned it and then fitted to it the sublime stanzas of his majestic hymn, "The God of Abraham praise". There were in all twelve stanzas and the hymn was divided into three parts of four stanzas each. (Quoted above are stanzas 1, 3, 4 and 12 of the original hymn.)

Olivers placed a text of Scripture at the top of the hymn, "I am thy shield and thy exceeding great reward" (Gen. 15: 1). The twelve verses of the hymn were published in Nottingham as an eight-page pamphlet, with the title, "*A Hymn to the God of Abraham. In three parts, adapted to a celebrated air, sung by the priest, Signor Leoni, etc, at the Jew's Synagogue in London; by Thomas Olivers*".

The Hebrew Yigdal rehearses in metrical form the thirteen articles of the Hebrew Creed and is sung on the eve of Jewish Sabbaths and Festivals. Some have regarded Olivers hymn as a free rendering or a paraphrase of the Hebrew Yigdal but there is only a minimal verbal resemblance between Olivers' version and the Hebrew original. Furthermore, its words are charged with Olivers' personal fervent devotion to God. James Montgomery judged that, "the man who wrote that hymn must have had the finest ear imaginable, for on account of the peculiar measure, none but a person of equal musical and poetic taste could have produced the harmony perceptible in the verse". Thomas Olivers was just such a person, talented as he was, both as a poet and as a musical composer. He named the tune "Leoni" after the chorister who sang it in the Jewish synagogue. A fine alternative tune, "Covenant" was later composed by John Stainer.

The content of this hymn has been a great support to many. Henry Martyn, ere he left England on 29th July 1805, learned its words and found in them a source of great consolation. And on the eve of his outward voyage to India, he wrote, "As often as I could use the language of it with any truth, my heart was a little at ease. There was something particularly solemn and affecting to me in this hymn, and particularly at this time".

This hymn is one of the finest hymns of adoration in the English language. Lord Selbourne has considered it, "one of the noblest hymns in existence, an ode of singular power and beauty". "There is not in our language", says James Montgomery again, "a lyric of more majestic style, more elevated thought or more glorious imagery".

This hymn gives to us **an appreciation of God** – absolute and independent in His Being, sovereign in His ways, possessed of majesty and power, infinitely holy, absolutely trustworthy, a God whom men can trust. Such a God was **Abraham's God**. Furthermore, says Olivers, "Abraham's God – **and mine!**"

> *I shall behold His face,*
> *I shall His power adore,*
> *And sing the wonders of His grace*
> *For evermore.*

"Majestic sweetness sits enthroned"

Samuel Stennett (1727-1795)

Samuel Stennett

In Eighteenth Century England, the pulpits of the Seventh Day Baptist Church, which observed Saturday rather than Sunday as their day of worship, were graced by a succession of talented and godly ministers by the name of Stennett. This succession of Stennetts covered five generations and their ministries extended for over a century. Samuel Stennett, the subject of this present sketch, belonged to that illustrious family.

Samuel's great grandfather, **Edward Stennett**, the first in the Stennett line, came from a respectable stock in Lincolnshire. He lived in the intolerant reign of Charles II and made his home at Wallingford

Castle. He was a medical doctor of no mean repute and was, besides, a preacher of the gospel. He preached regularly in his own home but as a dissenting minister he was subjected to many persecutions, often threatened, sometimes in great danger and for a time imprisoned for conscience sake. In later life he became pastor of the Seventh Day Baptist Church at Pinner's Hall, London and there he exercised a brief ministry until his death in 1689.

Samuel's grandfather, **Joseph Stennett**, was second in the Stennett line. He was son of the above Edward Stennett and was born at Abingdon in Berkshire in 1663. He was educated at Wallingford Grammar School and at the age of twenty-two moved to London. There he engaged in teaching for about five years and then for twenty-three years was pastor of the Seventh Day Baptists at Pinner's Hall. He was a renowned preacher, "the pulpit's honour, and the saint's delight", and besides preaching to his own congregation on Saturdays, he preached to other congregations on Sundays. Joseph was also a genuine poet, and wrote many hymns. He is reckoned as "the earliest Baptist hymnwriter whose hymns are still in common usage" and is remembered today as the author of the lovely hymn, "O blessed Saviour, is Thy love?"

Samuel's father, the third of the Stennett line, was also named **Joseph Stennett**. He was son of the above Joseph Stennett and was born in 1692. He was saved in his youth and gave most of his life to the ministry of the Seventh Day Baptist Church, first in Exeter and thereafter at Little Wild Street in London.

Samuel Stennett, the hymnwriter here considered, was of the fourth generation of the Stennett line. He was the younger son of the above Joseph Stennett and was born in Exeter when his father was Baptist minister there. When Samuel was ten the family moved to London, his father having been appointed pastor of the Baptist Chapel in Little Wild Street, Lincoln's Inn Fields. Samuel received a good education, first under the tuition of John Hubbard, Theological Tutor at Stepney and then of the distinguished linguist, Dr. John Walker, of the Mile End Academy.

Samuel was saved early in life. His conscience had been awakened to a sense of his personal spiritual need and, after a period of deep soul trouble, he found peace in trusting the Saviour. In one of his hymns he alludes to that transforming experience,

> *Come, ye that love the Lord*
> *And listen while I tell*
> *How narrowly my feet escaped*
> *The snares of death and hell.*

From the time of conversion Samuel showed a keen interest in spiritual things. He was baptized by his father and became a member of the Little Wild Street Baptist Church where he remained for over fifty years. At the age of twenty-one he became assistant to his father and on his father's death, ten years later, he was called to succeed him in the pastoral office. With a trembling heart he accepted the call and, for the next thirty-seven years, he exercised a faithful ministry in Little Wild Street.

Samuel was eminently qualified for the work. He was a man of remarkable qualities, a thinker, a linguist proficient in Latin, Greek and other languages, a scholar well versed in oriental literature and, besides, a skilful writer. In Rippon's register his abilities were recorded, "To the strength of natural faculties, vigour of imagination, and acuteness of judgment, he had added, from his earliest years, so close an attention to reflection and study that there was scarcely a topic in science or literature, in religion, or even politics, but he seemed to have investigated". In recognition of his scholarship the University of Aberdeen conferred on him a Doctorate degree at the age of thirty-six.

Samuel Stennett was one of the most outstanding and influential evangelical preachers of his day. His friend, Dr. Winter, stated that "Few preachers knew better than Dr. Stennett how to blend argument with pathos, how to convince the judgment and to touch the finest feelings of the heart". He was much respected by many of the statesmen of his day and, indeed, was much admired by and became a confidant of King George III. It is recorded that he was offered preferment and a place of prominence in the Church of England but he declined, saying, "I dwell among my own people". Samuel used his influence and ability in support of religious freedom and took a large part in the repeal of the Test and Corporation Acts, so unjust towards dissenters.

Samuel Stennett, in his private and family life, was a man of exemplary character. William Jones tells us that "He set the Lord always before him – had habitual recourse to prayer – and walked with God – and was ready to forgive. As a husband and father his deportment was alike upright and exemplary. Mrs. Stennett was a lady of unaffected piety and good nature, and they walked together as heirs of the grace of life for upwards of forty years". They had two children, a son, Joseph, and a daughter, Elizabeth. His son, Joseph, also became a minister of the Seventh Day Baptist Church and was the fifth and concluding generation of that remarkable succession of Stennett ministers.

Mrs. Stennett died on 16th March 1795. Her passing came as a severe blow to Samuel and was followed shortly afterwards by his own decease. After her death he was wont to quote, "the time of my departure is at hand" yet, in the interval, he continued with vigour and diligence in the things of God. He made sleepless nights an opportunity for meditation upon the Word of God and communion with his Lord. He prayed earnestly that God would give him an easy passage out of life. In his last illness, when given vinegar as a throat gargle, he tasted thereof and then commented with great emotion, " 'And in His thirst they gave Him vinegar to drink'. Oh! when I reflect upon the sufferings of Christ, I am ready to say, 'What have I been thinking of all my life?' What He did and suffered are now my only support!" At the close, some lines of his own composition meant much to him and were of the last from his lips,

Father, at Thy will I come,
In Thy bosom there is room
For a guilty soul to hide,
Press'd with grief on every side.

Thus Samuel Stennett passed away on 24th August 1795, in his sixty-eighth year. His body was laid to rest beside that of his wife in Bunhill Fields, City Road, London, where today an unusual yet striking tombstone marks the spot.

Samuel Stennett was a gifted writer. "He was a perfect master of the English language and, from his earliest appearance as an author, had accustomed himself to such accuracy both in preaching and writing, that he rarely allowed a careless, inelegant, or negligent expression to escape him on any occasion". Some of his works were published during his lifetime, as his *Sermons on Personal Religion*, his *Discourses on Domestic Duties*, his *Discourses on the Parable of the Sower* and his *Discourses on the Divine Authority and Various Use of the Holy Scriptures*, but most of his works not until after his death.

Samuel Stennett, besides, was a gifted poet. He composed at least some thirty-eight hymns. Most of these he contributed to Dr. Rippon's collection of 1787, but some appeared later in the Baptist *Psalms and Hymns*. Though some have judged his poetical genius not to be of the highest order, "having neither the originality nor the vigour of his grandfather's", yet his hymns were much appreciated and many are still in common use in Baptist congregations. A few have received wider recognition, as,

> "Jesus, O Name divinely sweet!"
> "On Jordan's stormy banks I stand" and
> "To Christ, the Lord, let every tongue".

This last hymn, entitled "Praise of Christ", is the best known and the most widely used of all Samuel Stennett's compositions. In its original form there were nine verses but in most hymnbooks a selection has been made. Most selections commence with the third verse, **"Majestic sweetness sits enthroned"**. Verses 6 and 7 of the original hymn were written as a parenthesis and these two verses are here omitted.

> *To Christ, the Lord let every tongue*
>   *Its noblest tribute bring:*
> *When He's the subject of the song,*
>   *Who can refuse to sing?*
>
> *Survey the beauties of His face,*
>   *And on His glories dwell;*
> *Think of the wonders of His grace,*
>   *And all His triumphs tell.*
>
> *Majestic sweetness sits enthroned*
>   *Upon the Saviour's brow;*
> *His head with radiant glories crown'd,*
>   *His lips with grace o'erflow.*
>
> *No mortal can with Him compare*
>   *Among the sons of men:*
> *Fairer is He than all the fair*
>   *That fill the heavenly train.*

> *He saw me plunged in deep distress,*
> *He flew to my relief;*
> *For me He bore the shameful Cross,*
> *And carried all my grief.*
>
> *To heaven, the place of His abode,*
> *He brings my weary feet;*
> *Shows me the glories of my God,*
> *And makes my joys complete.*
>
> *Since from His bounty I receive*
> *Such proofs of love divine,*
> *Had I a thousand hearts to give,*
> *Lord, they should all be Thine!*

Stennett is here occupied with **the beauties and the excellencies of the Saviour.**

> *No mortal can with Him compare*
> *Among the sons of men:*
> *Fairer is He than all the fair*
> *That fill the heavenly train.*

But that **One so worthy as He** should look upon **one so wretched as me,** moved Stennett's heart most deeply.

> *Had I a thousand hearts to give,*
> *Lord, they should all be Thine!*

"Behold the Lamb of God"

Thomas Haweis (1734-1820)

Thomas Haweis

In the early eighteenth century, spiritual life in Britain had reached a low ebb. Materialism had eaten deep into national life. The Established Church was in no fit state to meet the need of the day. The dissenting Churches were but little better. Nothing less than a revival of the Spirit of God could effectively deal with the situation. And God, in His great grace, was pleased to grant it. In the year 1734 revival started in America under the leadership of Jonathan Edwards. The following year (1735), in mainland Britain, saw the conversion of George Whitefield, Howell Harris and Daniel Rowlands, the year 1738 that of John and Charles Wesley. Thomas Haweis was born right on the threshold of this mighty evangelical awakening and figured greatly in its advancement right up to the close of the eighteenth century.

Thomas Haweis was born 1st January 1734 in the quaint old Cornish town of Redruth, noted then for its tin and copper mines. His father was a solicitor there, but through intemperance and imprudence had squandered the family estate and met with an early death. Thomas was only a small child at the time of his father's death. His mother, Bridgeman, was of the well-to-do Willyams family of Carnanton. After her husband's death she returned to Carnanton to care for a widowed brother. And there, at Carnanton, young Thomas and his cousin, John Oliver (Willyams) grew up together.

Thomas had "abundant educational advantages". He was privileged to be a pupil at Truro Grammar School under Master George Conon. Conon, a Scot from Aberdeen, was a believer in the Lord Jesus Christ and he firmly grounded his pupils, not only in the rudiments of Latin and of Greek, but also in the basic truths of the gospel. And though Thomas in his schooldays paid little heed to spiritual things, the good seed sown in those formative years was not sown in vain.

On leaving school, Thomas was apprenticed to a gentleman in the medical profession residing in Truro, "an eminent surgeon and apothecary". (Paucity of family finances had prohibited a more elaborate university training.) Thomas applied himself diligently to his profession, taking a great interest in the treatment of his patients. At that time a scourge of smallpox swept through the town of Truro and its district, and in the face of great difficulties and at no small danger to himself Thomas ministered faithfully to his patients. Afterwards he wrote a treatise on the management of smallpox.

While Thomas diligently attended to his profession, God was at work in the town of Truro. Master George Conon, his old schoolmaster, had been instrumental in leading the young curate, Samuel Walker, to Christ. And Samuel Walker, in turn, was greatly used of the Lord in his preaching and in pointing others to Christ. Of the sixteen hundred inhabitants in Truro at that time some eight hundred had enquired personally of Walker as to the way of salvation. Frivolity and moral looseness almost completely disappeared from the town, the playhouse and the cockpit were compelled to close their doors.

But Thomas, the promising medical student, all the while remained a scoffer. There was no fear of God before his eyes. He was "full of spirits, careless and indifferent about anything holy and heavenly".

Then God crossed his path in a most remarkable way. His sweetheart, a neighbouring clergyman's daughter, was snatched from his side by an attack of smallpox and one afternoon following her funeral he felt constrained to attend St. Mary's Church. Walker was the preacher. This proved to be the turning point of his life. As Walker preached that day on death and its consequences, "the arrow sped to its mark in Haweis' unregenerate heart". He thereupon sought the confidence of Walker and unburdened his heart. Indeed, that very day, he sought and found the Saviour.

Haweis' conversion caused no small stir in the town of Truro. Among his old comrades he soon became the object of ridicule and abuse. In consequence he made contact with Master Conon, his old schoolmaster, and found in him a refuge from the storm of opposition. Conon became to him a true shepherd, a spiritual father. Time spent with him was used for prayer when he learned "the use of his knees", for fellowship, for instruction in the Word of God and for spiritual upbuilding. And soon Haweis developed an interest in the salvation of others in the town.

Haweis' mind then turned to devoting his whole life to the ministry of the gospel. He had the necessary gift and ability. He had zeal. But his family had objections and he lacked the necessary resources. Walker advised that he remain at his profession till his apprenticeship expired. And meantime Conon and Walker undertook to direct and assist him in his studies, assuring him that if his "call" were of God, a door of opportunity would be opened to him. Gradually family opposition diminished and his path became clearer. Just then a visit to Truro by Joseph Jane, vicar of St. Mary Magdalene, Oxford, a fervent evangelical, shed more light on Thomas' path. Jane advocated for Thomas a course at Oxford and assured him that any associated outlay would be taken care of. In all this Thomas felt that the Lord was leading.

Thomas Haweis entered Christ Church, Oxford on 1st December 1755. On going there he determined that he would be no "idler among academic bowers", but soon found himself surrounded by temptations and indolence. He found great help in fellowship with other believers and they met together regularly for prayer and Bible study. Academically Haweis' attainments were above average and his studies progressed well. In October 1757 he was ordained deacon and duly appointed curate of St. Mary Magdalene in Oxford.

Right from the start Haweis' sermons were a bold declaration of the gospel of Jesus Christ and met with a storm of opposition, both from the student mob and from the University authorities. He was insulted. Stones were thrown through the windows of the church as he preached. Then some students, out of curiosity, went to hear him. Some who went to mock stayed to pray. Large crowds, both of gownsmen and of townsmen, flocked to the church. But a strong prejudice against Haweis and his message still remained and the ecclesiastical hierarchy took steps to evict all students from his church.

The climax came in 1761 when John Hume, the newly appointed Archbishop of Oxford, turned up the heat of persecution against him. He accused Haweis of kindling a flame in the University and declared that it must be suppressed. The outcome was that Haweis was expelled from Oxford, solely for the reason that he preached the gospel. Haweis then went to London.

In London Haweis was offered hospitality in the home of Martin Madan at Knightsbridge and there he was shown much kindness. He was given a post as assistant in the Chaplaincy of the Lock Hospital. The Lock, at that time, was the stronghold of London evangelism and linked with such names as Henry Venn, William Romaine, Martin Madan and Thomas Jones. Haweis now joined them. In the hospital he found his earlier medical training valuable as he ministered to the unfortunate patients, the majority of whom were victims of venereal disease. There was ample opportunity also for preaching. Besides a chapel in the hospital grounds, he was invited to preach in the evangelical chapels of the Countess of Huntingdon. In London many valuable contacts were made and there he remained till 1764 when he was inducted as "Rector of All Saints, Aldwincle" in Northamptonshire.

Aldwincle was a small village; the parish and the church were also small. But there Thomas Haweis lived and laboured for more than forty years. When he began his ministry he found the people totally ignorant of the truths of the gospel. On preaching his first sermon, one who was present commented, "He preached Christ uphill and down all the way through". And that initial sermon was the pattern for the years that followed. People flocked to hear him. Conversions were many and frequent, oftimes of the most unlikely people and sometimes of whole families. His care for the flock was exemplary. Homes were visited regularly, the sick and the aged were helped by his ministrations, both medically and spiritually. Family altars were reared in the homes of the people, for generally such had not been in existence before his coming. Each evening his home was open to his parishioners, and there they came to benefit from his exposition of the Scriptures. Thomas Haweis' early days at Aldwincle were happy and blessed days.

But soon the enemy got to work and Thomas found himself at the centre of a controversy pertaining to the legality of his holding of the living at Aldwincle. Accusations were levelled against him; scurrilous attacks were made upon his character. The year 1768 was dark and shadowed. Then there beamed into his life the sunshine of another life, that of Judith Wordsworth, and this helped dispel the shadows. They were married early in 1771. The parishioners termed them "the happy pair" and Judith proved an invaluable helpmate. In the following year Thomas returned to his university studies, this time to Cambridge, and from there, in July 1772, was awarded the degree of Bachelor of Laws.

The smallness of the parish at Aldwincle permitted Thomas, with periodic curate help, to absence himself from the parish for appreciable periods of time. In 1774 he was appointed Chaplain to the Countess of Huntingdon and this entailed preaching in her many private chapels throughout the land. He wrote of that appointment, "A great door and effectual is opened unto me". His itinerary took him to places as scattered as Brighton, London, Bath and Bristol.

All this burden of duty, however, took its toll upon Thomas' health and a break was needed. A spell in his native Cornwall reinvigorated him and he soon returned to his parish at Aldwincle. Then in 1786 he suffered a great loss in the unexpected death of Judith. "My heart fled daily to the Great Refuge. He supported me under the stroke of His hand. He allowed me to mourn but preserved me from murmuring". And he added, "I preached with flowing tears the Lord's day following her sepulture".

The winter following Judith's death was spent in Wales. A.S. Wood, his biographer, says, "It was here, in the land of song, that Haweis the hymnwriter was born. His sorrow taught him to sing". There he composed hymns, many with accompanying suitable melodies. Thomas was a great advocate of congregational hymn singing. Then two years later Thomas remarried. His second wife, Jennett Payne Orton, had been an acquaintance of many years. Prior to their marriage she had been the companion of Lady Huntingdon.

Thomas Haweis' zeal for the proclamation of the gospel knew no bounds, and in the year 1789 he sought to unburden an exercise he had carried for many years. He desired to train, equip and send out young missionaries with the message of the gospel. He wrote,

"For years I have planned, prayed for, and sought for an opening for a mission among the heathen". Thomas kindled a flame within the hearts of others in the city of London and this exercise led to the birth of the London Missionary Society. How his heart rejoiced to see the first expedition of some thirty young men, on board "The Duff" under Captain James Wilson, sail for the South Sea Islands to take the message of salvation "where His adorable Name hath never yet been heard, but the god of this world still reigns, the uncontrolled tyrant over the bodies and souls of men"!

In the year 1799 Haweis lost his second wife. His third marriage was in 1802 to Elizabeth Mc Dowall (Bessy), who proved a great comfort to him in his declining years. After forty-four years in Aldwincle Thomas and Bessy moved to Bath and there, for the remaining twelve years of his life, they made their home at Beauford Buildings. Then, after an illness of some six weeks, Thomas passed away at the ripe age of eighty-six. His body was laid to rest in Bath Abbey, where today a fitting memorial marks the spot.

The quietude of parish life at Aldwincle permitted Thomas to concentrate on his literary interests and the fruits of those labours have been left for us in his *Bible Commentary*, his *New Testament translation*, his *Life of William Romaine* and his *Church History* besides many other lesser works.

Thomas Haweis' contribution to hymnology has been noteworthy. In 1792 he published his *Carmino Christo; or, Hymns to the Saviour*, a collection of hymns by Isaac Watts, Philip Doddridge, Charles Wesley, John Newton, William Cowper, Joseph Hart and others. Its fullest edition (1808) contained two hundred and fifty-six hymns and included quite a number of his own composition. Few of his hymns are sung today apart from his **"Behold the Lamb of God"**, which is still widely used in gospel work.

Behold the Lamb of God,
Who bore a vile world's sin,
Look unto Him and be thou saved;
The promise takes thee in.

More marred than any man's,
The Saviour's visage see;
Was ever sorrow like to His,
Endured on Calvary?

BEHOLD THE LAMB OF GOD

Gaze on His thorn-wreathed brow,
Behold the crimson tide
Flow from His head, His hands, His feet,
And from His piercèd side.

O, hear that startling cry!
What can it's meaning be:
"My God, my God, O, why hast Thou
In wrath forsaken Me?"

O, 'twas because our sins
On Him by God were laid;
He, who Himself had never sinned,
For sinners, sin was made.

Thus sin He put away,
Thus justice satisfied;
And sinners all who Jesus trust
Through Him are justified.

> *For God so loved the world,*
> *He gave His only Son*
> *That whosoever Him believes,*
> *Eternal woe should shun.*

Thomas Haweis dearly loved the gospel. The proclamation of its message was his life-long burden.

For over sixty years he exulted to tell out its essential truth, "that man had sinned but Christ had died".

The Cross was ever central. The Cross was God's answer to sin. The Cross was the only answer to sin.

The load of sin! — The Lamb of God!
The load upon the Lamb!
"Behold the Lamb of God, which taketh away the sin of the world"
(John 1:29).

"Blest be the tie that binds"

John Fawcett (1739/40-1817)

John Fawcett

High up among the windswept moors of the Yorkshire Pennines on the slopes of Calderdale lies the little hamlet of Wainsgate. Naturally, it is bleak and barren; spiritually, it has been enriched by the life and ministry of John Fawcett. There, with a heart knit to the hearts of a poor, illiterate, yet warm-hearted rural community, John penned the words of the dearly loved hymn, "Blest be the tie that binds".

John Fawcett was born 6th January 1740 (possibly 1739) into a large family on a small farm at Lidget Green. In the eighteenth century Lidget Green was a distinct village in the West Riding of Yorkshire some miles east of Wainsgate. Today it is wholly absorbed within the city of Bradford. John was brought up in humble circumstances and, when he was twelve, his father died leaving his mother a widow with several young children. The early loss of his father caused John much grief and deep spiritual concern. He desired to be right with God. By candlelight he read Bunyan's "Pilgrim's Progress" and longed to become a "pilgrim". He perused Baxter's "Call to the Unconverted" and his "One Thing Needful". Oftimes he joined his older brother, who had similar concerns, for times of prayer in the barn.

At the age of thirteen John was apprenticed to a tradesman in Bradford where he remained for six years. The hours of his master's service were onerous, from 6 a.m. to 8 p.m. each day. About this time George Whitefield, the field preacher, came to Bradford and John resolved to attend his preaching. On his very first attendance Whitefield had taken as his text John 3:14, "As Moses lifted up the serpent in the wilderness, even so must the Son of Man be lifted up", and from it preached the gospel in the power of the Spirit of God. Under that message John was converted to God. Looking back on his experience, John afterwards recorded, "As long as life remains I shall remember both the text and the sermon". The light of the gospel had beamed into his soul, his fears were dispelled and he was filled with joy unspeakable. That memorable event was in the month of September 1755. John was then in his sixteenth year.

John immediately identified himself with the Methodist movement. He frequented George Whitefield's meetings held in Bradford City, where, in the mornings Whitefield preached to companies of some ten thousand people and in the afternoons and evenings to approximately twice that number. At those meetings the Spirit of God worked mightily, many prostrating themselves before God under conviction of sin and crying out, "What must I do to be saved?" And of those thus convicted, many found peace in believing.

At the age of nineteen John was baptized by immersion and afterwards threw in his lot with the Baptists of Bradford City. In the same year he married Susannah, daughter of John Skirrow of Bingley, a godly young woman who, though five years his senior, proved to be a real "helpmeet" in every way. All their years of married life were lived in humble circumstances and often on the breadline. John had but one ambition, to live his life for God. Shortly after his marriage he wrote,

> *Lord, teach me how to watch and pray,*
> *To keep my heart from day to day,*

> *To try each motive of the mind*
> *And check the rising lusts I find.*
>
> *Do Thou my sensual heart renew*
> *And pardon my transgressions too;*
> *Give strength to walk on duty's road,*
> *That narrow path that leads to God.*

John had aspirations after holiness of life and this led to his practice of rising early in the mornings for a time of prayer, self-examination, confession of sin, Bible study and meditation. On his twenty-second birthday he wrote again,

> *A fruitless branch I long have been;*
> *O! purge me now, and make me thrive;*
> *That I may flourish fresh and green,*
> *The days which yet I have to live.*

John procured a Hebrew Bible and this acquisition was both a treasure and a stimulus to deeper Bible study. He undertook public speaking and preached with conviction and boldness. At the close of 1763 he visited Wainsgate for the first time. Taking as his morning text, 1 John 3:2, "Beloved, now are we the sons of God" and as his evening text, Psalm 51:17, "The sacrifices of God are a broken spirit", he ministered warmly the precious truths of God to a struggling little company there. Their hearts were warmed and won. He was asked to go back and in the following year (1765) was pressed upon to settle amongst them and be their minister. He went and, though there was no parsonage in which to live (only "boarding around"), a burden of responsibility weighed heavily upon his heart. "O my soul! What a work hast thou entered upon!" He felt unworthy of his calling. Notwithstanding, he endeavoured to preach Christ among them and from house to house. Many travelled long distances to hear him. The Lord greatly blessed John's early labours at Wainsgate. Soon their place of assembly became too small and a gallery was added to the little meeting house. Those were days to be remembered. John rejoiced to see the new converts "walk in the truth" and diligently "watched for their souls".

John's labours, however, extended beyond the confines of Wainsgate. He preached in other parts of Yorkshire and Lancashire, going at times to the cities of Liverpool and London. In the latter he deputised at Carter's Lane for Dr. J. Gill, who, at that time was aged and infirm. Then, when Dr. Gill died in 1772, John was invited to take up permanent residence there and be their minister. The prospects in London were good, much better than among the little company at Wainsgate, both in terms of spiritual usefulness and in material return. (At Wainsgate his income never exceeded twenty-five pounds per annum, his frugal dwelling at the edge of the moors was inconvenient and exceedingly cramped for his growing family of young children.) He weighed matters up before the Lord and decided to go to London. Part of the furniture and books were sold, he preached his farewell sermon and preparations were made for departure. But the bond of mutual affection between him and the little flock would not suffer him to leave. He decided to stay. He would live and die among them. John never regretted his decision to stay with the little flock. In fact, when other calls to wider service came his way, (as in 1793, when, after the death of Dr. Caleb Evans, he was invited to succeed him as President of the Baptist Academy in Bristol) John gracefully declined each of these honours. His heart was knit to his own people.

At Wainsgate John experienced many trials. In 1774 a scourge of smallpox entered the home and four of his children were laid low with the plague. His second child, a boy of four, the darling of his mother, was taken. Just after his burial John penned the lines,

> *Deep in the grave his body sleeping lies*
> *'Till Jesus comes and bids the dead arise.*
> *His happy spirit dwells above the skies.*

Then the day following his boy's funeral, John himself was suddenly struck down with excruciating pain and scorching fever. After months of confinement, when both family and parishioners feared he was going to leave them, John entered the pulpit again and, though unable to stand, ministered to them an unforgettable message from Phil. 1:23,24, "I am in a strait betwixt two, having a desire to depart, and to be with Christ; which is far better: Nevertheless to abide in the flesh is more needful for you". Some eleven years later John buried his eldest daughter, aged nineteen, yet in her passing he was greatly comforted in that she belonged to Christ. Further sorrows followed, and in 1810, Susannah, his life-long partner, was taken from his side. Together they had shared intimately through life and John was at her side right to the close.

John, in his ministry, perceived a tremendous potential in youth and in this sphere he concentrated much effort. He conducted a large Sunday school in the neighbourhood. He acquired a schoolroom for the teaching of the Word of God. He set up a school to train young men for the Lord's service. Besides, he wrote a book for young children, *The History of John Wise*. This was read eagerly by the children and was greatly used of God. In 1778 he published his, *Advice to youth, on the advantages of early Piety*, and within its pages he spake from his heart to the hearts of his readers. He told them that as he was writing, "Death and eternity are before my eyes".

By the year 1777 further increase in the congregation at Wainsgate called for yet larger and better premises. A plot of ground was secured further down the valley at Hebden Bridge and there a new building, "Ebenezer", capable of seating five hundred to six hundred people, was erected for a total cost of five hundred pounds. There, at Hebden Bridge, John remained among his people for the remainder of his ministerial life. His closing message to them was taken from Nahum 1:7. "The LORD is good, a strong hold in the day of trouble; and He knoweth them that trust in Him". In that unforgettable message John recalled the goodness of God through all their days of trouble.

In the year 1810, the year of Susannah's death, John was pressed upon to speak at the Annual Baptist Association meeting in Bradford. He was poor in health, yet he consented to go. Joshua 23:14 was his text, "Behold, this day, I am going the way of all the earth". He entitled his message, *The important journey from this world to the next*. He was taking his final leave of the people of this world. He said, "Let no one in this congregation rest one day longer without knowing where he is going. Negligence in this argues a state of insensibility that wants a name". There was not a dry eye in the company. Hearts were melted. God had spoken.

John, after a few years of increasing feebleness suffered a sudden stroke at the close. He lingered a few days, then passed away peacefully into the presence of his Lord on the 25th July 1817. His last words were, "Come, Lord Jesus, come quickly". His body was laid to rest, beside that of his wife, Susannah, in the burial plot belonging to the old Wainsgate Church.

John, throughout life, had lived and ministered in obscure and humble circumstances. Notwithstanding, he has left for us a rich legacy in his writings, both prose and verse. *The Sick Man's Employ* was the outcome of his severe illness in 1774 when he hovered between life and death. *Advice to Youth, on the Advantages of Early Piety* was published in 1778, *The Cross of Christ – the Christian's Glory* appeared in 1793, *Christ, precious to them that believe* in 1799. His commentary on the Scriptures, *The Devotional Family Bible* (published in 1811) was the fruit of his lifelong study of the Scriptures, its preparation occupying the years 1807 – 1811. John composed verse periodically throughout life. His early compositions, written during his Bradford years, were published as *Poetic Essays* in 1767. His later verse, *Hymns adapted to the circumstances of Public Worship and Private Devotion* was published in 1782 and contained one hundred and sixteen pieces.

Of all John Fawcett's verse, one hymn stands out above the others. It is his **"Blest be the tie that binds"**. Of its writing, Josiah Miller in his "Singers and Songs of the Church" says, "This favourite hymn is said to have been written in 1772, to commemorate the determination of its author to remain with the attached people at Wainsgate. The farewell sermon was preached, the wagons were loaded, when love and tears prevailed, and Dr. Fawcett sacrificed the attractions of a London pulpit to the affection of his poor but devoted flock".

John entitled the hymn, "Brotherly Love". *"We have fellowship one with another"* (1 John 1:7).

> *Blest be the tie that binds*
> *Our hearts in Christian love;*
> *The fellowship of kindred minds*
> *Is like to that above.*
>
> *Before our Father's throne*
> *We pour our ardent prayers;*
> *Our fears, our hopes, our aims are one,*
> *Our comforts and our cares.*
>
> *We share our mutual woes,*
> *Our mutual burdens bear;*
> *And often for each other flows*
> *The sympathizing tear.*
>
> *When we asunder part,*
> *It gives us inward pain;*
> *But we shall still be joined in heart,*
> *And hope to meet again.*

The *"tie that binds"* together the children of God is a *"blest"* bond. It is a precious fellowship, *"like to that above"*, high and heavenly, intimate and trustful, pure and beautiful, ongoing and uninterrupted, unclouded and transparent. Its very foundation is love. It is to be treasured highly, cultivated diligently and guarded jealously. Indeed, if esteemed lightly or if other loves intervene, it will most certainly be lost.
Self is a great enemy.

"Little children — love one another"

" 'Twas on that night, when doomed to know"

John Morison (1746-1798)

John Morison

The ancient church of Canisbay lies some three miles west of John O' Groats and is the most northerly church on the Scottish mainland. It stands on a historic mound and commands an imposing view of the Pentland Firth. Saturated in history, it dates back to long before the Reformation, possibly to the sixth century. In recent years it has had the added distinction of the attendance of the late Queen Elizabeth, the Queen Mother, when in residence at the nearby Castle of Mey.

Canisbay Parish and its parishioners are unique, probably best portrayed in Elsie Cowe's verse, "Canisbay Parish".

Far to the North it lies,
Washed by the sea,
Spread under spacious skies,
Our parish Canisbay.

Peatland and fertile field,
Flagstone dykes for lea,
Havens with boat and creel,
Our parish Canisbay.

Surging seas of spume and spray,
Tides of treachery,
Stern cliffs stand amid the fray,
Our parish Canisbay.

Warm hearts and loyal friends,
Kindred, fidelity,
Open doors, and hands extend,
Our parish Canisbay.

Here at Canisbay, in the late eighteenth century, John Morison discharged a notable ministry.

John Morison, son of George Morison and Isobel Robertson, was born on his father's farm of Whitehill in the Parish of Cairnie, Aberdeenshire on 18th September 1746. He was educated at Ruthven School (near Cairnie) under Mr. John Davidson and Mr. John Dawson. The latter discerned in young Morison an unusual ability, and forecast that one day he would rise to fame. Though at that time Latin was not in the curriculum of the Society schools, John Dawson made an exception with Morison and taught him the rudiments of that language. But John's school days soon ended and he went home to help on the farm.

Then an interesting incident occurred and this changed the whole course of John's life. Its story has been related by James J. Calder M.A. minister of Cairnie, and afterwards recorded by Donald Beaton. "Like so many other Scottish lads who have risen to fame, Morison, after leaving school, was called to tend the cattle on the farm. He was, however, a much better scholar than a herd, and sometimes, as will happen with boys, his eyes closed in sleep and his charge wandered at will in forbidden pastures. On one of these occasions he dreamt that someone presented him with a beautiful volume entitled 'Goschen'. The lad was enraptured with the visionary gift, but on coming back to the world of reality he was confronted by his father, who upbraided him for negligence. His mother, however, on hearing the dream, with a mother's partiality and a woman's quickness of perception, encouraged her boy by saying to him, 'You'll get your book; for you will be sent back to school and herd no more' ". And so began again John's scholastic career which was later to take him to University.

John studied at King's College, Aberdeen and graduated M.A. in 1771. Then after serving as tutor to two well-known Scottish families, he went to Thurso in 1773 as Master of its parish school. There he met John Logan, who at that time was tutor to the Sinclair family of Ulbster. (The name of John Logan would afterwards be linked with John Morison in connection with "The Scottish Translations and Paraphrases".)

After a period of further study in Edinburgh, John was engaged as tutor to the family of Colonel Sutherland of Uppat. While there John Sinclair of Freswick, Sheriff of Caithness, presented him to the Parish of Canisbay as candidate for their expected ministerial vacancy and on 26th September of the following year (1780) John was ordained their minister. Indeed, Sinclair was so impressed with John's literary attainments and potential that he took a special interest in him. "After his settlement, so warmly was he interested in him, that he ploughed his glebe, and sowed it with seed taken from his own barn; cut and drove home his peats, and cut and stacked the whole of his crop".

At Canisbay, John Morison preached Christ. Though of a retiring disposition he was an able preacher. Among his parishioners he was highly honoured and greatly beloved. He in turn dearly loved them and laboured among them to the end that he might gather in a people to the praise of Christ's Name. He spent himself entirely for them, seeking not only their spiritual welfare but also their physical welfare and in this regard he instigated the erection of lighthouses at Duncansby Head and the Pentland Skerries to safely guide the fishermen through the treacherous waters of Pentland Firth.

After some eighteen years among those hardy fishermen and crofters of that Northern Shore, the ministry of John Morison came to a close. He was taken from them at the early age of fifty-one. He had succumbed to consumption, brought on by exposure to wet and cold, and passed away on 17th June 1798. Today, in the wall of Canisbay windswept churchyard, a sculptured stone stands to his memory.

John Morison's greatest memorial, however, stems from his

scholarship. Much has come from his pen. In early life he contributed poetical pieces to the Edinburgh Weekly Magazine under the signature of "Musaeus". His poems, *"Epithalamium on the marriage of Eliza"*, *"On the approach of winter"* and *"Lexina Indisposed, an ode"* have been highly praised. He wrote An Account of the Parish of Canisbay, a Topographical History of Caithness for Chalmer's "Caledonia" and translated Herodian's History from the Greek.

John Morison's work on "The Translations and Paraphrases", however, is his greatest literary work of all. In the early eighteenth century there was no such thing in Scotland as hymns and paraphrases. The Scottish Church had to content herself with the often-rugged verse of the Psalter. The question then came to be asked, "Can nothing be done to improve our congregational singing? — Might not the Psalms of the OT be supplemented by paraphrases of important passages from NT Scriptures?" A Committee was formed by the General Assembly to attend to this matter and in 1781 Dr. John Morison was added as a member. Prior to this appointment John had submitted twenty-four paraphrases and seven of these had been accepted. Of the seven John was the sole author of five; of the other two he was joint author with John Logan.

The best known of John Morison's paraphrases are Paraphrase No.30 and Paraphrase No.35.

Paraphrase No.30 is a paraphrase of Hosea 6:1-4 and has been judged by James Mearns, "one of the finest of the Paraphrases".

> *Come, let us to the Lord our God with contrite hearts return;*
> *Our God is gracious, nor will leave the desolate to mourn.*

It has been generally agreed that his viewing the frequent changing moods of the Pentland Firth from the end-window of his manse inspired his rendering of its second stanza.

> *His voice commands the tempest forth, and stills the stormy wave;*
> *And though His arm be strong to smite, 'tis also strong to save.*

But it is Paraphrase No.35, **" 'Twas on that night when doomed to know"**, a paraphrase of Matt. 26:26-29 that is the best known of all Morison's verse. Its original, as submitted by him to the Committee, received some alteration at their hand and it is this altered form that in widely used today.

'Twas on that night, when doomed to know
The eager rage of every foe,
That night in which He was betrayed,
The Saviour of the world took bread.

And after thanks and glory given,
To Him that rules in earth and heaven,
That symbol of His flesh He broke,
And thus to all His followers spoke:

My broken body thus I give
For you, for all; take, eat, and live:
And oft the sacred rite renew,
That brings My wondrous love to view.

Then in His hands the cup He raised,
And God anew He thanked and praised,
While kindness in His bosom glowed,
And from His lips salvation flowed.

My blood I thus pour forth, He cries,
To cleanse the soul in sin that lies;
In this the covenant is sealed,
And heaven's eternal grace revealed.

With love to man this cup is fraught,
Let all partake the sacred draught;
Through latest ages let it pour
In memory of My dying hour.

This paraphrase bears some resemblance to Andreas Ellinger's Latin hymn of the sixteenth century, translated later into English by William Archibald of Unst, Shetland. Some have suggested that Morison's paraphrase is but a modification of this but those authorities living nearer to his time attribute it solely to John Morison.

It is a great hymn. Duncan Morrison in 1890 said, "Any hymn that like this has maintained its place through the siftings of generations, — that has stood the crucible of the public taste and met the devotional feeling of the Church in its deepest and purest hours for one hundred years and more, has asserted its right to live". This is one of these hymns; it has stood the winnowing process of years. It is marked by purity, simplicity, solemnity, fidelity to the Scriptures and warm devotion.

Its theme is the institution of **the Lord's supper**.

The scene is an Upper Room in Jerusalem. It is our Lord's last night with His own. His actions are of solemn beauty and are set as a precious jewel against a dark background. "Jesus took bread, and blessed, and brake, and gave". "He took the cup, and gave thanks and gave". We hear Him say to His own, "Take, eat; this is My body". "Drink – this is My blood". In that act, simplicity and profundity combine. We may not understand all of its fullest import. Nevertheless, in simple obedience we keep it, *"in memory of His dying hour"*.

The request is His. The keeping is ours.

"O Lord, I would delight in Thee"

John Ryland (1753-1825)

John Ryland

"When", it has been finely said, "when, towards the close of the eighteenth century, it pleased God to awaken from her slumbers a drowsy and lethargic church, there rung out, from the belfry of the ages, a clamorous and insistent alarm; and in that arousing hour, the hand upon the bellrope was the hand of William Carey".

William Carey was a church pastor, first at Moulton, then at Leicester. Besides, he was a schoolmaster and a cobbler, and from these three vocations he earned an income of some thirty-six pounds a year. But when the hour arrived, Carey cast aside the shackles of prejudice and superstition associated with Church life. He had had a vision of a world in need and was determined to do something about it. He was firm in his resolve. Once as a boy he said to his mother, after retrieving a bird's nest from the top of a forbidden tree, "If I begin a thing, I must go through with it!" William Carey never looked back, but took as his life's motto, "Expect great things from God; attempt great things for God".

But William Carey was not alone in his enterprise for God; there were others with him. At that time there was a small group of godly Baptist ministers known as the Ministers' Fraternal of the Northampton Association. In one of their meetings Andrew Fuller remarked, "there is a gold mine in India, but it seems almost as deep as the centre of the earth", to which William Carey promptly replied, "I will venture to go down but remember that you (and here he addressed the others of the company) must hold the ropes". And hold the ropes they did! They entered into covenant that "they would never cease till death to stand by him". But none was more faithful in their commitment than John Ryland. For, from that day and right until the time of his death thirty-three years later, John Ryland upheld Carey as he laboured for God in India, in a multitude of practical ways, by regular correspondence and especially in prevailing prayer.

John Ryland was born in Warwick on 29th January 1753. His father, John Collett Ryland, was pastor of the Particular Baptist Church there, though he lived in the parsonage of the Established Church. When some complained to the parson about letting out the parsonage to an Anabaptist, the parson replied, "And what would you have me to do? I have brought him as near to the church as I can, but I cannot force him into it". But John Ryland, the elder, was not to be enticed. He was a man of conviction. He was, besides, a man of great learning, a master in the Hebrew and Greek languages, and saw to it that his family also had a thorough education.

John Ryland, the younger, the subject of this sketch, attended his father's academy. He was a child of outstanding mental ability and a genius at languages and literature. At the age of eleven his father stated of him, "He has read Genesis in Hebrew five times through; he read through the Greek Testament before nine years old. He can read Horace and Virgil. He has read through Telemachus in French". But it was John's mother who was his mentor in spiritual matters. She was a godly woman and taught young John his Bible history, as he sat upon her knee, from the illustrations on the Dutch tiles surrounding the parlour fireplace, like as Mrs. Doddridge had instructed her young son, Philip, some fifty years before.

When John was six his father assumed the Baptist pastorate in Northampton and the family moved there from Warwick. At the age of fourteen John experienced "a great spiritual change" and afterwards was baptized by his father in the river Nen near Northampton and received into the membership of his father's church. For several years John helped in his father's school while at the same time furthering his own education. By the age of eighteen he was an able preacher and was then ordained and appointed as co-pastor with his father in the Baptist Church at Northampton. Then, when his father moved to London, John succeeded him as sole pastor at Northampton.

John Ryland, the younger, had a remarkable ministry in Northampton. In many ways he was quite unlike his father who was "a vehement gruff Calvinist" and who, on one occasion, rebuked young William Carey for proposing that it be openly discussed, "Whether the command given to the apostles to teach all nations was not binding on all succeeding ministers to the end of the world?" To which the elder Ryland abruptly responded, "Young man, sit down. You're an enthusiast. When God pleases to convert the heathen, He'll do it without your aid and mine". But not so the younger Ryland. He had caught the vision of a needy world and was in the forefront of the Northamptonshire missionary exercise at that time.

The outcome of that enterprise was the birth of the Baptist Missionary Society. Its first meeting was held in a house in Kettering. John Ryland, the younger, and William Carey were founder members. Ryland at that time was thirty-nine, Carey was thirty-one and the others were of a similar age. William Carey became their first missionary. The young "enthusiast" took the gospel to the dark subcontinent of India, and for over forty years without a break, he engaged in preaching, establishing churches, founding schools and translating the Holy Scriptures. He advanced in the Indian languages to become Professor of Sanskrit, Bengali and Mahratta at Fort William College in Calcutta and, before his death, saw the translation, printing and distribution of some two hundred thousand Bibles (or portions thereof) in about forty Indian languages or dialects. And throughout all those years, back at home, John Ryland "held the ropes".

In the year 1794 John Ryland moved to Bristol to accept the Presidency of the Baptist College, following on the death of Mr. Caleb Evans. This included the pastorate of the historic Broadmead Chapel in Bristol and these two offices Ryland retained and filled admirably until his death in 1825. In the College and in the city of Bristol he wielded a tremendous influence for God. He maintained his vision of the need of a wider world and encouraged many young students in overseas missionary work. And on the death of Andrew Fuller in 1815 Ryland took over responsibility as secretary of the Baptist Missionary Society.

By his late sixties Ryland's health started to fail and each ensuing year found him getting weaker and weaker. Then, on 25th June 1825, he passed away peacefully to be with Christ, his last captured utterance being the phrase, "no more pain".

The passing of John Ryland brought a tremendous sense of loss to all that knew him. A faithful pastor, an outstanding preacher, a teacher with tremendous mental ability and of considerable learning, a tutor and an author had been taken from their midst. But that sense of loss was no more keenly felt than in the heart of William Carey in India. Ryland had baptized Carey in the river Nen and had been his most trusted human prop through all his years overseas. The loss was incalculable. Notwithstanding, Carey continued with the task that lay before him, for God was more to him than human props.

John Ryland had been revered through life as a man of fine scholarship and in recognition of that had been awarded a Doctorate by Brown University of Rhode Island, U.S.A. During his lifetime several of his prose works received publication and after his death a selection of his discourses was printed in two volumes, as *Pastoral Memorials*. John Ryland, besides, was a hymnwriter. Some of his earliest verse appeared while he was still in his teens and he continued to write verse up until the time of his death. His compositions first appeared in various magazines during his lifetime and were signed, "J. R., Jun." Then in 1862, Daniel Sedgwick collected together some ninety-nine of Dr. Ryland's hymns from the original manuscripts and these were published as, *Hymns and Verses on Various Subjects*.

John Ryland's hymns were plain and simple. Dr. John Julian

judged that "they lack poetry and passion". Nevertheless a few of them have survived. Two of the best known are, his children's hymn, "Lord, teach a little child to pray", composed at the request of Andrew Fuller's wife of Kettering for the use of her little girl, Sarah, who died at the age of six and a half, and his hymn, **"O Lord, I would delight in Thee"**.

This latter hymn was entitled, "Delight in Christ" and dated December 3, 1777. There were seven verses in all, though only five appear in most collections. Of its composition Dr. Ryland recorded in the original manuscript, "I recollect deeper feelings of mind in composing this hymn, than perhaps I ever felt in making any other". The complete hymn may be found in Dr. Rippon's collection. Six of its verses are to be found in the "Light and Love" hymnal and five in "The Believers Hymn Book".

> *O Lord, I would delight in Thee,*
> *And on Thy care depend;*
> *To Thee in every trouble flee,*
> *My best, my only Friend.*
>
> *When all created streams are dried,*
> *Thy fullness is the same;*
> *May I with this be satisfied,*
> *And glory in Thy Name!*
>
> *Why should the soul a drop bemoan,*
> *Who has a fountain near, –*
> *A fountain which will ever run*
> *With waters sweet and clear?*
>
> *No good in creatures can be found*
> *But may be found in Thee;*
> *I must have all things, and abound,*
> *While God is God to me.*
>
> *O that I had a stronger faith*
> *To look within the veil!*
> *To credit what my Saviour saith,*
> *Whose word can never fail!*

> *He, that has made my heaven secure,*
> *Will here all good provide;*
> *While Christ is rich, can I be poor?*
> *What can I want beside?*
>
> *O Lord, I cast my care on Thee;*
> *I triumph and adore;*
> *Henceforth my great concern shall be*
> *To love and please Thee more.*

Dr. Ryland judged the resources in Christ to be sufficient for his every need. They were both inexhaustible and available; there was no need for him to be poor.

"O blessèd God! how kind"

John Kent (1766-1843)

John Kent

John Kent was a Congregationalist. He was born into a large family in the town of Bideford in Devonshire in December 1766. His parents were poor materially, but rich in faith. They worked hard to meet the temporal needs of the family but their greater burden was the spiritual welfare of their children. They brought them up in the fear of the Lord and prayed much for them. God graciously heard their prayer and early in life four of the family trusted the Saviour. John was the youngest among that number but the circumstances of his conversion are unknown.

At the age of fourteen John was apprenticed to his father who was a shipwright in Plymouth Dock (now known as Devonport). John had a great thirst for knowledge and used all his spare time for the furtherance of his education as best he could. There were no resources for any formal education. However, John had been naturally endowed with a rich poetic talent and in his youth he started to compose verse.

John was of a cheerful disposition. He had boundless energy and packed much into life. He was a man of sincere conviction and high principle with an uncanny insight for detecting error or deceit. Any falsehood he immediately stripped of its deceptive garb and exposed it for what it was. John's Christian life was genuine and his manner of life bore testimony to its reality.

In the year 1803 John published his early verse, *A Collection of Original Gospel Hymns*. The unusual quality of his verse in this collection was much appreciated and its publication brought him into public notice as a hymnwriter. He continued to exercise this poetic talent throughout his busy life and, as he had opportunity, wrote many hymns and poems.

But John, ere he had reached his sixtieth birthday, was overtaken by blindness. He bore this heavy affliction with great fortitude and patience and regarded it as laid upon him by a wise and tender Father. Though obliged to lay aside his pen, he continued with his compositions for a further seventeen years; his little grandson became his amanuensis.

In later life John was severely tried by family bereavements but through it all he felt upheld by an Almighty hand. The year 1843 brought severe personal testing when he was afflicted by a painful and distressing illness and for several days at a stretch experienced unremitting and intense agony. Even in this he proved the promise of his Lord, "Thou art with me".

However, the end was drawing near. Several of his sayings from his last days of suffering have been placed on record and bear witness to the steadfastness of his faith. "I bless God that the promises of the gospel met me in all my wants, wounds and wretchedness". " 'We must all appear before the judgement seat of Christ'. That portion has cut me to the heart, while at the same time it has been my hope. If I am to stand by myself to give an account, I am lost, lost for ever; but it is the judgement seat of Christ; and He is my surety, and has paid all demands. I shall be tried by a covenant of grace, not a covenant of works; blessed be God for His great salvation".

The close came on 15th November 1843, but shortly before he

died he declared, "The war with Amalek will soon be over". Then he extended his hand and exclaimed, "I rejoice in hope; I am accepted – accepted!" and thus John Kent passed away triumphantly to be with his Lord. His seventy-seven years of earthly pilgrimage were ended.

John Kent was poor and uneducated through life, and for a period was blind, yet, despite such disadvantages, he was rich in faith, in talent, and in application, and left behind him a legacy in his verse. His 1803 publication, *A Collection of Original Gospel Hymns*, passed through several editions, and its last, the 10th edition, was published in 1861, after his death. This contained "The Author's Experience" in verse, two hundred and sixty-four of his hymns, fifteen longer poems and a short life of the author by his son.

Kent's hymns were somewhat different from those by other writers. Dr. John Julian judged them as "strangely worded, very earnest and simple, and intensely Calvinistic" and concluded that such features had restricted their use. Notwithstanding, some twelve of Kent's compositions were included by Charles H. Spurgeon in "Our Own Hymn Book" (1866) and fifteen were included by Charles B. Snepp in his "Songs of Grace and Glory" (1872).

In "The Believers Hymn Book" three of Kent's hymns appear.

"Hark! how the blood-bought hosts above". This hymn, entitled "Election", was first published in 1803.

> *Hark! how the blood-bought hosts above*
> *Conspire to chant the Saviour's love,*
> *In sweet harmonious strains!*
> *And while they strike their golden lyres,*
> *This glorious theme each bosom fires,*
> *That grace triumphant reigns!*

And Kent's singular theme throughout the four stanzas of the hymn is this, "Grace triumphant reigns!"

"O blessèd God! How kind". This hymn, entitled "Electing Love", also appeared in his 1803 publication.

> *O blessèd God! How kind*
> *Are all Thy ways to me,*
> *Whose dark benighted mind*
> *Was enmity with Thee;*
> *Yet now, subdued by sovereign grace,*
> *My spirit longs for Thine embrace.*

*How precious are Thy thoughts
That o'er my spirit roll!
They swell beyond my faults,
And captivate my soul;
How great their sum, how high they rise,
Can ne'er be known beneath the skies.*

*Preserved by Jesus, when
My feet made haste to hell;
And there should I have gone,
But Thou dost all things well;
Thy love was great, Thy mercy free,
Which from the pit delivered me.*

*Before Thy hands had made
The sun to rule the day,
Or earth's foundation laid,
Or fashioned Adam's clay,
What thoughts of peace and mercy flowed
In Thy great heart of love, O God!*

*A monument of grace,
A sinner saved by blood,
The streams of love I trace
Up to the fountain, God,
And in His sovereign counsels see
Eternal thoughts of love to me.*

This hymn, in its original form, commenced, *Indulgent God! how kind*, (indulgent being an old English word meaning 'forbearing'). There were initially six verses. (Verse No.5 is here omitted.) In its closing stanza John Kent ascribes everything of his personal salvation to the grace of God.

"Sovereign grace! O'er sin abounding". This hymn was entitled "Perseverance of the Faint" and was first published in 1827.

*Soverign grace! O'er sin abounding,
   Ransomed souls, the tidings swell;
'Tis a deep that knows no sounding;
   Who its length or breadth can tell?
      On its glories
   Let my soul for ever dwell*

And here, yet once again, the grace of God is Kent's great theme.

The grace of God was, in all probability, John Kent's favourite subject and its theme runs throughout much of his verse. In personal experience he had learned that salvation was by grace alone. The thought of grace to such a sinner as he filled his soul with deep gratitude; he spake of it oftimes to his family and as he did so tears coursed down his cheeks. And in each of these three hymns John Kent pours forth into verse his meditations on the grace of God.

A further composition, taken from his *A Collection of Original Gospel Hymns*, John had entitled **"Grace Triumphant!"** This longer poem was a memorial to the conversion and death of Jane Pitts, a character well known throughout the towns and villages of South Devon where she had lived. In early life she had plumbed the depths of sin.

> *Of human kind, the very curse and scum,*
> *Hopeless in this, and in the world to come;*
> *With God Himself an open war she waged,*
> *Nor heaven nor hell a single thought engaged:*
> *Deaf as the adder to the charming sounds*
> *Of mercy, through a Saviour's bleeding wounds,*
> *And blind to wisdom as th' encavern'd mole,*
> *She stumbled on, and sinn'd without control.*

Rays of Divine love then beamed into her darkened heart.

> *O love! Beyond the seraph's piercing eye,*
> *Where heights are lost, and depths unfathom'd lie,*
> *And length and breadth, alike are known no more,*
> *A sea without brim, bottom, brink or shore.*

The transformation in her life was beyond all telling. Jane had been "a five hundred pence debtor". Now she "loved much" and became a mighty witness for her Saviour, a living memorial to the transforming grace of God. And, when "her race was run", she took "her flight to glory and to God".

> *Saved as the dying thief, by grace alone,*
> *Who left the gibbet for a heavenly throne:*
> *At Jesu's feet her crown she humbly lays,*
> *For ever lost in wonder, love, and praise.*

> *No faith foreseen, or works, or duties done,*
> *Which thousands rest their souls immortal on,*
> *In whole, or part, the wonderous grace procured,*
> *God to Himself the glory all secured.*

Such is the grace of God, that where sin abounds grace does much more abound. Grace is both abounding and abundant. It is sovereign and it is sufficient. It not only saves but it will ultimately glorify, for this is grace's supreme and final prerogative.

When the old African woman's critics once remonstrated with her as to her total unworthiness of the salvation of God, she at once replied, "You do not understand the grace of God. When I get to heaven, the Lord will point to me and give the angels an object lesson on grace".

"An object lesson on grace!" up there in heaven — the anticipation of an old African woman.
But here and now on earth, **"A monument of grace!"** — the testimony of John Kent.

> *A monument of grace,*
>   *A sinner saved by blood,*
> *The streams of love I trace*
>   *Up to the fountain, God,*
> *And in His sovereign counsels see*
> *Eternal thoughts of love to me.*

"Our blest Redeemer, ere He breathed"

Harriet Auber (1773-1862)

Home of Harriet Auber, Hoddesdon
(Window X where hymn was inscribed)

"Our blest Redeemer, ere He breathed His tender last farewell" is a hymn by Harriet Auber. Throughout life Harriet wrote quite a lot of verse but only a fraction of her work was ever published and this is her only hymn that is sung much today. It is a hymn of great beauty, an excellent hymn on the person and work of the Holy Spirit of God. Though written initially by Harriet as she felt driven by a compelling impulse, in another sense it is the epitome of her long and beautiful life, a life nourished by the Holy Spirit and fruitful for God.

Harriet Auber came of Huguenot stock. Her great-grandfather, Pierre Auber, had fled, under persecution, from Normandy to England after the Revocation of the Edict of Nantes in 1685. Harriet was born in England, in the city of London on 4th October 1773. She was the second daughter of James Auber, rector of Tring in Hertfordshire. As a mark of her French ancestry she was christened Henriette, but throughout life she was known as Harriet.

Harriet lived her life in Hertfordshire, first at Broxbourne and then at Hoddesdon. When only a girl she got to know the Saviour and afterwards lived her life for His glory. She spent much time in communion with her Lord. She was of a gentle spirit and retiring disposition and lived a quiet and secluded life, away from the clamour of the world around her. In later years she shared the home at Hoddesdon with her intimate friend, Miss Mary Jane McKenzie, a lady of kindred spirit.

These two saintly ladies enjoyed each other's company. Both were writers. Miss McKenzie wrote prose and Miss Auber wrote poetry. Several of Miss McKenzie's devotional works received publication as, "Private Life", "Lectures on the Parables" and "Lectures on the Miracles". Harriet versified many of the Psalms and composed many poems and hymns. Thus Miss Auber and Miss McKenzie spent their days in the quietude of their Hoddesdon home.

Miss Auber lived till the ripe age of eighty-nine. She died in Hoddesdon on 20th June 1862 and was buried in the quaint old churchyard near to the home in which she had lived, and there she rests by the side of her dear friend, Miss McKenzie, who had predeceased her by a few years. They "were lovely and pleasant in their lives, and in their death they were not divided" (2 Sam. 1: 23). And for many years thereafter the memory of these two dear ladies was cherished with affection and veneration amid a wide circle of friends and relatives in Hertfordshire.

In the year 1829 a volume of verse entitled *The Spirit of the Psalms* was published anonymously. This was for the most part the verse of Harriet Auber but contained some verse by other writers besides. Harriet's contribution to this work included her versification of some of the Psalms and her verse on other devotional subjects. Interestingly, some five years later Henry Francis Lyte published another book with the same title and again this was a versification of selected Psalms. The publication of these two books about the same time and each bearing the same title, *The Spirit of the Psalms*, led, not surprisingly, to some confusion as to the authorship of some of the versified psalms. On the whole the Psalm renderings by Henry Francis Lyte survived the test of time much better than those by Harriet Auber. Notwithstanding, Harriet's work on the Psalter had merit and Dr. John Julian in his "Dictionary of Hymnology" considered several of her renderings as "full of gentle melody".

But not all of Harriet's verse has perished! One piece remains, her beautiful hymn on the Holy Spirit of God, **"Our blest Redeemer, ere He breathed His tender last farewell"**. This was one of two hymns written specially by Harriet for Whit Sunday and included in *The Spirit of the Psalms*. In its original there were seven stanzas.

> *Our blest Redeemer, ere He breathed*
> *His tender last farewell,*
> *A Guide, a Comforter bequeathed*
> *With us to dwell.*
>
> *He came in semblance of a dove,*
> *With sheltering wings outspread,*
> *The holy balm of peace and love*
> *On each to shed.*
>
> *He came in tongues of living flame*
> *To teach, convince, subdue;*
> *All-powerful as the wind He came –*
> *As viewless too.*
>
> *He came sweet influence to impart*
> *A gracious, willing Guest,*
> *While He can find one humble heart*
> *Wherein to rest.*
>
> *And His that gentle voice we hear*
> *Soft as the breath of even,*
> *That checks each fault, that calms each fear*
> *That speaks of heaven.*
>
> *And every virtue we possess,*
> *And every conquest won,*
> *And every thought of holiness,*
> *Are His alone.*

> *Spirit of purity and grace,*
> *Our weakness, pitying, see;*
> *O make our hearts Thy dwelling-place,*
> *And meet for Thee!*

It was some time after the publication of this hymn in 1829 before it came into wide general use, but once it became known it very rapidly gained popularity. It is sung today in almost every English-speaking country and has been translated into several languages. Its companion tune, "St. Cuthbert", by Dr. John B. Dykes, a notable English church musician of the nineteenth century, is most fitting and has contributed greatly to the hymn's wide acceptance.

An interesting story surrounds the circumstances of the writing of this hymn, to the effect that Miss Auber first wrote its words on a windowpane of her Hoddesdon home. It is commonly stated that a sudden rush of inspiration overwhelmed Miss Auber on that occasion and, with no pen and paper immediately to hand, she inscribed the lines on the glass pane of her bedroom window.

Not unexpectedly there has been some controversy over the authenticity of this story. In 1929, exactly one hundred years after the publication of the hymn, Miss Auber's great-niece, H. J. Harvey, wrote a letter to "The Times" denying the story. On the other hand weightier evidence in confirmation of the story has come from the Rev. Dawson Campbell, who lived for some years in Miss Auber's Hoddesdon home after her decease. He bore witness to the fact that the words were inscribed on the windowpane. And this engraved windowpane, we understand, remained in its place for some seventeen years after Miss Auber's death, then mysteriously disappeared and has never been traced.

But, though the inscribed windowpane has gone, the hymn remains. It has been termed by one writer, "a beautiful and timeless lyric". It is indeed a hymn rich both in its poetic beauty and in its Scriptural teaching. It is a fine treatise on the person and work of the Holy Spirit of God.

Of its seven stanzas the first three are historical, telling of the promise and of the coming of the Holy Spirit of God. The next three stanzas speak of this Divine person's work in the believer's life and are very practical. The concluding stanza is a fitting prayer.

The hymn commences with *our blest Redeemer* and His disciples on their last night together just prior to the Cross. The disciples were filled with sorrow at the thought of His approaching departure to the Father. Would they be left to face a hostile world alone? The Lord assured them that He would not leave them "orphans", but that "Another" would come to them when He had gone and would abide with them. This promised One would comfort them in their most trying circumstances. He would guide them through all of their unknown future, and in person He would be none less than "Another" of the Godhead, the Holy Spirit Himself. The fact that this One would definitely come to them was assured by the Saviour, "If I depart, I will send Him unto you" (John 16:7).

Harriet then speaks of the Holy Spirit's coming and in so doing uses three of Scripture's fitting symbols of His person – the dove, the fire and the wind. At the baptism of the Lord Jesus in the Jordan the Holy Spirit descended from the open heaven *in semblance of a dove* and rested upon the Beloved of the Father. Then, in fulfilment of the Saviour's promise, He came in full Pentecostal power upon the disciples as they tarried in Jerusalem, *in tongues of living flame* and *all-powerful as the wind*.

Harriet then weaves into her hymn Scripture's teaching concerning the Holy Spirit in Christian experience. This heavenly Guest comes to redeemed hearts to take up His residence. He is gentle and gracious in His manner, working patiently till all that is unholy be restrained. Fruit in the life, the fruit of the Spirit, evidences His Divine residence within. It is a lovely nine-fold cluster, "Love, joy, peace, longsuffering, gentleness, goodness, faith, meekness and temperance" (Gal. 5: 22,23). And all the while this Divine resident seeks nothing for Himself. Nor does He speak of Himself, only of the Lord Jesus. And He works within the heart to the end that everything of self may be brought to naught and Christ alone have the preeminence.

The seventh stanza is Harriet's concluding prayer and all true believers will voice their amen with its sentiment, that the heart become a worthier place of such a notable and so holy a resident.

> *Spirit of purity and grace,*
> *Our weakness, pitying, see;*
> *O make our hearts Thy dwelling-place,*
> *And meet for Thee!*

"Standing there amidst the myrtle"
("Wele'n sefyll rhwng y myrtwdd")

Ann Griffiths (1776-1805)

Ann Griffiths

    Ann Griffiths is perhaps the greatest woman poet to have written in Welsh. From a life of rural simplicity, circumscribed by the beautiful Berwyn Hills of Mid Wales and measured by a short span of twenty-nine years, she has left for Welsh speaking people a very rich treasure in verse. Much of this has been translated into English.
    Ann was born in the Spring of 1776, the third daughter and second youngest of the five children of John Evan Thomas and his wife, Jane Theodore of 'Dolwar Fach', a picturesque and remote farmhouse on the parish of Llanfihangel – yng – Ngwynfa in what was formerly known

as Montgomeryshire in Mid Wales.

Ann's father was a highly respected tenant farmer in that part, a man better educated than most men of his day and prominent in the life of the parish where he lived. Regular family devotions were held morning and evening in the home at 'Dolwar Fach' and the family, besides, attended regularly the Sunday services in the nearby Llanfihangel Parish Church. At these services, even the family dog took up its place in the pew and was known on occasions to have been the only Thomas member present!

Ann went to school for a short time, first the school of "Mas Owen y Sais" (Mrs. Owen, the English woman) and then to the church school where she learned the three "R's" (reading, writing and arithmetic). In all probability she learned some English. Ann, as a child, was very intelligent and vivacious, though not robust in health; later, as a young woman, she developed a great love for dancing.

Ann's mother died in 1794. By that time her two older sisters, Jane and Elizabeth, had already left 'Dolwar Fach' and consequently the responsibility for the running of the home fell to Ann, who was then only seventeen years of age.

At that particular period Wales was experiencing a great revival. The Methodist movement was sweeping throughout the Principality and Ann's eldest brother, John, was the first of the Thomas family to come under its influence. Through the reading of Richard Baxter's book, "The Saints' Everlasting Rest", he was awakened to his need of personal salvation. He consulted his parish clergyman who decried such an idea and advised that he indulge a little more in the normal pastimes of the day. The Spirit of God, however, had His way and John came to know the Lord Jesus as his personal Saviour. This saving grace extended to other members of the household and John Evan Thomas, the father, together with several members of his immediate family were soon rejoicing in personal salvation through the Lord Jesus. The people of the parish, however, belittled such things. Ann joined in the derision, even at times speaking mockingly of those who professed to have had such an experience.

Prejudices however, were soon broken down and in the summer of 1796 Ann came into her own personal experience of salvation. She had gone on a particular evening to attend a dance in the old town of Llanfyllin. There she met with a former family servant who persuaded her to go instead to the Independent Chapel to hear the visiting preacher, Benjamin Jones of Pwllheli. Ann went along and the sermon that evening left a profound impression upon her. She was convicted of her sinfulness before God and resolved to abandon the old life. This she did. She sought salvation and found it by complete reliance on the sacrifice of the Lord Jesus on the Cross. She was then twenty years of age.

A mighty change was effected in Ann's heart and life. From henceforth all her energies, formerly expended in the frivolities of the old life, were now to be used only for her Lord and Saviour. She had discovered in her Saviour the secret of true happiness and a new and eternal meaning to life.

In the year following her conversion Ann joined the fellowship of the Methodist Chapel at Pontrobert and there sat under the ministry of John Hughes. Two other great Welsh teachers of the time were also to greatly influence Ann's life. One was Thomas Charles of Bala and the other Thomas Jones of Denbigh. Thomas Charles held monthly 9 a.m. Sunday services at Bala, a distance of some twenty-two miles from Ann's home at 'Dolwar Fach'. Ann would endeavour to be present at those services, travelling on foot all those miles over the Berwyn hills, often in company with other young folk from her district, all longing to hear more of the Word of life. Then on the return journeys the sermons would be discussed, Ann often repeating them from memory, and together they would stop on the mountainside for times of prayer and praise.

Thomas Jones was an able teacher of the Word. He was the great scholar and writer of that revival period and from his publications Ann would glean the great doctrines of her new-found faith. Her greatest teachers, however, were the Spirit of God and her Bible. Day by day, amidst the pressing duties of the home and farm, she stored her mind and heart with its teachings and its precious truths became her constant meditation.

Ann's father died in 1804 and in October of the same year she married a young man from neighbouring Meifod named Thomas Griffiths, an elder in the Methodist Chapel at Pontrobert. Thomas came to live in the Thomas' home at 'Dolwar Fach'. A little daughter was born to them in the following July. The baby survived only two weeks and a fortnight later the broken-hearted young mother also died. Thus, in the month of August 1805, Ann Griffiths passed away from this world into the presence of her Lord. She was buried in Llanfihangel churchyard and there today, a red obelisk of Aberdeen granite (erected to her memory in 1864) marks the spot where her body rests awaiting the resurrection morning.

The hymns of Ann Griffiths have come down to us in a most remarkable way. Her compositions were not deliberately designed as hymns, rather they were the product of her heart's musings upon great spiritual truths as she went about her household duties. Oft she would have been seen at the spinning wheel in deep meditation, oblivious to all around her, her open Bible by her side and with tears streaming down her cheeks. Such musings Ann transmitted on scraps of paper or more usually by simple recitation to Ruth Evans, her housemaid and very close companion, desirous that she would set them to music and sing them. This Ruth would do. Ruth, however, though quite illiterate, had a phenomenal memory, and later, when married to John Hughes of Pontrobert, she dictated Ann's lines to him. This she was able to do with perfect accuracy while her husband wrote them down. The handwritten hymns were then passed on to Thomas Charles of Bala for printing and the first collection of Ann Griffiths' hymns in Welsh was published in 1806. (*Casgliad o Hymnau {1806})*

Ann Griffiths wrote entirely in Welsh. Some seventy-four of her hymns have been preserved. Her subject matter was the great truths of the Bible, every expression based upon a statement of Holy Scripture. In her verse she employed Old Testament figures to interpret the teachings of the New. She skilfully drew from many of the Old Testament books – the books of Moses, of Ruth and of Esther, the Psalms, the Song of Solomon, the prophecies of Jeremiah, of Hosea and of Zechariah.

Ann, in her meditations and verse, delved deep to secure great treasure. She was desirous that, in all her verse, she personally should not be seen, only her Redeemer. "Ann has disappeared behind her hymns", comments John Morgan. Ann's hymns were the spontaneous ebullitions of a heart inflamed with love, love to the Person of her Saviour who had loved her and saved her. That mighty fact filled her heart with wonder till she would sigh in holy aspiration, "O, to have faith to look with the angels above, into the plan of salvation!"

> *Let me drink forever deeply*
> *Of salvation's mighty flood,*
> *Till I thirst no more for ever*
> *After any earthly good.*

The mystery of the Incarnation captivated her mind, the unity of

God and man in Jesus Christ,

> *Two natures in one Person*
> *Inseparable henceforth*
> *True, pure and unconfounded*
> *In perfect unity*

And she felt that such sublime truths would occupy her thoughts eternally.

> *Entrance free, to dwell for aye*
> *In the courts of Three-in-One.*
> *A shoreless sea to swim for ever,*
> *Man as God and God as man.*

She wondered too with amazing and adoring wonder at the greatness of the Cross.

> *My mind was amazed at Who was on the Cross!*

> *The endless wonders wrought that day at Calvary!*

> *Life's author has been put to death*
> *The mighty Resurrection buried!*

The contemplation of the Cross was ever sweet to her heart.

> *When Mount Sinai roars in flame,*
> *Come and sup beside the Cross.*

Throughout the varied and pressing circumstances of life Ann proved the nearness of her Lord, ever faithful, yet sovereign in all His ways.

> *Wholly counter to my nature*
> *Is the path ordained for me;*
> *Yet I'll tread it, yes, and calmly*
> *While Thy precious face I see.*

Must I face the stormy river?
There is One to still the wave;
Jesus, my High Priest, is with me,
Strong to hold me, strong to save.

Time of cleansing, time of sifting,
Yet I'll serene and fearless stand,
The Man who is to be my shelter
Holds the winnowing-fan in hand.

Her spiritual union with Christ never ceased to thrill her soul. She was united to Christ and nothing could sever that bond. The thought to Ann was staggering. It captivated her thoughts. Such musings she expressed in verse in what is perhaps one of the sweetest of all her compositions, **"Wele'n sefyll rhwng y myrtwydd"**. Several translations of this hymn have been made into English but not without some loss of the richness of its Welsh original. The following is the rendering by Evan Richards. Its tune is Cwm Rhondda.

Standing there amidst the myrtle
My Beloved I can see;
In appearance unassuming,
Not as men of high degree;
Hail the morning
When no veil shall hide His face.

He is called the Rose of Sharon,
White and ruddy, oh! how fair!
None to Him among ten thousand
For one moment can compare;
Friend of sinners
He'll protect me on life's sea.

What have I to do with idols—
This world's idols, great and small?
Vouch I can that Jesus' friendship
Will eclipse their glory all;
May I ever
Dwell in His amazing love.

The Person of her Beloved wholly claimed the heart of Ann Griffiths for the few short years of her spiritual pilgrimage. She was, therefore, happy to renounce and abandon this world's worthless toys. Her Lord had displaced them completely.

The years of her life passed so swiftly, but she longed to be with her Saviour. Now, in experience, she has already *"hailed the morning"*, and today is delving more fully into the eternal mysteries she first began to contemplate in the simple homestead amid the Berwyn hills.

Ann Griffiths, the poet, has passed into history. The lamp of her testimony, however, still burns on. A. M. Allchin has termed her, *"The Furnace and the Fountain"*. She will never die. Her simple yet sublime life-story is indelibly inscribed in her verse and beautifully epitomized in lines by R. S. Thomas,

> *"Here for a few years*
> *the spirit sang on a bone bough*
> *at eternity's window, the flesh trembling*
> *at the splendour of a forgiveness*
> *too impossible to believe in, yet believing"*.

"Faint not, Christian, though the road"

James Harington Evans (1785-1849)

James Harington Evans

James Harington Evans had one of the most notable and God honouring ministries of the nineteenth century. But he never allowed himself to forget the depths of sin to which he had sunk nor the incurable depravity of his own heart. And when he came to the close of life he gave instruction that the text be inscribed upon his tombstone, "God be merciful to me, a sinner".

James Harington Evans was born in Salisbury, England, on 15th April 1785. His father was Priest-Vicar of Salisbury Cathedral. He was an only child and had a very special place in the affections of both his parents. He was a precocious child, always distinguishing himself in his mental abilities. As a child of three we find him taking his place in his father's school beside other boys, by far his senior. He surpassed them all and proceeded to become "head-boy" of the school.

But he was destined for the church. Father had decided that, and when he was only fourteen he accompanied his father on a visit to Oxford University. On arrival there, they were advised of a vacant scholarship at Wadham College and with some reluctance father consented to his son competing for the vacancy. Though much younger than any of his competitors, James gained the scholarship and in October 1799 entered Oxford University at the tender age of fourteen.

Though in mental capacity well above his years, at the same time he was only a youth and very vulnerable to the temptations and vices of university life. The older students sought to corrupt his young mind. James entered fully into the social round of things. His days were spent on the river and his nights at wine parties. But he soon found that there was a void within his heart which worldly pleasures could not fill. In May 1803, at the early age of eighteen, James took his B.A. degree and became known thereafter as "the boy-bachelor". Two years later he was elected Fellow of Wadham College.

James had been brought up in the Church of England, and at Oxford University it was compulsory for all students to attend Holy Communion four times a year. This caused James much heart distress for he knew that in himself he had no fitness to partake of the holy ordinance. The death of his mother caused him further deep thought. It was his first encounter with death and he was very attached to his mother. Such was the effect that his health gave way and a complete break became necessary. A spell at Cowes on the Isle of Wight resulted in restoration of health and James returned to Oxford, but now a subdued young man.

God was at work in James' heart, convicting him of his sin and his spiritual need. He resorted to prayer and started to read his Bible. He was searching for spiritual light. On vacation he shared his problem with his father but found that he could not help, merely recommending worldly pursuits as a solace for his sin-burdened heart. In his father's library, however, he happened on a copy of Philip Doddridge's "Rise and Progress of Religion in the Soul". This book shed light upon his problem and pointed him in the way of peace. But James went back to Oxford and back to the world.

As the time of his ordination approached serious thoughts troubled him again. He took Holy Orders in June 1808 and in the following year went as curate to Enville in Staffordshire. The rector there recommended that he study the sermons of Edward Cooper and, as he did so, he was led into the blessed truth of justification before God, by faith alone.

In the same year (1809) James got engaged to Caroline Joyce from Freshford House, near Bath. He then resigned the curacy of Enville and moved as curate to Milford in Hampshire. He was married the following year and right from the outset James and Caroline resolved to put God first in everything. God gave them a special burden for lost and perishing souls and, as James preached Christ crucified, God granted a spiritual awakening in the parish. The church was crowded at every meeting. Many turned to Christ for salvation and there were many enquirers, all with the one question, "What must I do to be saved?" In those days, salvation was the daily discourse among the parishioners, and the Bible the companion of the farmers going to the fields.

But the enemy soon got busy and James was given notice to quit the curacy of Milford. This caused him grief and much exercise of heart. In fact, it marked a great turning point in his ministry. Big questions had arisen in his mind and these demanded an answer. They concerned the scriptural position of the Established Church. After due consideration, James followed the Divine leading and seceded from the Church of England. So in January 1816 James and Caroline with their two infant children left Milford. Initially they went to Walford House near Taunton to share some time with another couple who had similar convictions. There they were baptized by immersion. However, James did not forget that back at Milford there was a company of young believers that needed help, and at great personal cost he organized the building of a hall there and the installation of a pastor to carry on the work from which he had been suspended.

Toward the close of 1816 James and his family moved to London. There he experienced the hand of God with him in the ministry of the gospel. Mr. Henry Drummond M.P. secured for him a site in John Street, Gray's Inn Lane and a chapel was built there. James commenced in John Street Chapel in October 1818. This proved to be his real life's work and continued right up until the time of his death.

But James' early days at John Street were very dark days. Attendances at the Chapel dwindled and there was no spiritual blessing. The problem was doctrinal and concerned the Persons of the Godhead. James had fallen into error on the Deity of the Lord Jesus and the Deity and Personality of the Holy Spirit, and in his error had published his *Dialogues on Important Subjects* (1819). This caused great alarm among many devout Christians, many whom he highly respected. So much so that he sought help. He desired only one course, the way of truth. He wrote to Dr. Wardlow of Glasgow asking for help. Dr. Wardlow's reply clarified his thinking, "that the Son and the Holy Ghost are, with the Father, truly, properly, personally God". James lost no time in confessing and retracting his error and went to every effort to do so. From the pulpit, through magazines and through his *Letters to a Friend* (1826) he unreservedly confessed his error. He bought up all the copies he could find of his 1819 *Dialogues* and consigned them to the flames. It had been a humbling time but great lessons were learned. God granted full restoration and soon rich blessing flowed at John Street Chapel, as souls were saved and young believers directed into ways pleasing to the Lord.

At John Street Chapel, James laboured fervently to build a church to the glory of the Lord Jesus. The purity of the church was paramount. Believer's baptism was practised and the Lord's supper observed each Lord's day. Among the flock James was a true shepherd, ever vigilant, and especially so for any tending to stray. Among the young he was as a father, loving and being loved. Among the sick and the dying he exercised a tender, yet faithful ministry. In the pulpit he was solemn and earnest in his preaching, and when helped of God impassioned and powerful. In public prayer he spoke to God with the simplicity and language of a child. Under James' ministry, many were blessed eternally. It was said, "Many were gathered around him, and ended their days in faithfulness". And one of the many was the beloved Robert C. Chapman who went to live at Barnstaple in Co. Devon.

The personal life of James H. Evans was "the faithful transcript of his ministry". His day started at 5:30 a.m. with prayer, meditation and study of the Word. Each day was packed full. Trifling matters, such as social intercourse were regarded as a waste of time. Like Paul, he had but one objective, "For to me to live is Christ" (Phil.1: 21).

By the year 1847 signs of strain started to show. James developed a severe chest infection and when this recurred the following year a complete break became necessary. He went north to Scotland and after five weeks in Edinburgh, moved on to Stonehaven. While there he suffered severe injuries when he was thrown from his horse-drawn carriage and never fully recovered. For some time complicating abscesses with accompanying delirium added to his distress but in his closing weeks he was completely restful. On Sunday 25th November he sent a message to his own people in London that he felt his sins and his deservings more than ever but, notwithstanding all, that he stood accepted in the Beloved, "In Jesus I stand: Jesus is a panacea". And in that confidence he passed away peacefully at 6:30 a.m. on 1st December 1849. His body was brought to London and buried in Highgate Cemetery.

James Harington Evans was a man of poetic talent. He dearly loved music and was endowed naturally with a strong singing voice. During his college years he spent many hours daily at the piano and violoncello, and through the years of his busy ministry found relaxation in singing hymns at the close of the day, accompanying himself on the organ or piano. At the commencement of his ministry in John Street (1818) he prepared a hymnal, *Hymns, Selected Chiefly for Public Worship*, for use in the chapel there. This contained one hundred and seventy-nine hymns including a few of his own composition. The hymnal went through five editions, the last appearing in 1843 with four hundred and fifty-one hymns. Very few of his own hymns are sung today but among his best known are, "As sinners saved, we gladly praise", "Change is our portion here" and "Faint not, Christian, though the road".

This last hymn, **"Faint not, Christian, though the road"**, appeared first in the 1833 edition of his hymnal and contained seven stanzas of four lines each. It was entitled "Patient Endurance" and based on the Scripture text, "For consider Him that endured… , lest ye be wearied and faint in your minds" (Hebs.12:3).

Faint not, Christian, though the road
Leading to thy blest abode
Darksome be and dangerous too,
Christ, thy Guide, will bring thee through.

Faint not, Christian, though in rage
Satan doth thy soul engage;
Take thee faith's anointed shield,
Bear it to the battle-field.

Faint not, Christian, though the world
Hath its hostile flag unfurled;
Hold the Cross of Jesus fast,
Thou shalt overcome at last.

Faint not, Christian, though within
There's a heart so prone to sin;
Christ, the Lord, is over all—
He'll not suffer thee to fall.

Faint not, Christian, though thy God
Smite thee with the chastening rod,
Smite He must, with Father's care,
That He may His love declare.

Faint not, Christian! Christ is near;
Soon in glory He'll appear;
Then shall cease thy toil and strife,
Death be swallowed up of life.

The metre and melody of this hymn are as the footfall of **a traveller on the heavenly roadway**. The way is difficult and beset by dangers, dangers without and within, dangers seen and unseen. The traveller's heart is appalled, and the danger of his fainting on the road becomes very real.

But right by his side is Another—a Companion for the roadway, a Protector, a Guide. This One once travelled the same road and did not faint, but endured and finished His course. His perfect example is a great incentive, His experience a great comfort. He is enough for the journey, and **the traveller may go safely through, right to the end of the road.**

"How sweet, my Saviour, to repose"

Henri Abraham César Malan (1787-1864)

Henri Abraham César Malan

The darkest hour is before the dawn. The early decades of the sixteenth century marked the close of the dark Middle Ages. A new day then dawned over the Continent of Europe as the light of the Reformation drove back the darkness of the night of ignorance and superstition. But soon that new light was enshrouded in another night, the night of skepticism and heresy. The eighteenth century in Europe was known as the "Age of Reason". The Bible was bitterly opposed and its truths held up to ridicule.

In France, Voltaire's curse was pronounced upon anything and everything religious. His favourite slogan, "Crush the infamous thing", echoed throughout the land. The Revolution, commencing in 1789, was devastating and the new regime that followed declared Christianity to be abolished. Church bells were pulled down and melted, church services were forbidden and the worship of God replaced by the "Worship of Reason". Atheism abounded everywhere.

In England, such unbelief and revolutionary change were stayed by a great movement of the Spirit of God, the Methodist revival under the Wesleys and Whitefield. England then sent missionaries to France and by the mid-nineteenth century a vigorous Methodist Church was established there, mainly through the efforts of Charles Cook. Merle d' Aubingé, the eminent historian, judged, "the work that John Wesley did in Great Britain, Charles Cook has done, though on a smaller scale, on the Continent". Besides, God raised up within Europe Adolphe and Frédéric Monod as preachers of the gospel. These two brothers saw a mighty work of God, particularly in France. Nonetheless, the greater part of the Continent remained untouched and spiritual darkness reigned.

In Switzerland, similar conditions prevailed and, by the eighteenth century, John Calvin was regarded as no more than a figure of history. Within the National Church heresies raised their ugly head. The great doctrines of the Trinity and of the Deity of Christ were discarded and replaced by Unitarianism. In the schools of theology rationalism prevailed. There was no place for the Word of God.

Then in the autumn of 1816, Robert Haldane, a well-to-do Scot who had been converted in 1793, arrived in Geneva. Though then over fifty years of age he set up a Bible School in the city, opened its doors to students and expounded to them Paul's Epistle to the Romans. Haldane's Bible School, under God, became the cradle of a great evangelical movement, "The Réveil", and César Malan was one of many young men whose lives were revolutionized by its influence.

The family of Malan had its roots among the Piedmont valleys of France. Then, when some of its members became victims of persecution, Pierre Malan fled to Switzerland. He settled in Geneva and there his son, Henri Abraham César Malan was born on 7th July 1787. César had his early education in Geneva and, after a short spell of apprenticeship in business at Marseilles, he returned again to his native city and entered the Academy of Geneva to study theology. In the Academy the heresies of the National Church prevailed, Rationalism and Unitarianism held sway. Malan was greatly influenced by such teachings and when he graduated from the Academy in 1810 at the age of twenty-three he was still in spiritual darkness.

The teaching of Haldane and "The Réveil" had caused no small stir in Geneva. Malan came under its influence. He heard the great truth of justification by faith and was soundly converted to God. As a result he became a devoted servant of Jesus Christ and right from the outset sought to declare publicly the great truths of the gospel. Initially he sought to reform the National Church from within. His sermon in Geneva on 19th January 1817, however, so incurred the wrath of the professors and theologians that he found himself on a collision course with dead orthodoxy. The opposing forces proved too strong for him and in the following year he was prohibited from preaching. But Malan was not to be silenced and in the year 1820 he built an independent chapel in his own garden and there continued his ministry. The chapel was soon filled to overflowing. Crowds came from far and near to hear his clear declaration of the great truths of the gospel, for Malan was a fervent and skilled evangelist.

Malan's evangelical zeal took him on visits to many parts of Switzerland and throughout the Continent of Europe and on these missionary tours large congregations attended his meetings. His special gift, however, was personal evangelism and wherever he went, whether on steamboat, on mountain trail or in hotel he ever sought opportunity to speak to the lost about the Saviour.

On visits to England, Malan was instrumental in God's hand in the conversion of two young women, both of whom later became hymn writers. Elizabeth Rundle Charles became the author of "Never further than Thy Cross" and Charlotte Elliott the author of "Just as I am, without one plea". Indeed, it was Malan's words to Charlotte that laid the basis for her outstanding hymn. When, as a young woman seeking salvation, yet not knowing how to come to Christ, Malan's words to her, "Charlotte, come just as you are", led not only to her spiritual birth but also to the birth of her hymn, "Just as I am, without one plea", some twelve years later.

Malan, throughout life, was an outstanding minister of the gospel. Though endowed with skills as a blacksmith, carpenter, mechanic and artist, at heart he was a soul-winner. Throughout life he had kept distinct from all church affiliations and organizations and in death he left no sect behind him. Indeed, one of his last instructions before the Lord called him home was for the demolition of his own chapel where he had preached for forty-three years. He died at Vandouvres on 14th May 1864, leaving behind a large family to mourn his passing.

It is, however, as a hymn writer and composer that Malan is recognized and remembered today. "The greatest name in the history of French hymns is that of César Malan of Geneva", writes H. Leigh Bennett in Julian's Dictionary of Hymnology. "Malan alone emulates the worth of production exhibited by Watts or Wesley. Like Watts, he gave the first great impulse towards the general recognition of hymns in public worship; like Charles Wesley, he was the poet and interpreter of a great religious movement craving devotional expression". Malan started to compose hymns shortly after his conversion and during his lifetime wrote the words and melodies of about a thousand hymns. The subject matter of his compositions was diverse but focussed largely on the great truths of the gospel. Though his critics frowned upon the literary defects in much of his verse, he wrote with "unaffected freshness and fervent sincerity".

The greater part of Malan's hymns was published during his lifetime. His first volume of thirty-five hymns, intended initially for family worship, appeared in 1825 and in the following year was enlarged to one hundred hymns and entitled, *Chants de Sion*. Further editions followed, and in its last publication of 1836 there were three hundred hymns. In the following year (1837) he published a collection of hymns for children and its latest edition, *Premiers Chants* (1853), contained one hundred and thirty-seven of his compositions. Some of Malan's hymns have been translated from the French into English. A volume of these translations by Ingram Cobbin appeared in 1825, *Hymns by the Rev. Caesar Malan—Translated into English Verse*, and in 1866 a further volume was published, *Lyra Evangelica*, by Miss Jane E. Arnold.

Perhaps Malan's greatest hymn, indeed, the one by which he is remembered today, is his, "Non, ce n'est pas mourir". This great hymn was translated into the German by Knapp and into the English by Dr. George W. Bethune, an eminent divine of the Reformed Dutch Church in New York. Bethune instructed that it be sung at his funeral. Its words are beautiful, its message triumphant and comforting.

> *It is not death to die,*
> *To leave this weary road,*
> *And, 'midst the brotherhood on high,*
> *To be at home with God.*

It is not death to close
　The eye long dimmed by tears,
And wake in glorious repose,
　To spend eternal years.

It is not death to bear
　The wrench that sets us free
From dungeon-chain, to breathe the air
　Of boundless liberty.

It is not death to fling
　Aside this sinful dust,
And rise, on strong, exulting wing,
　To live among the just.

Jesus, Thou Prince of Life!
　Thy chosen cannot die!
Like Thee, they conquer in the strife,
　To reign with Thee on high.

"How sweet, my Saviour, to repose" is yet another of César Malan's great hymns. The circumstances of its writing are unknown. In its English form it was arranged by Miss Jane E. Arnold (J. E. A.).

How sweet, my Saviour, to repose
　On Thine Almighty power!
To feel Thy strength upholding me,
　Through ev'ry trying hour!

　　Casting all your care upon Him,
　　Casting all your care upon Him,
　　Casting all your care upon Him,
　　For He careth, He careth for you.

It is Thy will that I should cast
　My ev'ry care on Thee;
To Thee refer each rising grief,
　Each new perplexity.

> *That I should trust Thy loving care,*
> *And look to Thee alone,*
> *To calm each troubled thought to rest*
> *In prayer before Thy throne.*
>
> *Why should my heart, then be distrest*
> *By dread of future ill?*
> *Or why should unbelieving fear*
> *My trembling spirit fill?*

This is a hymn born of personal experience and based upon the exhortation of the Apostle Peter,
"Casting all your care upon Him, for He careth for you". (1 Peter 5:7).

It is an exhortation with promise.
The promise, "He careth for you", is the Lord's part and is assured.
The exhortation, "Casting all your care upon Him", is our part and by no means easy.
Nevertheless, its outworking in daily experience proves exceedingly sweet.

> ***How sweet, my Saviour, to repose***
> ***On Thine Almighty power!***
> ***To feel Thy strength upholding me,***
> ***Through ev'ry trying hour!***

"Eternal Light! Eternal Light!"

Thomas Binney (1798-1874)

Thomas Binney

On Monday, 9th March 1874, the city of London bade a final farewell to one of its most honoured citizens. As the impressive procession made its way from Stomford Hill Chapel to Abney Park Cemetery at Stoke Newington, one thousand gentlemen, men of every opinion, walked in procession, two and two, after the hearse. Mourning coaches numbered thirty-three. Private carriages extended for one third of a mile. Vast crowds lined the route. An assembly of some five thousand people waited at the place of burial. They had all come to pay last respects to the beloved Thomas Binney, pastor of King's Weigh House Chapel, who for forty years had ministered the truth of God in their midst.

Thomas Binney was one of a long line of noteworthies from Northumbria. Born in Newcastle upon Tyne in 1798, he was essentially a self-made man. As a youth he was employed in a bookseller's shop and printing office. Throughout his teenage years he worked long hours, from seven o'clock in the morning till seven or eight o'clock in the evening and when work was demanding, from six o'clock in the morning till ten o'clock at night. Notwithstanding the business of those years, Thomas found time for study. He was an extensive reader, ever seeking the best authors. On two evenings a week he attended an elderly clergyman, from whom he learned the elements of Greek and of Latin. Thus Thomas Binney in his youth, by diligent application and economizing on every spare minute, laid a good foundation for life.

In due time Thomas entered Coward College at Wymondley in Hertfordshire and there studied under the tutorship of Thomas Morell. When college days finished he entered upon a brief pastorate in Bedford and then, in 1824, was appointed pastor of the St. James Street Congregational Church in Newport, Isle of Wight. For five years he enjoyed the seclusion of that island town and there his mind had opportunity to mature, for Thomas Binney was "a prince among thinkers". In Newport, Thomas came into contact with Albert Midlane. They shared much together and Midlane, in after years always attributed any degree of success that he had as a hymnwriter to his early encouragement from Thomas Binney. In his Newport years, Thomas wrote a biography of Stephen Morell, son of his former tutor at Coward College, a young man who had been cut down in the midst of a promising career at the early age of twenty-four.

In 1829 Thomas Binney went to London. He was then thirty-one years of age. He had been appointed pastor of King's Weigh House Chapel. Weigh House Chapel, at that time, was situated in Little Eastcheap. It was a small and insignificant building sited over some warehouses, yet much superior to the original King's Weigh House in Cornhill which had been nothing more than a kind of loft. In 1833 Thomas Binney laid the foundation stone for a new chapel at Fish Hill Street and the congregation moved there the following year. A sum of sixteen thousand pounds had been raised for the purpose and a handsome building was erected. But Weigh House was not renowned for its pretentious building, rather for its tradition of godly pastors, men of earnest piety, men from a heritage who had paid dearly for their convictions, men who ministered the truth of God in dark days.

Thomas Binney was another of that notable line and for forty years, with conviction, vigour and ability he carried high the banner for truth and religious liberty at Weigh House Chapel.

Thomas Binney, though inheriting a great tradition at Weigh House Chapel, was not bound by tradition. He was convinced that men were seeking something solid to believe in for life and death. He was convinced of the immortality and reliability of God's truth, that all else comes to naught, but that reality and truth live on. In his preaching he applied the truth of God directly to the consciences of men to arouse from slumber, but not before that same truth had passed through the avenue of their understanding. People felt compelled to listen to him for he made them to feel that he was dealing with their deepest, truest life.

In the pulpit Thomas Binney was always master of his subject. He did not read his sermons but with eye fixed on his audience and with masterly diction, though yet in familiar everyday speech, he transported his hearers to the very kernel of his message and then, for upwards of two hours, held their rapt attention. Thomas Binney had power in the pulpit. Furthermore, he had eloquence, not of the sensational or of the rhetorical kind, Binney's was the eloquence of the "real" and the "true". With him there was no falsehood.

Thomas Binney, in his ministry, was by no means an emotionalist, yet he firmly believed in "the victory of tears". In this he concurred with Augustine who had been wont to say, "I reckon that I have done nothing till I see the people weep". And the Weigh House congregation, under Binney's ministry, was often bathed in tears.

Thomas Binney's ministry was God-honouring; it bore the hallmark of reverence. Weigh House Chapel was usually crowded well before the appointed hour, thronged with listeners—attentive, silent, waiting. When Binney read from the Holy Scriptures it was with masterly emphasis, yet in a subdued and dignified tone. In prayer he addressed God with a bearing and an extraordinary devotion which betrayed to all his appreciation of the greatness of the One with whom he was speaking. There was "no familiarity, no bawling, no hurry; all was calmness, earnestness and quiet supplication".

But Thomas Binney, the man himself, was far greater than his ministry. He was a man of tremendous capacity, both of mind and of heart. His greatness of mind was evident in his oral and in his written ministries. The greatness of his heart was evident in daily life—his generosity with the needy, his consolation and sympathy with the sorrowing, his gentleness and patience with the erring and his deep delight in little children. Furthermore, Thomas Binney was a man of integrity, a man of influence, a man of deep conviction both of truth and of duty. Indeed, he was a man greatly beloved.

Thomas Binney, in his day, was regarded as a spiritual leader, a wise counsellor and guide. He had the transparency and strength of a prophet. And yet, he was a man of like passions as his fellows, for in his closing years when the pressures of life became intolerably heavy he succumbed to depression. In that circumstance, when his mind was beset with the tyranny of doubt as to his spiritual state, he was like an experienced sailor on a stormy sea—he knew where to lay hold. In his trial the Psalms were especially dear to him and of the 51st. Psalm he commented, "Wonderful that God should not despise the contrite and broken spirit that crawls into His presence; how men would despise it!" Through it all, the Saviour was the one subject on which he loved to dwell, and his whole soul rested on Him.

He died at his home in Upper Clapham. The close came on 24th February 1874 and as it approached a deep peace filled and flooded his soul. He spake of "a good God", of "the eternal world" and of "salvation". Thus he passed away to be with Christ.

Thomas Binney, though eminent as a powerful and eloquent preacher was scarcely less eminent as a writer. From a busy and crowded life more than twenty sizable works received publication. In them the subject matter was most diverse, yet throughout, his treatment and style were most vigorous.

Binney also wrote in verse, the greater part of which was distributed among friends and never received publication. One piece, however, **"Eternal Light! Eternal Light!"**, received attention and remains. It is said to be one of the most pure and most perfect hymns in any language. Binney wrote it when he was still in his twenties. Sitting one evening in his home in Newport he watched the setting sun go down. Then the moon appeared and the stars. He sat on in meditation, then retired to his desk and wrote,

> *Eternal Light! Eternal Light!*
> *How pure the soul must be*
> *When, placed within Thy searching sight,*
> *It shrinks not, but with calm delight*
> *Can live, and look on Thee!*

The spirits that surround Thy throne
   May bear the burning bliss;
But that is surely theirs alone,
Since they have never, never known
   A fallen world like this.

O how shall I, whose native sphere
   Is dark, whose mind is dim,
Before the Ineffable appear,
And on my naked spirit bear
   The uncreated beam?

There is a way for man to rise
   To that sublime abode;
An offering and a sacrifice,
A Holy Spirit's energies,
   An Advocate with God.

These, these prepare us for the sight
   Of holiness above;
The sons of ignorance and night
May dwell in the eternal Light,
   Through the eternal Love!

"Eternal Light!" is a great hymn. Its language is sublime. Binney transports us to the Divine presence. It is a vision of glory and of grace. Great twin truths tower high – **"God is Light"** and **"God is Love"**. As great and apparently opposing twin natural forces, the centrifugal and the centripetal, hold our universe in perfect poise, so the eternal throne is governed by "Eternal Light" and "Eternal Love". The one repels, the other attracts. The one excludes, the other includes.

"Eternal Light", uncreated, unsullied, forever burning – it penetrates, searches and excludes the sinner. "Eternal Love", at tremendous cost, finds the way and the banished sinner is welcomed and embraced. And, in that welcome and embrace at the eternal throne, "Eternal Light" cannot but acquiesce.

Together and forever they stand, inviolable and immutable, **"Eternal Light"** and **"Eternal Love"**.

"Jesus is our Shepherd"

Hugh Stowell (1799-1865)

Hugh Stowell

Hugh Stowell was born in Douglas on the Isle of Man, on the 3rd December 1799. His father, Hugh Stowell (Sen.) was rector of Ballough in the north of the Island, but shortly after Hugh's birth the family moved to the vicarage at Kirk Lonan and there Hugh spent his boyhood. Mr. Howard who knew the family well described Hugh as "a sweet little boy, very social and friendly and quite at home with everybody". However, like many other boys, he was inquisitive. One day he ventured into one of the Manx churches during the service. The preacher there was trying to impress upon his hearers the cordiality of the invitation to the gospel feast (Luke 14). As Hugh listened he was greatly taken with the zeal of the preacher as in the flourish of his native Manx dialect he exclaimed, "Come, for all things are now ready; there you will find mountains of porridge and rivers of new milk!"

When Hugh was about twelve there were deep concerns regarding his health. He was delicate, listless and had a persistent cough. Consumption (pulmonary tuberculosis) was feared. However, after a period of rest and horse riding with friends at Kirk Braddon, his cough subsided and he returned home, virtually restored to full health again.

When Hugh was only a boy he got to know the Saviour and thereafter took a great interest in the salvation of others. He visited a neighbouring lad who was sick and taught him to read. He then got him a Bible. This became the boy's delight and on Hugh's last visit to see him, the dying lad's countenance lit up with joy as he exclaimed, "Glory and praise to God; I'm going home! I'm going home!"

Mr. Howard tells us too of life in the vicarage at Kirk Lonan. It was "an abode of harmony, peace and love". Within its walls the things of God took precedence over every other aspect of life. Mr. Stowell (Sen.) was noted for his simplicity of life, his sweetness of disposition and his fervent piety. Hugh's mother was cheerful in her manner, and kind. However, in the disciplining of the home, she exercised a gentle firmness. She was looked upon as "one of the tenderest and best of mothers", and her untimely death, when Hugh was fourteen, was one of his deepest sorrows.

Hugh received his early education at home under the instruction of his father and then was placed under the tuition of John Cawood of Bewdley. At the age of nineteen, he proceeded to St. Edmund Hall, Oxford. Thomas Watson, an Oxford colleague recounted of Hugh's college days, "His course was characterized by a beautiful uniformity throughout.—In Christian fellowship and love, it may be truly said of him, 'Once a friend, a friend for ever'. He was ever ready to stretch out the warm hand of friendship; and the grasp of his hand was the interpreter of his heart". In college studies Hugh was very successful. Moreover, in the University debating chamber he excelled, and there displayed "almost unrivalled powers as a public speaker". He spoke extempore and was entirely at home in defending the great evangelical doctrines of his faith.

Hugh graduated from Oxford in 1822. In the following year he was ordained and after ordination was appointed curate in the Coltswold village of Sheepscombe. He vividly remembered his first Sunday there, arriving with only one prepared sermon and the disastrous outcome as he sought to deliver it at the morning service. As he surveyed the faces of his rural congregation, he could read their thoughts, "What sort of a stripling have we got? This may be all very good, but it is above our comprehension". He went home very downcast, then after lunch settled down to prepare his evening sermon. His eye rested upon a text of Scripture that weighed heavily upon his heart. He meditated upon it and in the evening preached its message to the people of Sheepscombe from a full and overflowing heart and observed, as he did so, tears trickling down an aged face. "From that time to this", he testified, "I have never preached a written sermon".

In the following year, Hugh moved to the curacy of Huddersfield and after a brief time there, accepted a call to the Church of St. Stephen in Salford. Salford thereafter became his home and the centre of his ministry. At the time of his going there he had the reputation of being "an extemporaneous fire brand". This initially gave concerns to his licensing Bishop, but the people of Salford warmed to him and shortly after his arrival they built for him a new church by voluntary subscription, Christ Church in Salford. Hugh was greatly loved by all. Once when his father visited him, in what proved to be a farewell visit, and the parishioners spoke to the venerable old man of the esteem in which his son was held, "Ah!" said he, "they are administering poison to my son out of a golden dish!"

Hugh Stowell was one of the most eloquent and forceful preachers of his day. Charles Bullock refers to his style, "In the pulpit and on the platform, he was an Apollos in eloquence, and a John in love". "He made the pulpit, as it should be, not a philosopher's desk, or a professor's chair, but the source of well-directed appeals to the conscience and the deepest emotions of the heart". In his preaching he possessed remarkable power. "His words came fresh from the anvil of the heart". But withal, his ministry was ever marked by simplicity and "the common people heard him gladly".

In his stand for the truth of God, Hugh faced strong opposition from many quarters. He received anonymous and threatening letters but these he usually consigned to the fire, and often without reading them. When someone once suggested that he respond to a scurrilous personal attack in a newspaper publication, he gracefully replied, "No, I treat him as a chimneysweeper whom I might meet in the street with a sack of soot on his back: I give him as wide a berth as possible".

Hugh's gifts and qualities earned for him a wide reputation and this, in turn, led to invitations from other parishes. His heart, however, was wed to Salford. Among his own people he was a true shepherd, ever vigilant among the flock. If a sheep went missing, the absence would be followed by prompt visitation. In times of need and of sickness among the flock, he selflessly moved in and out of the homes of the people, totally regardless of any danger from contagious illness. His sympathetic heart was evident to all.

Thus Hugh ministered diligently and faithfully among the people of Salford for forty years. The burden of his ministry, however, took its toll on his health and in 1862 he was obliged to pull rein. His medical attendants advised him to desist from preaching. He went to Grasmere in the Lake District for a period of rest but while there he developed a severe bout of diphtheria and had to return home. This was complicated by congestion of the lungs and, in spite of treatment, his condition gradually deteriorated and it pleased God to call him to his eternal rest on Sunday, 8th October 1865.

His son was with him in his last illness and testified, "His mind was entirely filled with holy and heavenly things". Almost every word he spoke was a prayer, couched in the language of Holy Scripture. At the close he confessed himself to be the chief of sinners and passed away repeating the lines of Charlotte Elliott's hymn,

> *Just as I am – without one plea,*
> *But that Thy blood was shed for me,*
> *And that Thou bidd'st me come to Thee –*
> *O Lamb of God, I come!*

His funeral was a most impressive sight. The whole of the borough of Salford was in mourning. The city of Manchester seemed to "sit solitary". The funeral procession was a mile long, multitudes thronged the roadway to the church and the indications of sorrow were deep and fervent. "Few indeed were they who refused the tribute of a tear". Thus concluded the earthly and notable ministry of Hugh Stowell.

Hugh Stowell, during his lifetime, published a number of works, and after his death much of his personal ministry went on record as, *Sermons by the Rev. H. Stowell* (1869). However, Hugh Stowell is best remembered for his hymns. In 1831 he published his *Selection of Psalms and Hymns*. This contained two hundred and thirty three hymns, nine of which were of his own composition. A later edition of this same work contained a further thirty-four of his personal hymns. Then, following his death, in the year 1868, all of his hymns, some forty-seven in number, were collected and published by his son.

Two of Hugh Stowell's hymns are still widely used today and are great favourites, his hymn on prayer, "From every stormy wind that blows", and his delightful little hymn, **"Jesus is our Shepherd"**, on the shepherd care of the Lord Jesus.

Jesus is our Shepherd, wiping every tear;
Folded in His bosom, what have we to fear?
Only let us follow whither He doth lead –
To the thirsty desert or the dewy mead.

Jesus is our Shepherd; well we know His voice;
How its gentlest whisper makes our hearts rejoice!
Even when He chideth, tender is His tone,
None but He shall guide us, we are His alone.

Jesus is our Shepherd; for the sheep He bled;
Every lamb is sprinkled with the blood He shed;
Then on each He setteth His own secret sign –
"They that have My Spirit, these," saith He, "are Mine".

Jesus is our Shepherd; guarded by His arm,
Though the wolves may raven, none can do us harm;
If we tread death's valley, dark with fearful gloom,
We will fear no evil, victors o'er the tomb.

Jesus is our Shepherd; with His goodness now,
And His tender mercy, He doth us endow;
Let us sing His praises with a gladsome heart,
Till in heaven we meet Him, nevermore to part!

This hymn is essentially a children's hymn. Indeed, most of Hugh Stowell's hymns were children's hymns. Hugh Stowell dearly loved children. He had nine children of his own and through life devoted a large part of his time to Sunday school work in Salford. Many of his hymns were written for the Sunday school children, for their Anniversary Services in Christ Church. "Jesus is our Shepherd" is one of these "anniversary hymns" and was written in the year 1849.

JESUS IS OUR SHEPHERD

"Jesus is our Shepherd" is one of the sweetest and tenderest hymns in the English language. In rich pictorial language the author selects and gathers together many of the portraits of the Shepherd and His flock from both Old and New Testaments and renders them into simple verse, from the perspective of a child. And just as a child might relate to earthly parents, so the child of God relates to his heavenly Shepherd.

> I belong to Him – "sprinkled with His blood".
> I am loved by Him – "folded in His bosom".
> I am safe with Him – "guarded by His arm".

> **What a Shepherd!**

> Intimacy and fidelity, the hallmarks of His care! Security and serenity, the portion of His flock!

"Nearer, my God, to Thee"

Sarah Flower Adams (1805-1848)

Sarah Flower Adams

A harsh punishment, even in 1799! At least, so it seemed. Benjamin Flower, the proprietor and editor of the weekly "Cambridge Intelligencer", had been sentenced to a six-month prison sentence and a hundred pound fine for what appeared a rather menial offence. His crime was the publication of an article in defence of the French Revolution in which criticism was made of a certain Bishop Watson of Llandaff. But Benjamin Flower was a man of principle, a great advocate of civil and religious liberties and he stood by his publication. In consequence he was committed to Newgate gaol. But he had sympathizers and in the gaol he received many visitors. Among these was Eliza Gould, a young woman from Dodbroke in Devon. Benjamin and Eliza shared kindred sympathies. In the prison a close attachment was formed which blossomed into love and led to their marriage after Benjamin's release. Strange circumstances indeed! But the unjust sentence and the prison term served the purposes of God and thus, in God's great plan, Benjamin and Eliza, the parents of Sarah Flower Adams, were brought together.

Benjamin and Eliza set up home together, first in the city of London and later in Harlow, Essex. They had a family of two girls. Both were born at Harlow, Eliza on the 19th April 1803 and Sarah on the 22nd February 1805. Tragically their mother died in 1810, shortly after the birth of a baby boy who also died, and Benjamin Flower was left with the upbringing and education of his two girls. This he attended to dutifully. In the home there was daily religious observance for Benjamin was a devout man. Affection was not allowed to interfere with discipline. The girls' education, though fragmentary, was of the best. Their father sought out for them the leading masters in Harlow and personally devoted to them such time as he could afford.

The two sisters, Eliza and Sarah, grew up together. In childhood, they were closely attached and remained so throughout life. Both were very talented and in many ways their talents complemented each other. Eliza was a gifted composer, Sarah a poetess of great sweetness. Sarah composed verse and Eliza set it to music. They pooled their talents and worked closely together. They assisted their minister, W. J. Fox of South Place Chapel, Finsbury, London in his compiling of a new hymn book, "Hymns and Anthems" (published in two parts, in 1840 and 1841). For this publication Eliza composed the music of sixty-two and Sarah the words of thirteen of the hymns.

Together, Eliza and Sarah dutifully cared for their father in the closing years of his life and then, when Eliza fell sick and wasted away from consumption at the early age of forty-three, Sarah nursed her till the close. In so doing, Sarah herself became a victim of the same condition and passed away less than two years later. Thus both sisters died at the early age of forty-three. At both funeral services the hymns and music that were sung were of the sisters' own composition. Both were laid in the same grave and on the side of the tombstone were inscribed the words, "They were lovely and pleasant in their lives and in their deaths they were not divided".

However, for a little, the paths of the two sisters did part. Sarah married in 1834 and she and her husband, William Bridge Adams, made their home at St. John's Wood in the city of London. William was an eminent civil engineer, a pioneer in railway carriage construction, and with some repute also as a writer.

Sarah spent the closing years of her life in the city of London and there she passed away on 14th August 1848. "She wore away, almost her last breath bursting into unconscious song as the gentle spirit glided from its beautiful frame". One week later her body was brought from London and laid to rest, with that of her sister and parents, in the Baptist Cemetery, Foster Street in Harlow. At her funeral service the company of mourners sang her own composition, "Resignation" ("He sendeth sun, He sendeth shower"). Its concluding lines bespeak an inner peace,

> *Where falls the shadow, cold in death*
> *I yet will sing with fearless breath,*
> *As comes to me in shade or sun,*
> *"Father, Thy will, not mine, be done".*

In speaking of Sarah, Leigh Hunt termed her, "a rare mistress of thought and tears". Mrs. E. Bridell Fox, a near relative, recorded of her, "Sarah was tall and singularly beautiful, with noble and regular features; in manner she was gay and impulsive, her conversation full of sparkling wit and kindly humour". Mrs. Fox went on to say of Sarah's poetical compositions, "They were the spontaneous expression of some strong impulse or feeling at the moment; she was essentially a creature of impulse—she wrote when she felt the spirit moved her".

This "spontaneous expression of strong impulse" is particularly evident in Sarah's *Vivia Perpetua*, a dramatic poem portraying the conflict between heathenism and Christianity. The poem has a third century setting in Carthage and in it Sarah's heroine suffers martyrdom. In the poem there are five Acts. At the close of Act 3, "Part in Peace" is sung in a dimly lighted sepulchre by Perpetua and a small group of Christians who had just heard that the edict has been issued for their arrest. And so, before parting, and possibly never to meet again, they all sang,

> *Part in peace! Christ's life was peace –*
> *Let us live our life in Him!*
> *Part in peace! Christ's death was peace –*
> *Let us die our death in Him!*

> *Part in peace! Christ promise gave*
> *   Of a life beyond the grave,*
> *Where all mortal partings cease*
> *   Brethren, Sisters! Part in Peace.*

And again, on the night just before martyrdom, they all sang the same words in the prison.

However, Sarah Flower Adams is best remembered for her immortal hymn, **"Nearer, my God, to Thee"**.

> *Nearer, my God, to Thee,*
> *   Nearer to Thee!*
> *E'en though it be a cross*
> *   That raiseth me:*
> *Still all my song shall be,*
> *Nearer, my God, to Thee –*
> *   Nearer to Thee!*
>
> *Though like a wanderer,*
> *   The sun gone down,*
> *Darkness be over me,*
> *   My rest a stone;*
> *Yet in my dreams I'd be,*
> *Nearer, my God, to Thee –*
> *   Nearer to Thee.*
>
> *There let the way appear,*
> *   Steps unto heaven;*
> *All that Thou send'st to me*
> *   In mercy given:*
> *Angels to beckon me*
> *Nearer, my God, to Thee –*
> *   Nearer to Thee!*
>
> *Then with my waking thoughts,*
> *   Bright with Thy praise,*
> *Out of my stony griefs,*
> *   Bethel I'll raise:*
> *So by my woes to be*
> *Nearer, my God, to Thee –*
> *   Nearer to Thee!*

Or if on joyful wing
  Cleaving the sky,
Sun, moon, and stars forgot,
  Upwards I fly:
Still all my song shall be,
Nearer, my God, to Thee –
  Nearer to Thee!

Many years after Sarah's death Bishop E. H. Bickersteth wrote a most fitting sixth verse but this was never incorporated. Nevertheless, its sentiment is very beautiful.

There in my Father's house,
  Safe and at rest,
There in my Saviour's love
  Perfectly blest;
Age after age to be
Nearer, my God, to Thee
  Nearer to Thee!

The circumstances surrounding the writing of Sarah's hymn are not known but the original manuscript was dated November 1840. It was included, together with twelve other of her hymns in Fox's "Hymns and Anthems" (1841) and for years was confined to the comparative obscurity of South Place Chapel in London. Then, after Sarah's death, it became the possession of a wider world and is today included in the hymnbooks of almost all denominations on both sides of the Atlantic. Its words have been translated into many European and other languages.

Several tunes have been composed for this hymn. The English composers, John B. Dykes and Sir Arthur Sullivan, set the words to music and these tunes, "Horbury" and "St. Edmund", are still used today. However, it is the American tune, "Bethany", that is most closely linked with the hymn. Lowell Mason, the distinguished Boston musician, composed this lovely tune and of the occasion of its composition he recounted, "one night, lying awake in the dark, eyes wide open, through the stillness of the house the melody came to me and the next morning I wrote down the words of 'Bethany' "

Few hymns have received such general approval and acclaim. It is a timeless favourite. A great many people, in the dark experiences of life, have voiced its words. President Mc Kinley, as he lay dying from a murderer's shot in Buffalo, New York, quoted them as his last testimony. In the American Civil War, the little drummer boy whose arm had been shot off by a canon sang them ere he passed away on the battlefield at Fort Donelson. And on the fateful night of the sinking of the Titanic, 14th April 1912, their plaintive strains floated over the icy Atlantic waters just before the ill-fated vessel, and with her over fifteen hundred souls, was engulfed in its waters.

Sarah's hymn finds its background in Jacob's experience at Bethel (Gen. 28). There God met with Jacob on his very first night away from home and the place where he lay down to sleep was sanctified by the Divine presence. Jacob termed it, "the house of God", "the gate of heaven". That night was a great milestone in Jacob's experience for on that night God came very near to him and on that night Jacob made his father's God his own God. "God Almighty" became "the God of Jacob".

"Happy is he that hath the God of Jacob for his help" (Psa.146: 5).

The hymn's refrain, **"Nearer, my God, to Thee – Nearer to Thee!"** voices the soul's inner longing.
Its words are the loftiest and purest of all human aspirations.
Indeed, the hymn is **a most hallowed prayer.**

"What raised the wondrous thought?"

George Vicesimus Wigram (1805-1879)

George Vicesimus Wigram

George V. Wigram was born into a well-to-do family. His father, Sir Robert Wigram, was a wealthy merchant and shipowner of London and Wexford. George was the twelfth son and twentieth child in the family, and because of the latter was given the middle name of Vicesimus (derived from the Latin meaning twenty).

George lived his youth in the lap of luxury. He had a great desire to see the world and, while still a teenager, embarked on a military career in the British army. Then God crossed his path in a most remarkable way and this changed his whole course in life. Of that spiritual experience George has left the record in his own words.

"Good instructions as to the content of the Bible were mine at school, at seventeen, under a John the Baptist ministry; but I never knew the gospel till, at nineteen, I went abroad, full of the animal pleasures of a military life. I and my comrade spent a long and tiring day on the field of Waterloo in June 1824 (note; this was nine years after the battle). Arriving late at night at — I soon went to my bedroom. It struck me, "I will say my prayers". It was the habit of childhood, neglected in youth. I knelt down by my bedside, but found I had forgotten what to say. I looked up as if trying to remember, when suddenly there came on my soul a something I had never known before. It was as if some One, infinite and almighty, knowing everything, full of the deepest, tenderest interest in myself, though utterly and entirely abhorring everything in and connected with me, made known to me that He pitied and loved myself. My eye saw no one: but I knew assuredly that the One whom I knew not, and never had met, had met me for the first time, and made me to know that we were together. There was a light, no sense or faculty my own human nature ever knew: there was a presence of what seemed infinite in greatness – something altogether of a class that was apart and supreme, and yet at the same time making itself known to me in a way that I as a man could thoroughly feel, and taste, and enjoy. The Light made all light, Himself withal: but it did not destroy, for it was love itself, and I was loved individually by Him. The exquisite tenderness and fullness of that love, the way that it appropriated me myself for Him, in whom it all was, while the light from which it was inseparable in Him discovered to me the contrast I had been to all that was light and love. I wept for a while on my knees, said nothing, then got into bed. The next morning's thought was "Get a Bible". I got one, and it was thenceforward my handbook. My clergyman companion noticed this, and also my entire change of life and thought. We journeyed on together to Geneva, where there was an active persecution of the faithful going on. He went on to Italy, and I found my own company—stayed with those who were suffering for Christ".

George's conversion experience was real. In due course he resigned his commission and in 1826 entered Queen's College, Oxford with view to entering the Church of England. George's brother, Joseph Cotton Wigram, was already in the Church of England and in due course would be distinguished there as the Bishop of Rochester. At

Oxford, George was a very distinctive student. He was, in fact, the only young man at College at that time that kept a close carriage, and for which he hired a pair of horses.

At college George met with fellow students with similar spiritual interests, young men saved by the grace of God and studying for the ministry of the Church. They had much in common and together they shared their convictions as to the teaching of the Word of God. Among them were W. Jarrett, also of Queen's College, and James L. Harris and Benjamin W. Newton, both of Exeter College. As they read and studied the Scriptures together, doubts were sown in some hearts as to the scriptural position of the Established Church for which they were then studying. And when they qualified later, though most of his friends were ordained in the Church of England, it appears that the Bishop of London judged George V. Wigram too evangelical for ordination.

By the year 1830 George's college colleagues, James L. Harris and Benjamin W. Newton had moved back to their home county of Devon and there John Nelson Darby who had come from Dublin joined them. George also moved to Devon and in his association with Darby found in him a man of kindred spirit. They became fast friends and that friendship and loyalty lasted through life. These young men were joined by Captain Percy Francis Hall and together they hired a disused chapel in Plymouth (Providence Chapel). There they publicly expounded the teachings of the Word of God and commenced to observe the Lord's supper after the simple New Testament pattern. Their desire was to honour the simple teachings of God's Word. The Scriptures of Truth and the Spirit of God were their only guide.

George then moved back to the city of London and there he was instrumental in establishing similar testimonies to the Name of the Lord Jesus. For many years he personally was associated with the testimony at Rawstorne Street. There he taught the truths of the New Testament relative to salvation, church gathering and the coming again of the Lord Jesus. Besides, George's public labours took him further afield, to the rural areas of County Devon, to Ireland where he saw the formation of a testimony in Cork, to the British West Indies, to British Guyana and to New Zealand.

George was a diligent student of the Holy Scriptures and skilled in their original languages. He perceived a great need of some aid to the study of the Scriptures for those with little or no knowledge of the original languages and forthwith set to work with the help of other scholars in compiling "The Englishman's Greek Concordance of the New Testament". After eight years of diligent labour this work was published in 1839. The financial outlay had been considerable but George saw it through, humbly commenting on the expenditure involved (some fifty thousand pounds at that time), as only "passing through my hands". Then there followed in 1843 "The Englishman's Hebrew and Chaldee Concordance of the Old Testament". Both these works were monumental and have proved invaluable to successive generations of the people of God.

In the 1840's George undertook the editorship of "The Present Testimony", a magazine which replaced the earlier "Christian Witness" initially edited by James L. Harris. Therein he personally contributed many articles, including a valuable series on the Psalms in which Divine names are clearly distinguished.

George had an interest in hymnology and in 1838 he edited a small hymnbook, *Hymns for the Poor of the Flock*. Then in 1856, when a larger work became necessary, George undertook its compilation and entitled it, *Hymns and Spiritual Songs (Selected)*. In his personal account of its compilation George stated that his objectives had been, to "retouch as little as possible, and with as light a hand as possible", while at the same time allowing no falsity of doctrinal or dispensational truth to remain. This 1856 compilation included a number of hymns of George's own composition.

George kept busy in his labours for the Lord right to the close of life. Though he had been born into a family with means, he lived modestly. He travelled widely in the work of the Lord and sometimes was accompanied by his wife and unmarried daughter, Fanny Theodora. Fanny was a nurse and oftimes ministered to the sick and needy as her father proclaimed the gospel. Like her father, she too was poetical and has left for us the little hymn of worship, "Worthy of homage and of praise".

In the closing years of life George was no stranger to sorrow. In the month of September in the year 1867 he lost his dear wife. She had accompanied him to the city of Montreal where he was ministering the Word of God and there she died, "in perfect peace – the peace of God Himself". Then in March 1871 he lost his devoted daughter, Fanny. In both these losses George never questioned the ways of God but was totally resigned to the will of God. But not least of his sorrows was the heartbreak of witnessing a rift in that great work of God in which he had been instrumental at its foundation. Nevertheless, his spirit soared above his sorrow.

> *How bright, there above, is the mercy of God!*
> *And void of all guilt, and clear of all sin,*
> *Are my conscience and heart, through my Saviour's blood:*
> *Not a cloud above – not a spot within.*
>
> *Christ died! then I'm clean: not a spot within.*
> *God's mercy and love! not a cloud above.*
> *'Tis the Spirit, through faith, thus triumphs o'er sin:*
> *Not a cloud above – not a spot within.*

And into the reality of that unsullied realm of which he had written, George V. Wigram passed personally on 1st January 1879, at the age of seventy-three.

Very few of George V. Wigram's hymns survive today. Nevertheless his compositions have been worthy of the Lord. He had an intellect capable of lofty thought and was besides "one accounted familiar with the sanctuary". These features are evidenced in his composition, **"What raised the wondrous thought?"**

> *What raised the wondrous thought,*
> *Or who did this suggest, –*
> *The church should be to glory brought,*
> *And with the Son be blest?*
>
> *O God, the thought was Thine,*
> *Thine only could it be,*
> *Fruit of the wisdom, love divine,*
> *Peculiar unto Thee.*
>
> *For, sure, no other mind,*
> *For thoughts so bold, so free,*
> *Greatness or strength could ever find;*
> *Thine only could it be.*
>
> *The motives, too, Thine own,*
> *The plan, the counsel, Thine;*
> *Made for Thy Son, bone of His bone,*
> *In glory bright to shine.*

O God, with great delight
Thy wondrous thought we see;
Upon His throne, in glory bright,
The bride of Christ shall be.

Sealed with the Holy Ghost,
We triumph in that love;
Thy wondrous thought has made our boast,
Glory with Christ above!

Truly, it is **A SUBLIME THOUGHT! – Christ and His church, so indissolubly linked together, and destined to be glorified together!**

But it is **A DIVINE THOUGHT! – nor could it have originated in any human heart, only in the Divine heart of infinite wisdom and immeasurable love!**

"Holy Saviour! we adore Thee"

Samuel Prideaux Tregelles (1813-1875)

Samuel Prideaux Tregelles

In the mid-nineteenth century God worked mightily within the hearts of many of His people through His Word and the operation of His Holy Spirit. Great New Testament truths were rediscovered and their practical teachings implemented. Many of the people of God dissociated from the known churches of the day and gathered simply to the Name of the Lord Jesus after the New Testament pattern. A new hope was born within hearts, that of the personal coming again of the Lord Jesus. Such a wealth of truth was shared among the saints by oral and written ministry; sometimes it was expressed in verse. In the forefront of the movement were such well-known names as J. N. Darby, R. C. Chapman, J. G. Deck, J. Denham Smith and Sir Edward Denny. Another name, perhaps less well known, yet nonetheless an important figure in the movement, was that of Dr. Samuel P. Tregelles.

Samuel Prideaux Tregelles, the son of Samuel Tregelles and Dorothy Prideaux, was born into a Quaker home at Wodehouse Place, Falmouth, on 30th January 1813. At the age of twelve he entered Falmouth classical school and there he attended for three years. He proved to be a brilliant scholar with a phenomenal memory and exhibited a great flair for languages. His headmaster, discerning his academic ability, encouraged him to proceed to university but, because of his links with "The Society of Friends", this was not possible. His practical minded father, who was a merchant, decided that he should see something of the hard reality of life and sent him, at the age of sixteen, as an apprentice to The Iron Works at Neath Abbey in Glamorganshire in South Wales. There he was employed for six years.

As a young man Samuel drifted from his early upbringing. He had knowledge of the Scriptures and his acutely discerning mind perceived a gross misapplication of Holy Scripture in the practising religious world around him. This greatly disturbed him, indeed, almost to the point of infidelity. At the age of nineteen he visited Plymouth and there encountered Benjamin Wills Newton, who had married his cousin. Newton was the instrument in God's hands in Samuel's conversion. Newton showed to his inquiring mind the authority and accuracy of Holy Scripture, whereupon Samuel searched the Scriptures anew and in them he found the Saviour. The experience of personal salvation brought peace to his heart and from that moment he sought to serve the Lord.

Samuel's flair for languages and his academic ability could not be suppressed and though still employed in the Iron Works, he filled every moment of his spare time in studying Greek, Hebrew and Chaldee. His concern for the spread of the gospel in Wales induced him to learn the Welsh language and though still in secular employment he found time to make known the gospel's glorious message both in English and Welsh in many parts of the Principality.

Samuel had the conviction that an emphasis should be placed on the authority of the Holy Scriptures and that this would help counteract the traditions and practices of religious systems around him. Besides, the influences of Mormonism and Atheism were spreading among the people. He therefore prepared and gave a scholarly lecture on the authorship of the books of the New Testament and this helped to meet the need of the day. Eben Fardd translated the lecture into Welsh and this one-shilling booklet encouraged people to confidently study the Holy Scriptures for themselves.

Samuel's spiritual interests were now such that the Iron Works could no longer hold him and in 1835 he returned to Falmouth. There he was ostracized by his family because of his loyalty to Christ, but he supported himself by taking pupils. During the two-year period that followed he associated with the assembly of the Lord's people meeting at Plymouth.

Samuel was asked to help in the production of *the Englishman's Greek and Hebrew Concordances*, a work launched by G. V. Wigram in 1831, and this involvement set Samuel on a career which was to place him at the forefront of Biblical textual critics. His great ambition was the production of a reliable Greek text of the New Testament and in this great task he set to work single-handed. In the year 1837 he moved to London and in the following year announced his proposals. He was then only twenty-five years of age.

Samuel's studies took him to the great centres of learning in Europe. In 1845 he visited Rome and there spent five months. He gave himself to the study of the *Codex Vaticanus* and although not allowed to transcribe any part of it, it is said that he made an occasional note on his fingernails. From Rome he went to Florence, Modena, Venice, Munich and Basle. In 1849 he moved to Paris but an attack of cholera forced him to return home to England. In 1850 he visited centres in Germany, at Leipzig, Dresden, Wolfenbuttel and Utrecht.

The years that followed were spent at home labouring in the manuscripts. With skill, diligence and honesty he worked tirelessly and the resultant *Greek Text* stands today as a monument to his scholarship and application. His objective was to produce a Greek text resting entirely on the direct evidence of the most ancient documents existing at that time. He steadfastly refused to alter anything by conjecture and he left it to later scholars to translate and explain the text.

His monumental work was published at intervals between 1857 and 1872 and in all there were six parts. While in the act of revising Part 6 he suffered a stroke. This resulted in paralysis and he never walked again. Nevertheless, he continued the task from his bed and in the introduction to the final section (1872) he stated, "It is with exceeding satisfaction and thankfulness that I am able to put the last part of my Greek Testament into the hands of subscribers, thereby finishing my responsibility in connection with so much of God's Word, a work which has only deepened my apprehension of its Divine authority". Of this monumental work C. J. Ellicott, bishop of Gloucester and Bristol, has remarked, "The edition of Tregelles will last, perhaps to the very end of time, as a noble monument of faithful, enduring and accurate labour in the cause of Truth; it will always be referred to as a trustworthy collection of assorted critical materials of the greatest value and as such it will probably never be superceded".

Tregelles' scholarship was recognized and acknowledged. At the age of thirty-seven the University of St. Andrews conferred on him a Doctorate of Laws. In 1862, on Lord Palmerston's recommendation, he was granted a Civil List Pension of one hundred pounds. In his closing years he was invited to serve on the Revised Version Committee but for health reasons he had to decline that invitation.

On April 24th, 1875, Samuel P. Tregelles passed away to be with Christ at the early age of sixty-two. In his passing there went from among men a strong yet gentle personality, a scholar largely self-taught but of rare brilliance and ranked by many as the greatest Biblical scholar of the nineteenth century, a staunch evangelist, one deeply devoted to his Lord. The Western Morning News commented of him, "Tregelles must rank as the most learned man ever associated with the city of Plymouth". His body was laid to rest in Plymouth Cemetery, there to await the resurrection morning. A commemorative bronze plaque marked his late home, No.6 Portland Square in Plymouth, where he had lived from 1846 up until the time of his death. This simple memorial stood for many years but sadly no longer exists.

Samuel Tregelles' literary legacy has been vast. Besides his *Greek New Testament*, other works have come from his pen – some textual, some prophetical, some historical, and some doctrinal. The British Museum Catalogue lists some forty-seven items of "Works by S. P. Tregelles". Poems and hymns have also been part of his legacy. His versified compositions are rich and full, bowing the heart in adoring worship and lighting the horizon with the glowing hope of the coming again of the Lord Jesus and the resurrection morning. The subject matter of his hymns is very diverse, as a glance at the following titles will suggest – "Thanksgiving for Divine Mercies", "The Second

Advent", "Peace in Jesus", "Praise for Electing Grace", "Christ the One Oblation", "Heaven anticipated", "Complete in Jesus", "Jesus, our Strength and Safety", "Jesus, the Name over all", "The Sacrifice of Praise", "The Dead in Christ" and "Communion of Saints".

Samuel P. Tregelles' hymns, however, have had limited usage but some six of his hymns have been included in the *Believers Hymn Book* and of these perhaps the one best known is **"Holy Saviour! we adore Thee"**. He entitled it, "The Second Advent desired". It was one of his earliest compositions and first appeared in *Hymns for Poor of the Flock* in 1838.

> *Holy Saviour! we adore Thee,*
>   *Seated on the throne of God,*
> *While the heavenly hosts before Thee*
>   *Gladly sound Thy praise abroad –*
>   *Thou art worthy!*
>   *We are ransomed by Thy blood.*
>
> *Saviour! though the world despised Thee,*
>   *Though Thou here wast crucified,*
> *High the Father's glory raised Thee,*
>   *Lord of all creation wide –*
>   *Thou art worthy!*
>   *We now live, for Thou hast died.*
>
> *And though here on earth rejected*
>   *'Tis but fellowship with Thee.*
> *What besides could be expected,*
>   *Than like Thee our Lord to be?*
>   *Thou art worthy!*
>   *Thou from earth hast set us free.*
>
> *Haste the day of Thy returning*
>   *With Thy ransomed Church to reign:*
> *Then shall end the days of mourning,*
>   *We shall sing with rapture then –*
>   *"Thou art worthy!*
>   *Come, Lord Jesus, come, Amen."*

HOLY SAVIOUR! WE ADORE THEE

This is a hymn of adoration and praise.

Christ in glory is its theme throughout,
as rejected by earth, vindicated by the Father, adored by heavenly hosts,
loved and longed for by the Church.

"Thou art worthy!" is its recurring refrain.
The hearts of the heavenly hosts, of the Father and of the Church
are in perfect accord.
Heaven's song is one.

"The wanderer no more will roam"

Mary Jane Walker (1816-1878)

Tombstone of Dr. Edward and Mary Jane Walker
(Cheltenham Cemetery)

In the seventeenth century, when the Huguenots, under persecution, fled from France, a family of them, by the surname of Deck, settled in the South of England. Some of that family later moved to East Anglia and engaged in farming. One of their descendants, John Deck, (born in 1761), became postmaster in Bury St. Edmunds in Suffolk. He was a man of influence and affluence and later became Mayor of the town. John Deck and his wife had a family of eight children. Their eldest son, James George, became well known as a hymnwriter. Mary Jane, the subject of this sketch, was a younger member of that family.

John Deck and his family, in early years, were dutiful members of the Church of England. Then, when the gospel reached them, John and his wife were saved. Thereafter they sought to bring up their family in the fear of the Lord. Mrs. Deck was a praying woman, a mother whose one burden in life was the salvation and spiritual welfare of her children. She adopted the practice of regularly setting aside time each day to be alone with God to pray for the family. God graciously heard her cries and she had the unspeakable joy of seeing all her family of eight children led to Christ and consecrating their lives to His service.

Mary Jane Deck was born on 27th April 1816. Of her early years not much has been left on record, but we know that when she was only a girl she started to write hymns and poems. In this, perhaps, she was encouraged by James George, her older brother. Many of Mary Jane's early pieces first appeared in leaflet form but these had limited circulation.

In the year 1848 Mary Jane married Dr. Edward Walker, who later became rector of St. Mary's Parish Church in Cheltenham, Gloucestershire. She was then thirty-two years of age. Edward was a godly evangelical rector. He had been educated at Lincoln College, Oxford and after brief ministries on the Isle of Man, in Manchester and in Salford, he commenced his labours in Cheltenham in 1857, first as curate, then becoming rector in 1863. After a brief ministry in Cheltenham of only fifteen years Edward died at the early age of forty-nine, but such was his godly influence in that town that, at the time of his death and funeral, almost every trading establishment put up its shutters and thousands of townspeople followed his funeral cortege through the crowded streets to the cemetery on the outskirts of the town. Dr. Edward Walker was regarded as, "one of the most pious, earnest, conscientious and truth-loving men that have ever held the rectory of Cheltenham". "Few men were loved as he was". A marble plaque to his memory was later placed in St. Mary's Parish Church, the inscription thereon concluding, "—He ceased not to teach and to preach Jesus Christ and Him crucified".

Edward and Mary Jane Walker had a family of three sons, all bearing the father's name, Edward, as one of their forenames. The eldest and the youngest sons died in early life. The second son, James (James Edward) was a student at Oxford at the time of his father's death. Under the circumstances the bereaved congregation of St. Mary's subscribed the generous sum of two thousand, five hundred pounds in order that Mrs. Walker and her son should not be left in any financial difficulty. James thereby was enabled to continue his studies and on graduation he returned to Cheltenham. There he established "The Walker Memorial Church" in Whaddon Lane where he faithfully ministered for thirty-four years. The order of the Whaddon Lane Church followed that of the Church of Scotland. Its original building was an iron structure but this was replaced some years ago by a permanent red brick building on the same site and is known today as Cheltenham Evangelical Free Church. As a minister James was greatly beloved. As a son he was deeply devoted to his mother, writing of her years afterwards as "a gentle, but deeply tried Christian".

Mary Jane in her widowhood continued to live in Cheltenham, in a small terrace house at No.15 Pittville Villas. She outlived her husband by six years and during that period she identified herself with a company of believers in the Lord Jesus, gathered simply to His Name and meeting in the Old Corn Exchange in the centre of Cheltenham. There she found a spiritual home and there she remained until the time of her death. She passed away to be with Christ on 2nd July 1878 and is buried beside her husband in the Walker family burial plot in Cheltenham Cemetery. Some fourteen years later, her eldest sister, Margaret Deck, was laid to rest in the same plot.

Dr. Edward Walker in his lifetime had a great interest in hymnology. He compiled and edited a volume of hymns and poems, entitling it, *"Psalms and Hymns for Public and Social Worship"*. In this collection there were quite a number of hymns from the pen of his brother-in-law, James George Deck, but, more interestingly, there were nine hymns with the initials "M. J. W." appended. These had come from the pen of his wife, Mary Jane Walker and some of them had been written before their marriage.

Among the nine hymns of "M. J. W." in her husband's collection there were some precious compositions,

> "I journey through a desert drear and wild", ("The Journey of Life"),
> "Jesus, I will trust Thee, trust Thee with my soul", ("Trust in Jesus"),
> "O spotless Lamb of God, in Thee", ("Passiontide"), and
> "The wanderer no more will roam", ("Reconciliation with God").

Mary Jane wrote, besides, many other poems and hymns. One of her poems, "In the heart of London city", was later set to music and is now used as a hymn. Its touch is tender and beautiful, its theme singular and telling, "I have CHRIST! – what want I more?" In its adaptation as a hymn some words have been altered, a refrain has been added and one verse has been omitted.

Similarly, her hymn, "I journey through a desert drear and wild" is incomplete in most hymnals. This incomplete hymn is used today by saints gathered at the Lord's supper to direct their hearts into the perfect pathway of the Lord Jesus. Nevertheless, its writer had probably originally intended it as linked with life's experience, as suggested by its title, "The Journey of Life", and indicated by its closing stanza,

> *Thus while I journey on, my Lord to meet,*
> *My thoughts and meditations are so sweet,*
> *Of Him on whom I lean, my Strength, my Stay,*
> *I can forget the sorrows of the way.*

Indeed, the hymn was probably born out of her own personal experience for she was "a deeply tried Christian".

Mary Jane's hymn, "Jesus, I will trust Thee" has been used of the Lord more than any other of her compositions. Its words have often been the language of the burdened soul in coming to the Saviour and include not only conversion's initial experience, but also the soul's repose right to the close. Indeed, its opening stanza was the closing song of the beloved Frances Ridley Havergal, just a few moments before she died.

> *Jesus, I will trust Thee, trust Thee with my soul;*
> *Guilty, lost, and helpless, Thou canst make me whole:*
> *There is none in heaven, or on earth like Thee:*
> *Thou hast died for sinners – therefore, Lord, for me.*

And, on that occasion, Frances substituted her own personal words, "hast made" in the second line, instead of Mary Jane's original words, "canst make".

But Mary Jane Walker's composition, **"The wanderer no more will roam"** is altogether unique.

> *The wanderer no more will roam,*
> *The lost one to the fold hath come,*
> *The prodigal is welcomed home,*
>   *O Lamb of God, in Thee!*

Though clothed in rags, by sin defiled,
The Father hath embraced His child;
And I am pardoned, reconciled,
  O Lamb of God, in Thee!

It is the Father's joy to bless,
His love provides for me a dress,
A robe of spotless righteousness,
  O Lamb of God, in Thee!

Now shall my famished soul be fed,
A feast of love for me is spread,
I feed upon the children's bread,
  O Lamb of God, in Thee!

Yea, in the fullness of His grace,
He puts me in the children's place,
Where I shall gaze upon His face,
  O Lamb of God, in Thee!

I cannot half His love express,
Yet, Lord, with joy my lips confess,
This blessed portion I possess,
  O Lamb of God, in Thee!

And when I in Thy likeness shine,
The glory and the praise be Thine,
That everlasting joy is mine,
  O Lamb of God, in Thee!

Mary Jane Walker wrote this hymn in the year 1845, three years before her marriage. She was then twenty-nine years of age. Her brother, James George Deck, tells us that it was written on his suggestion that "the manner of God's love in receiving sinners needed to be known as well as our way of coming to Him". The hymn was intended as a complementary hymn to that of Charlotte Elliott's "Just as I am, without one plea", written some nine years previously. If Charlotte Elliott's great hymn is *the sinner's acceptance of the Divine invitation*, then Mary Jane Walker's hymn is truly complementary, *the Divine acceptance of the returning sinner*. Both hymns have the same metre and both have a similar repetitive fourth line in each stanza, *"O Lamb of God, I come!"* and *"O Lamb of God, in Thee!"*.

The background imagery of Mary Jane's hymn is from Luke 15, the father's welcome of the prodigal. The picture in the Gospel is painted in vivid colour. It was painted by the Saviour. None other but He could tell out the fullness of the father's heart. In that scene there was no withholding. The prodigal's prodigality was put behind forever, the loneliness of the far country was exchanged for the father's embrace, the filthy rags for the best robe, the want and the husks for the fatted calf and the humiliation of slavery for the place of a son.

And a Father's unstinted welcome and heaven's bounty still await the returning prodigal.
On this ground, *"O Lamb of God, in Thee!"*.

"Jesus loves me! This I know"

Anna Bartlett Warner (1822-1915)

Anna Bartlett Warner

Henry W. Warner, a well-to-do New York lawyer, lost almost everything in the financial panic of 1837 and in order to satisfy his creditors was compelled to sell off his luxurious Long Island home. In November of the previous year he had acquired the valuable and strategically placed property of Constitution Island on the Hudson River which he had seen and appraised while on a visit to his brother, Thomas, who was then chaplain and professor at the United States Military Academy at West Point. Mrs. Warner had died the previous year and when the Long Island home was sold, Henry Warner, with his two daughters, Susan and Anna, moved to "Wood Crag" on

Constitution Island. And in order to make a home for the father and the two girls, Henry's sister, Aunt Fanny, went with them. Anna was then a delicate introspective adolescent of fifteen years of age. Susan was four years her senior.

The lifestyle of the Warner girls, both of whom were well educated, was now to be totally different from aforetime. The wealth and ease, with which they had grown up, must of necessity be left behind. Daily bread must be won by daily work, their life of luxury exchanged for a life of simplicity and relative frugality. Susan, on looking back on that experience, afterwards wrote, "We left home, silk and satin dresses, carriage house and servants, to don calico and to do work with our hands that we had always considered menial".

The two sisters did all they could to supplement the family income. They embarked on many ventures, from making flags and ceramics to inventing games, and in all their efforts were encouraged by Aunt Fanny. Both girls were avid readers and one day Aunt Fanny suggested that they write a book. They agreed and soon Susan's first novel, *The Wide, Wide World,* under her pen name, "Elizabeth Wetherell" was ready for publication. Just at that time resources in the Warner home were very sparse; there were only sixty-three dollars in hand to settle debts of over a hundred dollars. Susan's book was submitted to several publishers but all turned it down. Then, at last, it found a sympathetic reader in Mrs. Putnam, mother of George Putnam, the proprietor of The Putnam Publishing Company. Mrs. Putnam insisted that the family company publish the book. The book proved to be a great success. It turned out to be a best seller and soon outsold every other novel of its day except Harriet Beecher Stowe's "Uncle Tom's Cabin".

This initial success started off the two girls on a literary career and, in the years that followed some seventy books came from their pen, some by Susan, and some by Anna and some as a joint effort. Like the Flower sisters, Eliza and Sarah, of Harlow, England, the Warner sisters, Susan and Anna, worked closely together in their literary productions. They had complementary talents, Susan was the chief novelist and Anna was the chief poet. However, Susan did write some verse and Anna wrote some novels. Anna wrote under the pen name of "Amy Lothrop".

In the year 1859, Susan and Anna collaborated in writing another novel, *Say and Seal,* its story woven around three principal characters – John Linden, Faith Derrick and little Johnny Fox. Mr. Linden was

Johnny's Sunday school teacher. Towards the end of the story little Johnny is very sick and feverish. When asked what he wants, "Walk – like last night". Mr. Linden takes the little fellow in his arms and walks back and forth. Little Johnny is soothed and quieted. Then suddenly he pleads, "Sing" and, as Faith listens, Mr. Linden starts to sing words that neither Faith nor little Johnny had ever heard before.

> *Jesus loves me! This I know,*
> *For the Bible tells me so;*
> *Little ones to Him belong,*
> *They are weak but He is strong.*
>
> *Jesus loves me – He who died*
> *Heaven's gate to open wide;*
> *He will wash away my sin,*
> *Let His little child come in.*
>
> *Jesus loves me, loves me still,*
> *Though I'm very weak and ill;*
> *From His shining throne on high*
> *Comes to watch me where I lie.*
>
> *Jesus loves me – He will stay*
> *Close beside me all the way,*
> *Then His little child will take*
> *Up to heaven for His dear sake.*

A few hours later, after Mr. Linden had read to him from the Book of Revelation, God took little Johnny to Himself, at the same time Mr. Linden remarking to Faith, "We were permitted to show him the way at first, but he is showing it to us now".

William B. Bradbury, organist of the New York Baptist Tabernacle, later set the words to music and added the lines of its simple yet immortal chorus

> *Yes, Jesus loves me! Yes, Jesus loves me!*
> *Yes, Jesus loves me! The Bible tells me so.*

The Warner home at "Wood Crag" on Constitution Island was the birthplace of Susan and Anna's compositions and there, for more than fifty years, the two sisters laboured tirelessly in their literary efforts. Besides, in the living room of their home, they also carried on a Sunday school and Bible class for the cadets of the West Point Military Academy and many of Anna's simple hymns were written originally for her class of cadets.

Susan passed away in 1885. Anna lived till 1915 and at her death, Constitution Island was willed over to the United States government to become a permanent part of the West Point Military Academy. Both sisters were buried at West Point with full military honours on the instruction of the American President and at Anna's funeral service the Military Band played the strains of her own hymn, "Jesus loves me!", at the graveside. And today, Constitution Island and "Wood Crag" are fitting memorials to the two Warner sisters.

Anna's real life work was the writing of hymns and the translating of hymns. In her lifetime she compiled and edited two volumes of verse, *Hymns of the Church Militant* (1858) and *Wayfaring Hymns, Original and Translated* (1869). These two volumes contained both her own compositions and her translated hymns. Anna's translation work is of distinct merit. Most were from the German and some forty-seven of these have been listed in Julian's Dictionary of Hymnology. They are worthy hymns, wide ranging in their subject matter and beautifully translated.

Anna's own compositions were written mostly for children and are marked by simplicity. Though most of them are no longer sung, two remain, her popular children's hymn, "Jesus loves me", and her "We would see Jesus". The words of this latter hymn are very beautiful. Its lines initially appeared in her novel, *Dollars and Cents* in 1852 and then independently as a hymn in her first collection of 1858. Its lines were the fruit of her meditation on the text of Scripture, "We would see Jesus", from John 12: 21.

We would see Jesus, for the shadows lengthen
Across this little landscape of our life;
We would see Jesus, our weak faith to strengthen
For the last weariness, the final strife.

We would see Jesus, the great rock foundation,
Whereon our feet were set by sovereign grace;
Not life, nor death, with all their agitation,
Can thence remove us, if we see His face.

> *We would see Jesus, other lights are paling,*
> *Which for long years we have rejoiced to see;*
> *The blessings of our pilgrimage are failing;*
> *We would not mourn them for we go to Thee.*
>
> *We would see Jesus, this is all we're needing;*
> *Strength, joy, and willingness come with the sight;*
> *We would see Jesus, dying, risen, pleading;*
> *Then welcome day and farewell mortal night.*

As a hymnwriter, Anna B. Warner is remembered today for her popular children's hymn, "**Jesus loves me!**" With its lines of simplicity she has endeared herself to the hearts of children the wide world over. The hymn, soon after its writing, became a favourite throughout America, finding its way into almost all hymnals. Very soon afterwards it was included in many English compilations. It has since been translated into more languages than probably any other hymn in the world and has been used of the Lord in the salvation of many children.

Jacob Chamberlain, a missionary among the Hindus in Southern India translated it into the Telugu language and taught it to the children of the day school. Some time afterward, when riding through the village streets on horseback, he discovered one of the boys singing its words in Telugu at the top of his voice to a group of native men and women.

> *Jesus loves me! this I know,*
> *For the Bible tells me so.*

"Sonny, where did you learn that song?" called out one of the men.
"Over at the Missionary School" the boy replied.
"Who is that man Jesus and what is the Bible?" asked the native.
"Oh, Jesus is the name of Him who came into the world to save us from our sins, and the Bible is the book from God. That is what the missionaries taught me".
And so the native boy witnessed to his own people of the precious name of Jesus and told them of the precious Word of God.

The strength of this hymn, "Jesus loves me!" lies in its simplicity. Alfred, Lord Tennyson once said, "In a good hymn you have to be simple and practical. The moment you cease to be commonplace and put in any expression out of the common, it ceases to be a hymn". Anna B. Warner put in nothing complicated. Its words are simplicity all the way. And yet in its words there is deep profundity of truth.

> ***Jesus loves me! this I know,***
> ***For the Bible tells me so.***

There is no simpler truth than this, yet none more sublime, none greater, and none more sweet.
Thereon, the child may place its simple trust, and the greatest intellect confidently enter eternity.

"It is a thing most wonderful"

William Walsham How (1823-1897)

William Walsham How

Whittington in Shropshire, an English farming village almost on the Welsh border, was the reputed birthplace of the famous fourteenth century Dick Whittington, Lord Mayor of London. Many of the stories surrounding him were of doubtful authenticity. Then centuries later, in that same village, another children's story was born. William Walsham How told that story in verse and there is no doubt about its authenticity. It is the story of the Cross. It is altogether and absolutely true.

IT IS A THING MOST WONDERFUL

It is a thing most wonderful,
Almost too wonderful to be,
That God's own Son should come from heaven,
And die to save a child like me.

And yet I know that it is true;
He chose a poor and humble lot,
And wept, and toiled and mourned and died
For love of those who loved Him not.

I sometimes think about the Cross,
And shut my eyes, and try to see
The cruel nails and crown of thorns,
And Jesus crucified for me.

But even could I see Him die,
I could but see a little part
Of that great love which like a fire
Is always burning in His heart.

I cannot tell how He could love
A child so weak and full of sin;
His love must be most wonderful,
If He could die my love to win.

It is most wonderful to know
His love for me so free and sure;
But 'tis more wonderful to see
My love for Him so faint and poor.

And yet I want to love Thee, Lord;
Oh, light the flame within my heart,
And I will love Thee more and more,
Until I see Thee as Thou art.

William Walsham How was descended from an old Cumberland family. He was born at College hill, Shrewsbury in Shropshire on 13th December 1823. His father, William Wybergh How was a solicitor there. William's mother died when he was only two. His father remarried and the second Mrs. How subsequently proved to be an endearing stepmother.

William grew up in Shrewsbury and there went to school, under the headmastership of the notable Dr. Butler. When he was eighteen he entered Wadham College in Oxford to study law but while there became interested in theology. He graduated B.A. in 1845 and after a theological course in Durham was ordained in the Church of England. He served as curate, first at St. George's, Kidderminster, then at Holy Cross, Shrewsbury. While at Shrewsbury, he married Frances Ann Douglas, a clergyman's daughter.

In 1851 William was appointed rector of Whittington and there he ministered for twenty-eight years. During those years he became Rural Dean of Oswestry, then honorary canon and later chancellor of St. Asaph's Cathedral. In 1879 William was appointed Suffragen Bishop of East London, with the accompanying title, "Bishop of Bedford". There in London he served amidst the poverty, squalor and overcrowded slums of the East End. In 1887 Mrs. How died and this influenced William's decision to move from London and accept the first Bishopric of Wakefield in Yorkshire. There he laboured for nine years until the time of his death on 10th August 1897.

William died at Lennane in Co. Mayo in the West of Ireland. He had gone there to Killary Harbour on a fishing holiday when serious illness overtook him. His body was brought back and laid to rest beside that of Mrs. How in the Garden of Remembrance in Whittington. A tall cross bearing the symbol of the Good Shepherd was later erected there to his memory and is known today as How's cross.

But William Walsham How was much more than an ecclesiastical academic moving up through the ranks of the Church of England. He was a man of great personal piety, one who lived for others. Selfish ambition had no meaning for him. Through twenty-six of the twenty-eight years of his Whittington ministry he kept a diary, but never once did he record any of the many offers of preferment which came his way during those years. He just quietly and politely declined them, one by one – the colonial bishoprics of Natal (1867), of New Zealand (1868), of Montreal (1869), of Cape Town (1873) and of Jamaica (1878), and in his own country, the attractive livings of Brighton and of Windsor, the canonry of Winchester and the bishoprics of Manchester and of Durham.

In London's East End, William's life style was simple, unlike that of his fellow bishops who resided in their palaces and rode in their carriages. He lived among the people. He travelled with them in their public transport. He visited them in their lodging houses and Salvation

Army halls. Though the slums appalled him, he dearly loved the people and the people loved him. The children trusted him and adored him for they knew he had a large place for them in his heart. And among the common people of London's East End, How became known as "The People's Bishop", "The Omnibus Bishop", "The Poor Man's Bishop" and "The Children's Bishop". It was this last title that delighted him most of all.

Bishop How was a shepherd of the common people. He had inscribed upon his pastoral staff the words of St. Bernard, "Pasce verbo, pasce vita" ("Feed with the Word, feed with the life"). Both these injunctions he sought to fulfil and it was his life as much as his preaching that commended the gospel and drew people to Christ. And yet at the same time William Walsham How exerted substantial influence in society's higher ranks. He was known among the leaders of the nation, by the Prime ministers of his day and by Queen Victoria herself. When it came to her Diamond Jubilee in 1897 How was approached to compose something suitable to be sung in St. George's, Windsor and for that occasion he wrote "O King of Kings, whose reign of old" and Sir Arthur Sullivan set the words to music.

How was truly a man of the people. But more, he was also a man of nature. He lived close to nature and she was his constant companion through life. From his boyhood days in Shrewsbury, when he started fishing for trout in the river Severn with a bent pin, right to the close of life in Connemara, he dearly loved the hours spent by the riverbank. How, besides, had a life-long interest in botany. In boyhood he kept a fernery. At school he and his friends organized a small horticultural society and held regular exhibitions. Nature's ever-changing seasonal flowers were a deep delight to him. In the towns and cities it was not so much the exotic exhibits of flowers that enthralled him, but rather the commonplace blooms raised in boxes on windowsills or in back yards that brought him most pleasure. And in all his natural pursuits his constant companion was his spaniel dog.

Nor was the fishing rod How's only skill. His pen he also plied with great dexterity and to great effect and many publications were the result. His *Commentary on the Four Gospels* for the S.P.C.K. set of volumes of the Bible combined clear exposition with spiritual depth. His *Plain Words* (both *Four Series* and *for Children*), his *Pastor in Parochia* and *Lectures on Pastoral Work* were practical and helpful.

But it is as a hymnwriter that William Walsham How is remembered today. Indeed, he has been judged by many as the greatest hymnwriter of the nineteenth century. In verse he "painted lovely images inwoven with tender thoughts". His compositions started when he was only a boy. One of his first serious efforts "The Resurrection", was written when he was scarcely thirteen and for that work he based his thoughts on a captivating natural illustration, the transformation of the caterpillar to a beautiful emancipated butterfly.

How wrote in all about sixty hymns. Many are still in use today, several are of the highest quality. They embody his own ideal of a hymn, "a good hymn should be like a good prayer – simple, real, earnest and reverent". Of his verse, Dr. John Julian has said, "Combining pure rhythm with directness and simplicity, Bishop How's compositions arrest attention more through a comprehensive grasp of the subject and the unexpected light thrown upon and warmth infused into facts and details usually shunned by the poet, than through glowing imagery and impassioned rhetoric. — Those compositions which have laid the firmest hold upon the church, are simple, unadorned, but enthusiastically practical hymns, the most popular of which, "O Jesus, Thou art standing", "For all the saints, who from their labours rest", and "We give Thee but Thine own" have attained a foremost rank. — He has sung us songs which will probably outlive all his other literary works".

His "O Jesus, Thou art standing" was written after his reading of a poem, "Brothers, and a sermon", by Jean Ingelow. Its theme is that of Holman Hunt in his painting, "The Light of the World", of the Saviour standing, knocking and pleading at a closed door (Rev. 3:20).

> *O Jesus, Thou art standing*
> *Outside the fast-closed door,*
> *In lowly patience waiting*
> *To pass the threshold o'er.*
> *Shame on us, Christian brothers,*
> *His Name and sign who bear,*
> *O shame, thrice shame upon us*
> *To keep Him standing there!*

His "For all the saints, who from their labours rest", on the fellowship of saints, was in all probability written in his study in Whittington Parish Church. It is widely known and perhaps his most popular hymn.

His "We give Thee but Thine own" is a fine hymn. In it he regards giving to God as much more than monetary giving; it extends to

IT IS A THING MOST WONDERFUL 179

embrace our wider debt to God and the needy world around us where there are so many broken and empty hearts in need of solace and salvation.

His hymn, "O Word of God Incarnate" is one of the best hymns existing today on the Bible.

> *O Word of God incarnate,*
> *O Wisdom from on high,*
> *O Truth unchanged, unchanging,*
> *O Light of our dark sky,*
> *We praise Thee for the radiance*
> *That from the hallowed page,*
> *A lantern to our footsteps,*
> *Shines on from age to age.*

But it is How's children's hymn, **"It is a thing most wonderful"**, that has won such a special place within so many hearts. Its words were written in 1872 and headed with the Scripture text, 1 John 4:10, "Herein is love, not that we loved God, but that He loved us, and sent His Son to be the propitiation for our sins". In its original it had five verses, a further two verses How added later. Its tune, "Herongate", was the composition of Ralph Vaughan Williams, one of the great composers of the twentieth century.

This great hymn tells of the wonder and the response within the heart of a child on beholding the Cross.
The greatest intellect may look at the Cross and wonder. He is baffled. He questions all and turns away.
The simplest child, on beholding it, is also filled with wonder but does not try to analyse. It simply trusts.
How precious to the heart of the Saviour is the faith of "one of these little ones which believe" (Mt.18: 6)!

"Low in the grave He lay"

Robert Lowry (1826-1899)

Robert Lowry

The name of Robert Lowry takes a high and honoured place in the realm of sacred song. By calling, he was a Baptist minister, and as such served several churches in the Eastern States of America. He was, besides, a hymnwriter and a musician of the first rank. He wrote hymns with their accompanying music and in addition composed tunes for the words of others. Both his words and his tunes are widely sung today.

Robert Lowry was the son of Crozier Lowry and was born in Philadelphia, Pennsylvania on 12th March 1826. He became a believer and a follower of the Lord Jesus when he was seventeen. Afterward, he proceeded to the University of Lewisburg in Pennsylvania and from there graduated with honours in the year 1854.

After ordination as a Baptist minister, his first charge was at West Chester in Pennsylvania. Thereafter he served other Baptist churches, both in New York City and in Brooklyn, New York. He had outstanding qualities as a preacher and in 1876 was appointed Professor of Rhetoric at his parent University of Lewisburg. After six years in that honoured position he resigned his professorship and returned to the pulpit. He always regarded preaching as his chief calling. It was his first love. His last ministerial charge was at Plainfield, New Jersey and there he laboured until the time of his death. He passed away on 25th November 1899 at the age of seventy-three and is buried in Hillside Cemetery, Plainfield.

Robert Lowry, from his twenty-eighth year until the close of life, was a faithful minister of Christ. He was also a man of rare administrative ability and a thorough Bible student. But notwithstanding such abilities and application it was his contribution to sacred song that has been his treasured legacy to succeeding generations. Indeed, it has been well said that "Robert Lowry's preaching reached thousands with the gospel but his simply stated hymns have moved and inspired millions for more than a century".

Dr. Robert Lowry was a self-effacing man and always regarded his musical talent as something of a "side issue". At one stage in his career he was known to say, "I felt a sort of meanness when I began to be known as a composer". Notwithstanding, he brought all the wealth of his musical talent to the work of God. His name was intimately associated with the production and publication of some of the most popular Sunday school hymn books in the United States of America, as *"Happy Voices"* (1865), *"Chapel Melodies"* (1868), *"Bright Jewels"* (1869), *"Pure Gold"* (1871), *"Royal Diadem"* (1873), *"Tidal Wave"* (1874), *"Fountain of Song"* (1877) and *"Welcome Tidings"* (1877), and in the year 1868, after the death of William Bradbury, the Biglow Publishing Company selected Dr. Robert Lowry as the Company's music director.

There are many well-known hymns that are sung today to tunes composed by Dr. Robert Lowry. And in each case his music is most fittingly wedded to the words. He has given to us the fitting marching metre for Dr. Isaac Watts' great hymn "Come, ye that love the Lord". (It is noteworthy that more than a century lapsed between the composition of its words and its music.) He has also given to us the music for Sylvanus Dryden Phelps's great devotional hymn, "Saviour, Thy dying love"; for Fanny Crosby's "All the way my Saviour leads me"; for Edward Payson Hammond's "Christians, go and tell of Jesus"; for Annie Sherwood Hawks' "I need Thee every hour" and for Anna B. Warner's "One more day's work for Jesus". And in each case the tune has been greatly responsible for the acceptance and success of the hymn.

Dr. Robert Lowry did much of his writing and composing on Sunday evenings. He found that after the mental strain of services his mind simply refused to rest and he thereupon occupied himself with musical compositions. Once, when asked about his method of writing hymns, he replied, "I have no one method. Sometimes the music comes and the words follow — I watch my moods, and when anything strikes me, whether words or music, no matter where I am, at home or on the street, I jot it down — my brain is sort of a spinning machine, I think, for there is music running through it all the time. I do not pick out my music at the keyboard. The tunes of nearly all the hymns I have written have been completed on paper before I tried them on the organ. Frequently the words of the hymn and the music have been written at the same time".

Dr. Lowry has left for us several compositions in which both the words and the music were written simultaneously. His most popular hymn, "Shall we gather at the river?" (Mutual recognition in the hereafter), was written on a sultry July afternoon in 1864 during the height of an epidemic when he was pastor in Brooklyn. Many were passing away, parting from their loved ones at the river of death. Families and friends were asking the question, "Shall we meet at the river of life?" Dr. Lowry responded in verse, giving to them the hymn, as we know it today, "Shall we gather at the river?" It immediately met with warm approval, and later, when he visited England in 1880 for Raike's Centenary, an occasion when Sunday school workers from many countries came together, he received a tremendous ovation when introduced as its author.

His hymns, "Weeping will not save thee" (Salvation through faith) and "What can wash away my stain?" (Precious blood of Jesus) are great favourites in gospel work. Their simple statements of truth declare the way of salvation with perfect clarity. The former hymn tells us that salvation is not had by weeping, or by working, or by waiting, but only through faith in Christ.

> *Faith in Christ will save thee—*
> *Sinner, trust God's risen Son,*
> *Trust the work that He has done,*
> *To His arms now quickly run—*
> *Faith in Christ will save thee.*

The latter hymn is introduced by the question, "What can wash away my stain?" and is then immediately answered with clarity, "Nothing but the blood of Jesus". This answer then becomes the theme phrase of the little hymn, sometimes as the reply to a question posed and sometimes as affirmation of a stated truth.

> *Nothing can for sin atone;*
> *Nothing but the blood of Jesus.*
> *Naught of good that I have done;*
> *Nothing but the blood of Jesus.*

These great gospel truths so clearly stated have helped many seeking souls to find the way of salvation.

Apart from his evangelical hymns, Dr. Lowry has written a lovely hymn of praise to God,

> *Praise ye Jehovah! Come with songs before Him,*
> *Maker, Redeemer, mighty Lord of all;*
> *While all the angels joyfully adore Him,*
> *Let all the world before His footstool fall.*

and a lovely hymn on the Bible,

> *While we look within Thy word,*
> *Show Thy face to us, O Lord;*
> *In these pages may we see,*
> *Every lesson points to Thee.*

But it is Dr. Robert Lowry's hymn on the resurrection of Christ, **"Low in the grave He lay"**, that is ranked by many as his best composition. He composed both its words and its music on an evening in the year 1874. The completed hymn then appeared the following year (1875) in "Brightest and Best", a publication edited by Dr. Lowry and William H. Doane.

> *Low in the grave He lay –*
> *Jesus, my Saviour,*
> *Waiting the coming day –*
> *Jesus, my Lord.*

> *Up from the grave He arose*
> *With a mighty triumph o'er His foes;*
> *He arose, a victor from the dark domain,*
> *And He lives for ever with His saints to reign;*
> > *He arose! ... He arose!*
> > *Hallelujah! Christ arose!*

> > *Vainly they watch His bed –*
> > > *Jesus, my Saviour,*
> > *Vainly they seal the dead –*
> > > *Jesus, my Lord.*

> > *Death cannot keep his prey –*
> > > *Jesus, my Saviour,*
> > *He tore the bars away –*
> > > *Jesus, my Lord.*

When the "hour" of the Saviour's cross was past, His precious body was reverently laid in a rock-hewn sepulchre *"waiting the coming day"*, "the third day" of which He so often had spoken. Then –

> *Up from the grave He arose*
> *With a mighty triumph o'er His foes;*
> *He arose, a victor from the dark domain,*
> *And He lives for ever with His saints to reign.*

In every realm the Saviour triumphed and every enemy was completely routed.

Physically He triumphed. The sentry, the seal, the stone, the sepulchre were all in vain when the mighty Victor started His upward march to the everlasting throne, leaving behind Him, as a tattered spider's web, every pernicious design of the enemy. (Matt. 27: 66 – 28: 6).

Morally He triumphed. Hitherto sin and death had reigned with undisputed sway. But, in the presence of holiness, death was rendered impotent. He *"tore its bars away"* and stepped forth from its *"dark domain"*, for "it was not possible that He should be holden of it" (Acts 2: 24).

Personally He triumphed. His bodily resurrection was the indisputable proof of the greatness of His Person and declared Him "the Son of God with power". (Rom. 1: 4) The sign He had given to

His would-be critics was fulfilled and was unmistakable, "Destroy this temple and in three days I will raise it up again" (John 2: 19).

Infernally He triumphed. Through incarnation and through death "The Mighty God" stooped to enter the strong man's domain and there, in enemy territory and with the enemy's sword, "He destroyed him that had the power of death, that is, the devil" (Heb. 2: 14).

Eternally He triumphed. In rising from the dead He took with Him the key. And now He is "alive for evermore" (Rev. 1: 18).

The Saviour's triumph stands complete.

**He arose! He arose!
Hallelujah! Christ arose!**

"There is a Name I love to hear"

Frederick Whitfield (1827-1904)

Frederick Whitfield

The treasure stores of hymnology are rich with compositions on the name of Jesus. This precious Name, given by God the Father to the Son of His love in incarnation, has filled and flooded the hearts of the people of God throughout the ages. Amid the vicissitudes of life overflowing hearts have poured forth the strains of its music. Truly this Name is a melody most sweet!

In the dark Middle Ages the name of Jesus filled and completely ravished the heart of Bernard and, within the monastery at Clairvaux, he penned the lines of his immortal "Jesu dulcis memoria", a forty-two stanza poem on the lovely name of Jesus.

> *Nor voice can sing, nor heart can frame,*
> *Nor can the memory find*
> *A sweeter sound than Thy blest Name,*
> *O Saviour of mankind!*

In the eighteenth century, John Newton, the once profligate sea captain and foul blasphemer, poured forth in verse his heart's appreciation of the lovely Name which he had once despised.

> *How sweet the name of Jesus sounds*
> *In a believer's ear!*
> *It soothes his sorrows, heals his wounds,*
> *And drives away his fear.*

Then, just over a century ago, Frederick Whitfield added his contribution to the already rich store. Indeed, his composition, **"There is a Name I love to hear"** has been a worthy addition. In early life he penned its lines. In later life he proved its truth, as, amid the trials and sorrows of life, the name of Jesus became to him as a soothing balm.

> *There is a Name I love to hear,*
> *I love to speak its worth;*
> *It sounds like music in mine ear,*
> *The sweetest Name on earth.*

> *It tells me of a Saviour's love,*
> *Who died to set me free;*
> *It tells me of His precious blood,*
> *The sinner's perfect plea.*

> *It tells me of a Father's smile*
> *Beaming upon His child;*
> *It cheers me through this "little while",*
> *Through desert, waste and wild.*

> *It tells me what my Father hath*
> *In store for every day,*
> *And, though I tread a darksome path*
> *Yields sunshine all the way.*

> It tells of One whose loving heart
> Can feel my deepest woe,
> Who in my sorrow bears a part
> That none can bear below.
>
> It bids my trembling soul rejoice,
> It dries each rising tear;
> It tells me in a "still small voice",
> To trust and never fear.
>
> Jesus! the Name I love so well,
> The Name I love to hear;
> No saint on earth its worth can tell,
> No heart conceive how dear.
>
> This Name shall shed its fragrance still
> Along life's thorny road,
> Shall sweetly smooth the rugged hill
> That leads me up to God.
>
> And there, with all the blood-bought throng,
> From sin and sorrow free,
> I'll sing the new, eternal song
> Of Jesus' love to me.

Frederick Whitfield was born at Threapwood on the Welsh border of Cheshire in the year 1827. He was the youngest of the family of Thomas and Jane Whitfield. Frederick grew up in a godly home and early in life he learned of his spiritual need before God. Then, when he was only a boy, he trusted the Saviour.

When Frederick was in his twenties he entered Trinity College, Dublin. The city of Dublin at that time was astir with a spiritual awakening. Frederick came under its influence and threw all his youthful energies into the movement. In 1859 he graduated B.A. from Trinity College and in the same year was ordained in the Church of England. This marked the beginning of Frederick's notable ministry for God, a ministry that covered a period of forty years. These forty years were divided into three distinct periods and spheres — the first six years (1859-65) in the West Riding of Yorkshire, the next ten years (1865-75) in and around the city of London, and the concluding twenty-four years (1875-99) in Hastings on the south coast of England.

Frederick's Yorkshire ministry commenced in Wharfedale, in the town of Otley. There, as curate, he ministered for two years and while there made his first publication, *Voices from the Valley*, a volume of sermons deriving its title from the lovely Wharfedale valley in which he lived. At the close of his Otley ministry Frederick married Sarah Garforth. He then moved to Kirby-Ravensworth, where as vicar he ministered for four years.

In the year 1865 Frederick moved to the London area and over the next ten years held several appointments, including those of senior curate of Greenwich and vicar of St. John's, Bexley. During the early part of his London ministry Mrs. Whitfield died and Frederick was left, a young widower with three small boys. After five years of widowhood, he found a suitable partner in Miss Sophia Butler and remarried.

In 1875 Frederick was appointed vicar of St. Mary's-in-the-Castle, Hastings, and in this appointment he followed on the ministry of the eloquent Thomas Vores. This was Whitfield's greatest ministry and continued right up until his retirement in 1899. In his preaching he was faithful to the Word of God and in return God granted His blessing. Notable features of Frederick's Hastings ministry were the regular Bible Readings, conducted by himself, and an annual convention, patterned after the convention at Keswick.

After twelve years of remarriage, the second Mrs. Whitfield also died and Frederick was again left with a young family. The eldest girl in that family, Miss Emily Banks Whitfield, is remembered for her close association with the Mt. Hermon Missionary Training College at Streatham Common; another daughter was the author of her father's life-story, *Memorial of the Rev. Frederick Whitfield, B.A.*.

In the year 1899, Frederick, because of failing health, retired from his ministry at St. Mary's and went to live at Norwood in South London. He loved preaching and in his retirement occasionally deputized for others. His last message was given in St. Matthew's Church, Croydon. Then, on 13th September 1904, he took his leave of earth and passed away to be with Christ. His body was laid to rest beside that of his beloved Sophia, in Kensal Green Cemetery, London. Thus concluded the earthly life of Frederick Whitfield, a life marked by a genuine humility and deep devotion to Christ.

Frederick Whitfield throughout life was a prolific writer, both in prose and in verse. Some thirty sizeable works have come from his pen. His better known prose publications include, *Voices from the Valley*, *Spiritual unfolding from the Word of Life*, *Gleanings from Scripture*, *Truth in Christ*, *The Word Unveiled* and *Counsels and Knowledge from the Words of Truth*.

Whitfield's verse appeared in three of his publications – *Sacred Poems and Prose*, *The Christian Casket in Prose and Verse* and *Quiet Hours in the Sanctuary*. Of his hymns a number still survive and four are included in The Believers Hymn Book – "I need Thee, precious Saviour", "I saw the Cross of Jesus", "Jesus, O Name of power divine" and "There is a Name I love to hear".

This last hymn, **"There is a Name I love to hear"** (entitled "The Name of Jesus") is one of the sweetest that have come from the pen of Frederick Whitfield. He wrote it when in his twenties during his college days in the city of Dublin. The hymn first appeared in the year 1855 on hymnsheets and leaflets, and within ten years of its publication became widely known. It became a great favourite in America and has been translated into various languages.

Frederick Whitfield had known life's sorrows. He was twice bereaved of his dear life's partner and on each occasion left with three young children. The depths of his heart's sorrow were real and are disclosed in lines which he penned in his second bereavement,

> *Oh! lighten, Lord, this darkened life,*
> *Lord, shine upon my way!*
> *A broken heart, a darkened home,*
> *O God! Is this Thy way?*

The way for Frederick Whitfield was dark. Yet in the darkness he proved the solace of the lovely Name of Jesus, smoothing life's rugged hill and shedding fragrance upon its thorny road.

Truly, the Name of Jesus is **a lovely Name.** It fills the heart of the child of God and sings itself along life's pathway. Frederick Whitfield, in his hymn, has termed it, **the sweetest name on earth.**

Besides, the Name of Jesus is **a lordly Name.** It fills all heaven. There every heart is bowed at its mention. Indeed, the Divine author of Holy Scripture has ranked it, **the highest name in heaven.**

> "God also hath highly exalted Him and given Him a Name
> which is above every name;
> that at the Name of Jesus every knee should bow, —
> and every tongue confess that Jesus Christ is Lord, to the glory of
> God the Father". (Phil. 2: 9-11).

"'Midst the darkness, storm and sorrow"

Emma Frances Bevan (1827-1909)

Emma Frances Bevan

Just over a century ago the hymn, "'Midst the darkness, storm and sorrow", appeared in Frances Bevan's collection, "Hymns of Ter Steegen*, Suso and Others" with the initials "P.G." appended. In this two volume collection of beautiful hymns and poems Mrs. Bevan included, besides her translations from the German of such notable authors as Gerhard Tersteegen, Heinrich Suso, Johann Tauler, Paul Gerhardt and others, quite a number of hymns of her own composition. As a hymnwriter, she preferred anonymity and, rather than sign her own name or use a pen name, she often appended merely the initials

*Mrs. Bevan always wrote the name, Tersteegen, as two words.

of the house where the hymn was written. The initials "P.G.", appended to "'Midst the darkness, storm and sorrow", indicate that Mrs. Bevan wrote the hymn at her Princes Gate home in London, rather than pointing to a Paul Gerhardt authorship.

Emma Frances Bevan came from an old Lancashire Whig and notable clerical family, the Shuttleworths of Gawthorpe Hall near Preston. She was born at Oxford on 25th September 1827, the eldest daughter of Rev. Philip Nicholas Shuttleworth. At the time of Frances' birth, her father was Warden of New College, Oxford. In 1842 he was appointed Bishop of Chichester but died two years later, leaving Frances fatherless at the early age of seventeen.

In early life Frances was a high churchwoman. At the age of twenty-seven, she attended Bible Readings in the home of R. C. L. Bevan of Fosbury Manor, Wiltshire and Trent Park, Middlesex and there she met with Christians, well taught in the Word of God. Those Bible studies made a lasting impression upon Frances and proved to be a turning point in her life. Two years later Frances married R. C. L. Bevan, at that time a widower and chairman of the family-banking firm, later to become Barclays' Bank. The Bevans were a well-to-do family, descended from Quaker and evangelical Anglican stock. Soon after marriage Frances identified herself with a company of Christians at Barnet, gathered simply to the Name of the Lord Jesus, and there she found a spiritual home.

Where the heart of God is resting,
I have found my rest.

Frances was highly educated. She was no mean Hebrew scholar and took modern languages in her stride, speaking German and French fluently. As a young girl she had had a German governess as a teacher and later in life was closely attached to the family of the scholarly Baron Von Bunsen, the Prussian ambassador to England. Such early and life-long influences led to her study of German literature and translation of many German hymns.

After marriage, Frances and her husband made their home at Trent Park, but later in life the family spent increasing periods of time at Cannes in the south of France. After her husband's death in 1890, Frances spent practically all her time on the Continent, the summers at Territet in Switzerland and the winters at Cannes. Frances died at her home in Cannes on 13th February 1909, at the age of eighty-one.

'MIDST THE DARKNESS, STORM AND SORROW

She is buried at Cockfosters in England, interred there in the family vault outside Christ Church. Her tombstone bears the Scripture inscription, "Waiting for the coming of our Lord Jesus Christ" 1 Cor. 1:7.

Further glimpses into Frances's life story have been given us in two little biographies, written by herself, *"Reminiscences of Ada Frances Bevan"*, the touching story of her eldest child who died at the age of four, and *"Recollections of R. C. L. Bevan"*, a memoir of her husband who, as a devoted Christian, lived his life simply, yet beautifully for God.

Frances had read deeply in the German mystics and pietists of the Middle Ages and in her interesting volumes, *"Three Friends of God"* and *"Sketches of the Quiet of the Land"*, has portrayed something of the background of these German hymnists. She says, "How distinct was their witness to the truth of the gospel may be easily seen by comparing their writings with those of the true servants of God who remained under the influence of Roman Catholicism only. A comparison of Thomas à Kempis with Johann Tauler will serve as an instance in this contrast. In the case of the latter, the present possession and enjoyment of eternal life; in the case of the former an earnest and true desire to attain that possession. In the latter forgiveness, peace and joy, the starting point; in the former the goal to be reached by strenuous effort".

Frances is best remembered today for her excellent translations of many old German hymns of the Middle Ages. In the introduction to her *"Hymns of Ter Steegen, Suso and Others"* one has said, "There is found in them that mystical touch, that indefinable quality that reaches the inmost recesses of the soul, and calls forth the deepest longings of the spirit. By her beautiful translations, Mrs. Bevan has taught us something of that wealth of hymnology found in the German language". And of that wealth the late Philip Schaff has judged, "It surpasses all others in wealth. These hymns are an eloquent witness for the all-conquering and invincible life-power of the evangelical Christian faith. Those possessed of the greatest vigour and unction, full of the most exulting faith and the richest comfort, had their origin amid the conflicts and storms of the Reformation; or the fearful devastations and nameless miseries of the Thirty Years War (1618–1648)".

Frances published her translations in several volumes, *"Songs of Eternal Life"* (1858), *"Songs of Praise for Christian Pilgrims"* (1859), *"Service of Song in the House of the Lord"* (1884), two volumes of *"Hymns of Ter Steegen, Suso and Others"* (1894 and 1897) (These were judged as decidedly the best to have come from her pen) and *"Come. A Selection of Gospel Hymns"* (1902).

In these collections Frances hid her own poetic compositions among her translations. Her personal contributions were indeed hidden treasure, but in true humility she concealed them. She desired only the exaltation of her Lord. The initials, which she appended to her verse, denoted the place where the hymns were written. Some of these have been identified, as, "T.P."= Trent Park, "P.G." =Princes Gate, "F.M."= Fosbury Manor, "V.M.C." =Villa Madeleine, Cannes, "C.P.C." =Chalet Passiflora, Cannes and "W.R." = Wykeham Rise. Others still await identification.

In Frances' two volumes of *"Hymns of Ter Steegen, Suso and Others"* there are upwards of sixty of her own beautiful hymns and poems. A few of these have received wider circulation. "Marvel not that Christ in glory" is taken from her six stanza hymn commencing, "I was journeying in the noontide" and entitled, "Beyond the Brightness of the Sun" (Acts 22:11). "We thank Thee, Lord, for weary days when desert springs were dry" is the commencement of her very beautiful piece, entitled, "Companionship". Her poem, "The Gospel according to Paul", contains lines which are familiar to many and have often been quoted in connection with overseas missionary work,

> Christ, the Son of God, hath sent me
> Through the midnight lands;
> Mine the mighty ordination
> Of the piercèd Hands.

But the best known and best loved of all Frances' verse is her, **"'Midst the darkness, storm and sorrow"**. She entitled it, "The Bride" (John 14:3). In its original there were fourteen stanzas of four lines each. These have been rearranged into seven eight-line stanzas.

> 'Midst the darkness, storm, and sorrow,
>   One bright gleam I see;
> Well I know the blessèd morrow
>   Christ will come for me.
> 'Midst the light, and peace, and glory
>   Of the Father's home,
> Christ for me is watching, waiting,
>   Waiting till I come.

Long the blessèd Guide has led me
    By the desert road;
Now I see the golden towers,
    City of my God.
There, amidst the love and glory,
    He is waiting yet;
On His hands a name is graven
    He can ne'er forget.

There, amidst the songs of heaven,
    Sweeter to His ear
Is the footfall through the desert,
    Ever drawing near.
There, made ready are the mansions,
    Radiant, still, and fair;
But the Bride the Father gave Him
    Yet is wanting there.

Who is this who comes to meet me
    On the desert way,
As the Morning Star foretelling
    God's unclouded day?
He it is who came to win me
    On the Cross of shame;
In His glory well I know Him
    Evermore the same.

Oh the blessèd joy of meeting,
    All the desert past!
Oh the wondrous words of greeting
    He shall speak at last!
He and I together entering
    Those fair courts above –
He and I together sharing
    All the Father's love.

Where no shade nor stain can enter,
    Nor the gold be dim,
In that holiness unsullied,
    I shall walk with Him.

> *Meet companion, then, for Jesus,*
> *From Him, for Him, made–*
> *Glory of God's grace for ever*
> *There in me displayed.*
>
> *He who in His hour of sorrow*
> *Bore the curse alone;*
> *I who through the lonely desert*
> *Trod where He had gone;*
> *He and I, in that bright glory,*
> *One deep joy shall share–*
> *Mine, to be for ever with Him;*
> *His, that I am there.*

Its title, **"The Bride"**, is most fitting for it is "the Bride" who speaks throughout. Separation and loneliness are her present lot, yet faith, love and hope spring eternal. Well she knows **her Beloved** will come for her, and she anticipates the moment. The night will then be over, the desert will be but a memory.

Then, — **He and I, together and forever.**

And with such meditation "The Bride" quickens her step toward that nuptial day!

"My Chains are snapt"

Margaret Ledlie Carson (1833-1920)

Margaret Ledlie Carson

Margaret Ledlie Carson was descended from sturdy Ulster stock.

Alexander Carson, her paternal grandfather, was a renowned Baptist pastor in Tobermore, Co. Derry. Having seceded from the Presbyterian Church in the year 1805, he became a prominent figure in the evangelical movement in Ulster at that time. He was a man of outstanding genius, a "fearless saint and scholar", one who forsook all to follow Christ. Witherows says of him, "Carson was a great, strong-minded, lion-hearted man. Difficulties could not daunt him. He was not to be turned aside from what he considered the way of duty because of perils in the path. He took care to do what he thought right, and left it to God to take care of the consequences". Alexander Carson and his beloved wife, Margaret Ledlie, had a family of thirteen children and their unspeakable joy was to see their prayers abundantly answered in the salvation of each one of them.

George Ledlie Carson, father of our present subject, was the second son in that large family of thirteen, and was born on 20th January 1803. Despite financial constraints, George received a good education, qualified as a medical doctor and set up practice in the town of Coleraine. He was, besides, pastor of the Baptist Church there and the proceeds of his medical practice enabled him to be self-supporting in his ministry. In 1823 he married a young widow, Mary Thomson Hanna, of Kilcronaghan, Tobermore in Co. Derry. They had a family of eight children. George's life span, however, was short; he died in his thirty-sixth year. On his eighteenth birthday, he had written a six-stanza poem. Its lines were very personal and very poignant. Indeed, they were almost prophetic.

> *Full eighteen years this day are gone*
> *Since first I saw Aurora dawn.*
> *When eighteen more have rolled away*
> *Shall purple morning dawn on me?*
> *Or shall I e'er that time has come*
> *Lie sheltered in the silent tomb?*
>
> *If destined to an earlier fall*
> *May I be ready at His call*
> *Ready to hide among the dead*
> *My vile, my base, my guilty head*
> *Ready to meet the bar of God*
> *Pure, just and clean through Jesus' blood.*

Margaret Ledlie Carson, our present subject, was the fifth child and third daughter of Dr. George and Mary Carson of Coleraine. Margaret was only five years of age when her father passed away, yet she had very definite memories of him and later in life put one of these memories into verse.

> *In memory's cell a shadowy portrait lies,*
> *I try to grasp it, try to catch those eyes*
> *In which I gazed in all my childish glee,*
> *While they beamed back bright streams of love for me.*

But O, 'tis vain; no feature can I trace;
A shadowy form, but not the dear, dear face,
And yet his voice, his touch, I don't forget;
And O that prayer, it lingers with me yet.

At twilight's hour I sat upon his knee,
'Twas then his soul went out in prayer for me;
"O let", he said, "Thy heavenly grace descend
On this white head in blessings without end".

His earnest tones I hear, the words he said
While his hand rested on my infant head,
And then he drew me closer, closer still,
While silent prayer his yearning heart did fill.

That was my father. Others speak of him
With quivering lips, and eyes with tears bedim,
But as for me, this one bright memory lies
A precious gem unseen by mortal eyes.

And do I never weep, have I no tears
For him who loved me 'mid unconscious years,
Yes; tears of joy, of truest ecstasy,
Gush forth, my father, while I think of thee.

I think of thee in that lone twilight hour,
A mighty prince, one who with God had power,
And did prevail, for O thy God did send
On that white head, "the blessings without end".

Early in life Margaret got to know the Saviour. She owned Him as Lord of her life and lived only for His glory. She took a deep interest in the salvation of others and throughout life proved to be a remarkable soul-winner. Her amiable and cheerful personality, combined with a deep spirituality, fitted her as a person whom the Lord greatly used. During the 1859 Revival she was instrumental in leading many to Christ and thereafter her interest in personal evangelistic work never waned. Her home was the spiritual birthplace of many.

Besides getting to know the Saviour, Margaret also, early in life, got to know her Bible. She was a very keen student of the Word, largely self-taught, but did carry on a large correspondence with many of the great teachers among the early brethren. Charles Henry Mackintosh

(C.H.M.) in particular was a close friend. Margaret was "steadfast, unmovable" in her stand for the truth of God. She would never allow anything that savoured of doctrinal error to go unchallenged. She was mighty in the Scriptures and skilled in the use of her pen and would fearlessly engage in combat any opponent of the truth of God. The opponent would be laid low, while she herself would emerge from the battle unscathed and undaunted. In this regard she exhibited the qualities of her grandfather, Alexander Carson.

Margaret L.Carson was a lady of not insignificant means. For most of her life she lived in the family home built by her father at No.4 Bath Terrace, overlooking the Arcadia in Portrush. But everything she possessed she held in trust for her Lord. She was a generous giver and helped forward greatly the work of missions. It has gone on record that she helped greatly to finance the building of the original Portrush Gospel Hall at Bath Street.

In the eventide of life Margaret enjoyed the companionship of a nephew in her home at Bath Terrace, besides the friendship of many friends. From there she passed away to be with the Lord on 24th February 1920 at the ripe age of eighty-seven years. Her body was laid to rest four days later in the family burying ground some thirty miles distant, in the little churchyard of Dromore outside Desertmartin in Co. Derry.

Margaret Ledlie Carson (or M.L.C. as she frequently signed herself) composed many hymns and poems. A volume of these in her own handwriting still survives. A selection was made from them in 1913 and published as *A Few Hymns and Poems by M. L. Carson*. Her compositions in the main were based on Scriptural subjects and include such pieces as, "David and Goliath", "The Leper", "The Victory", "Lord, I believe, and he worshipped Him", "His coming", "The dying thief", "S.o.S. 7:10", "The Lamb", "The man in the tombs", "The love of God", "I'll by no means clear the guilty" and "Cast not away your confidence". Among her compositions there also appears, again in her own handwriting, a most interesting poem of sixty-six verses, entitled "The books of the Bible" and therein, in each of the four line stanzas, she succinctly summarizes the content of each book of the Bible.

The best known, by far, of all M.L.C.'s compositions is her hymn, **"My chains are snapt"**. She entitled it "The Victory". It appears near the beginning in her handwritten book of hymns and hence and in all probability, was written in the early part of her life. The original composition consisted of eight verses (Facsimile, page 201). Margaret added a ninth verse at a later date and it appears in the 1913 publication

The Victory

My chains are snapped, the bonds of sin are broken
And I am free.
Oh, let the triumphs of his name be spoken
Who died for me.

O death, O hell I do not dread thy power,
The ransom's paid
On Jesus in that dark and fearful hour
My debt was laid.

And Oh! he bore it, bore sin love unbounded
That none may know.
He bore the cross and by his death confounded
Our every foe.

Oh! that he suffered, all his heart strings rending
For my found soul,
From him to Elom his anguished soul's ascending
In prayer the while.

O God of love, Thine own, thy heart's fond treasure
Thou didst not spare.
Yet thou alone, the infinite, couldst measure
His sufferings there.

We'll shout aloud, we'll tell the wondrous story
Through earth and sky.
Thou gav'st thy Son, thou gav'st the Lord of glory
For us to die.

But Oh! thy joy when from the dead returning
That cherished One.
Hell stood aghast, 'twas Gods own Son returning
That lonely tomb.

Yes he is risen — believe the joyful story
The Lord's on high
And we in him are raised to endless glory
That ne'er can die.

as the second last stanza,

> *O lift your heads, ye gates! Ye eternal doors,*
>   *Be opened wide,*
> *Far! Far above the heavens, the Victor soars,*
>   *The One who died.*

When Margaret wrote her original poem of eight stanzas she asked her friend, C.H. Mackintosh, for his comment. C.H.M. judged it good, but felt that it was incomplete without mention of the coming again of the Lord Jesus and he himself composed and appended a closing stanza.

> *We wait to see the Morning Star appearing*
>   *in glory bright,*
> *This blessèd hope illumes with beams most cheering*
>   *The hours of night.*

Thus the five-stanza hymn, as it appears today in most hymnals, consists of four stanzas written by M. L. C. and a closing stanza written by C. H. M.

> *My chains are snapt, the bonds of sin are broken,*
>   *And I am free;*
> *O! let the triumphs of His grace be spoken,*
>   *Who died for me.*
>
> *O death! O grave! I do not dread thy power,*
>   *The ransom's paid;*
> *On Jesus, in that dark and dreadful hour,*
>   *My guilt was laid.*
>
> *Yes, Jesus bore it – bore, in love unbounded,*
>   *What none can know;*
> *He passed through death, and gloriously confounded*
>   *Our every foe.*
>
> *And now He's risen, proclaim the joyful story,*
>   *The Lord's on high!*
> *And we in Him are raised to endless glory,*
>   *And ne'er can die!* (M. L. C.)

We wait to see the Morning Star appearing,
   In glory bright;
This blessèd hope illumes, with beams most cheering,
   The hours of night. (C. H. M.)

The hymn title **"The Victory"** is fitting. It tells of the mighty triumph over sin, death and the grave in the vicarious death, glorious resurrection and triumphant ascension of the Lord Jesus.

The appended closing stanza by C.H.M., speaking of the coming again of the Lord, perfects "The Victory".
"Then shall be brought to pass the saying that is written, Death is swallowed up in victory".
"O death, where is thy sting? O grave, where is thy victory?"
"But thanks be to God, which giveth us **the victory through our Lord Jesus Christ".**

(1 Cor. 15:54,55,57.)

"Crowned with thorns upon the tree"

Henry Grattan Guinness (1835-1910)

Henry Grattan Guinness

Henry Grattan Guinness turned his back on a lucrative life style and lived his life for God. As one of the most talented gospel preachers of the nineteenth century he was instrumental in pointing many souls to the Saviour. As founder of a missionary training college he helped to equip scores of young men and women for the Lord's service overseas and as one of the greatest prophetic scholars of his time he published works which influenced the British nation and beyond. On the human side of the story, the industry, determination and accomplishment that marked his path stemmed from a renowned ancestry, the Guinness family, of whom it has been said, "Never has the struggle between

God and mammon been so obviously fought out as in the Guinness tribe". Thus, while many of that distinguished family were renowned in this world, Henry Grattan Guinness lived for another world.

Henry Grattan Guinness was the grandson of the first Arthur Guinness, founder of the brewery at St. James' Gate, Dublin, and of Olivia, cousin of Henry Grattan, Ireland's foremost orator and politician. Henry was born in Monkstown, Dublin in the year 1835, the firstborn son of John Grattan Guinness and Jane Lucretia. He was named after his celebrated ancestor, Henry Grattan.

Henry's father died when Henry was just a boy. His mother, a member of the notable D'Esterre family, was a remarkable woman, a woman of excellent qualities, very talented in music and art, a spiritual woman, yet at the same time intensely practical. When she and the family moved to Cheltenham in England, she there performed acts of charity throughout the neighbourhood, visiting the sick and gathering the children to the ragged school. Often with open Bible in hand she spoke to people in the street of eternal things. In the town of Cheltenham she established an institution for the reclamation of fallen women. Her labours for God and for the underprivileged, however, were not much appreciated by those in authority and she met with a great deal of opposition. Notwithstanding, she was not easily daunted or turned aside.

Henry spent most of his youth in Cheltenham. In many ways he was a loner, a dreamer. He had an instinctive love for nature and for books and would often be found either strolling alone through the countryside or sitting in some quiet corner completely absorbed in a book. Henry also had his vices and as a young teenager frequented the taverns of the town. But above all else Henry loved adventure. It was his consuming passion, and at the age of sixteen he went off to sea, sailing as a midshipman to Mexico. The excitement of storms absolutely thrilled him and he was never happier than when at the wheel of a ship in the midst of a storm. Then something happened and this completely changed the whole course of his life.

Back home in Cheltenham, Henry waited up one night for his brother Wyndham returning from sea. It was late when Wyndham arrived and together they shared a room. Before going to sleep Wyndham told Henry of his latest and greatest experience, not of adventure in a storm at sea, but of finding a safe haven for his storm-tossed soul. Wyndham had been converted; he had found the Saviour. That night the Spirit of God spoke very clearly to Henry's heart. As he looked back, he saw only a wasted aimless life. He longed for the conscious reality of knowing Christ personally in his life and on that very night he put his trust in the Lord Jesus, making Him his personal Saviour. Henry was then nineteen years of age and from that night forward things were different.

Shortly after conversion Henry returned to Ireland. There, in the land of his birth, he observed the empty religious formality and superstition of the people and he resolved to do something about it. He started to preach the gospel, wherever he got men and women to listen, in the open air, in the market places, at cross roads or in the fields. He told them of their need of a new birth and of the Saviour whom he had found. Out in the West of Ireland he met with a great deal of opposition and frequently had to flee from his place of preaching under protection of a bodyguard.

Henry then moved back to England and there he preached the same message — in chapels, in the open air and at various venues in the city of London. He was a fluent public speaker and when helped of God had the ability to gather and hold a crowd. He loved preaching. As a young man still in his twenties he preached the glorious gospel throughout the cities and towns of England. He also visited France, Switzerland, Wales and Scotland but his most notable experiences were back in Ireland during the 1859 Revival. In the city of Dublin at that time he preached to thousands of people of all denominations and on many occasions, members of the clergy, judges, M.P.'s and professionals came to hear him. He told them of the folly of living only for the material things of this world and of the need for a new birth. Those were days of much blessing, days to be remembered.

In the city of Dublin Henry met with Hudson Taylor, who at that time was home on furlough from pioneer missionary work in China. Henry was deeply impressed by what Hudson Taylor told of the work of God in that land and confided to him of his exercise to go back with him to China. But Hudson Taylor, on inquiring as to Henry's age and learning that he was already thirty, told him that he was too old. Nevertheless he impressed upon him the need for someone to establish a base in the homeland for the training of young men and women for overseas missionary work. This encounter with Hudson Taylor left a deep impression on Henry.

Henry married in October 1860. His wife, Fanny Fitzgerald, proved to be a very congenial partner for him in every way for, whereas Henry was somewhat absent minded, Fanny was very practical and saw to the day to day running of the home and the bringing up of the family. But soon after marriage, a change of emphasis was noted in Henry's ministry. He gave less and less time to public preaching and devoted more time to the study of the Scriptures. The prophetic Scriptures fascinated him. He interpreted world history in the light of Scripture and had a special interest in the Jewish nation as part of the Divine programme. Through the generosity of a friend he undertook a four-month tour of the land of Palestine and the Middle East and was deeply impressed by what he saw. And the impressions made had a lasting effect on Henry's later ministry.

Henry made his home in the city of London. The time had come for his vision of a missionary training college to become a reality. He commenced a centre for students in the East End of London, at Stepney Green. The work was established on the basis of faith. No fees were asked of the students but instead they were required to participate in the running of the home as no servants were employed there. Besides their studies and duties in the home the students also engaged in mission work in the East End of London and as the result mission halls were established throughout the city. Henry felt that if students could not cope with life among the slums of London then they could not cope with missionary work in China. Henry's institute for students then later moved to a more suitable venue at Harley House. Henry and Fanny shared in the daily frugality of the home and looked solely to the Lord to meet their needs. Thus, while many of Henry's relations in the city of London and back in Ireland lived in the lap of luxury, he and Fanny lived near or on the breadline.

Material possessions mattered little to Henry. His interests were heavenly. He had but one earthly treasure, an eight-inch diameter telescope, and on this he inscribed (in Hebrew lettering), *"Holiness unto the LORD"*. Henry spent long nights at his telescope, absorbed in the study of the universe. His astronomical studies were closely linked with his study of prophecy for he was convinced that the apocalyptic books of the Bible were in a form of astronomical code. His complex charts on astronomy became a standard reference for astronomers of that time and his valuable contributions in this field of science led to honorary fellowships from the Royal Geological Society (F.R.G.S.) and the Royal Astronomical Society (F.R.A.S.).

As life advanced Henry gave more and more time to the study of prophecy and the fruit of his studies he committed to writing. *"The approaching end of the Age"* appeared in 1878. In 1886 he published *"Light for the Last Days"* and therein pointed out the significance of the year 1917 for the Jewish nation. Then followed, in the year 1888, *"The Divine Programme of the World's History"*. In all, some nine important publications came from his pen and these prophetic works greatly influenced the British nation. Lord Salisbury and Arthur James Balfour (who later became Britain's Foreign Secretary at a significant time in Israel's history) both studied them closely and expressed great interest in their content.

During the 1870's Jewish immigrants began to arrive in the East End of London. Five young Jews, converted to Christ but a short time before, arrived one day at Harley College. The Zionist cause was just emerging and these five young men desired to study the Scriptures with Henry Grattan Guinness. Although the college was full, they were not turned away. One of the five was a young man named David Baron, who later helped to found the Hebrew Christian Testimony to Israel and produced literary works ranked among the foremost pertaining to the nation of Israel and its place in prophecy.

In the year 1897 Fanny, on whom Henry had leaned so much, developed a stroke and in the following year passed away to be with Christ. For a time Henry was devastated but was greatly helped when his daughter took him once again to the Holy Land. There he gave numerous addresses to the delegates of the Zionist Conference in Jerusalem on the subject so dear to his heart, "the place of the Jewish nation in the purposes of God".

When Henry returned home to London, he further communicated with A. J. Balfour regarding his prophetic publications. It is noteworthy that the Balfour Declaration was signed in the year 1917 some years after Henry's death. That historic document stated that, "His Majesty's government view with favour the establishment in Palestine of a National Home for the Jewish people". Nor was this the only important date that Henry had discerned as significant for the Jewish people. At the close of Ezekiel's prophecy in his large black Bible, he had inscribed the year 1948.

The closing years of Henry's life were packed full—travelling, writing and lecturing, especially on his favourite subject, 'The Second Coming of the Lord Jesus'. His last written work, *"On This Rock"* was published in 1909, the year preceding his death. One day as the close approached he said to his latter wife Grace, "Grace, can I sink through a rock!" Well he knew the certainty of his foundation in Christ, and with unshakable confidence Henry passed away peacefully into the presence of his Lord, on Midsummer Day (21st June) 1910. His body was laid to rest in Abbey Cemetery, overlooking the city of Bath, and there a fitting memorial, sited underneath a spreading copper beech tree, marks the spot today.

Henry Grattan Guinness was not a prolific hymn writer but very occasionally expressed himself in verse, and that seemingly only when his heart was deeply moved. Once, when he visited a grave of the Spanish Inquisition, the Quemadero at Madrid, his heart was deeply touched by what he saw and he was moved to write "Tell me, thou murderess black, what mean these bones?" But Henry beheld a greater sight. He beheld the Cross of Christ. His heart was transfixed and he penned the lines,

> *Crowned with thorns upon the tree,*
> *Silent in Thine agony;*
> *Dying, crushed beneath the load*
> *Of the wrath and curse of God.*
>
> *On Thy pale and suffering brow,*
> *Mystery of love and woe;*
> *On Thy grief and sore amaze,*
> *Saviour, I would fix my gaze.*
>
> *On Thy pierced and bleeding breast*
> *Thou dost bid the weary rest;*
> *Rest there from the world's false ways,*
> *Rest there from its vanities.*
>
> *Rest in pardon and relief*
> *From the load of guilt and grief;*
> *Rest in Thy redeeming blood,*
> *Rest in perfect peace with God.*
>
> *Sin-atoning Sacrifice,*
> *Thou art precious in mine eyes;*
> *Thou alone my rest shall be,*
> *Now and through eternity.*

Before the Cross, Henry's meditation overflows in verse and he addresses his lines to **the silent Sufferer.** His heart is deeply moved as he looks upon the Crucified. Depths of suffering at first appall him, at length his heart is quieted. The mystery of woe is a mystery of love, the silent Sufferer is **the sin-atoning Sacrifice**. The sight is glorious. Christ crucified is exceedingly precious and is Henry's pillow of rest,
'*now and through eternity*'.

"The gospel of Thy grace"

Arthur Tappan Pierson (1837-1911)

Arthur Tappan Pierson

 The accession of Princess Victoria to the British throne in 1837 marked the beginning of a new era in world evangelization. Mission fields began to be explored and many doors were opened for the first time to the Lord's messengers. Arthur T. Pierson was quick to perceive these newly opened doors. He took advantage of them and became a great advocate of worldwide evangelism in the late nineteenth century. But, first of all, Arthur T. Pierson was a fervent minister of the gospel and through his preaching thousands of men and women were led to the Saviour. He was, besides, a man mighty in the Scriptures, a gifted teacher, one of the great Bible expositors of his generation.

Arthur T. Pierson was born of God-fearing parents on 6th March 1837 in Chatham St., New York, U.S.A. He was the youngest of four boys and the ninth child in a family of ten. His mother, Sally Ann Wheeler, had been one of a family of fourteen. His father, Stephen Haines Pierson, was a capable and careful accountant in New York City, a devout man whose trust was in God. He named his youngest boy after his very close friend and associate, Arthur Tappan, a greathearted merchant in the city and one who had shared closely with him in the ups and downs of life

Stephen and Sally Ann Pierson brought up their family in the fear of the Lord. Though times were difficult materially and poverty never far away, the parents and children met daily at the family altar. The Pierson family was associated with the Old Spring Street Church where Dr. Wm. M. Patton was pastor. At the services there, life-lasting impressions were made on the heart of young Arthur as to the inspiration of the Scriptures, the Deity of Christ and the work of the Spirit of God in spiritual regeneration.

As a boy, Arthur was sent to a nearby private school for his education. Then, at the age of eleven, he entered the Mount Washington Collegiate Institute and there he was introduced to the classical subjects of Greek and Latin, which proved useful in later life. By the time he was twelve he had started to read the New Testament in Greek and this he continued to do, to great profit, for the remaining sixty-two years of life.

At the age of thirteen Arthur went to boarding school at Tarrytown on the Hudson. On his leaving home, his father imparted to him two things—first, a Scripture text as a life motto, "In all thy ways acknowledge Him, and He shall direct thy paths" (Prov.3: 6), and then a piece of sound advice, "My son, you are going among strangers and will find some who think it a clever thing to call in question your faith and your father's faith and teachings. Whatever else you think or do, stand true to God and always give Him the advantage of your doubt". And these parting communications were never forgotten.

At Tarrytown young Arthur was converted. He had gone to some revival meetings at the local Methodist Church and one night he trusted Jesus Christ as his personal Saviour. Some of his fellow boarders who had also been to the same meeting quickly got back to the school bearing the news, "Pierson is converted". His room mates, some ten or twelve of them, waited for him to see what he would do. That night, before turning into bed, young Pierson knelt down and silently prayed. For a time the boys were quiet. Then they started to snigger. Soon a pillow came flying at his head. He continued to pray; the boys picked up the pillow and never thereafter disturbed him during his quiet times with God.

Arthur decided to prepare himself for Christian ministry and at the age of sixteen entered Hamilton College at Clinton, New York. There he proved himself a talented young man and won many honours—in classics, poetry, English composition, debating and oratory. Some of his essays and poems were submitted for publication and this marked the beginning of his career as an author. His first interests at the college, however, were spiritual, and he had the great honour and joy of leading many of his class to the Saviour. While at Hamilton he met a young lady, Sarah Frances Benedict, who later became his wife. She, like himself, was a committed Christian and from their very first meeting they were mutually attracted to each other.

After four years at Hamilton, Arthur entered Union Theological Seminary and there he spent the next three years. His principal and tutors there were men of scholarship but, more so, they were men of deep personal godliness and this left a lasting impression upon the young student. During those years he held a Bible class in a nearby church and this gave him great encouragement, not only as the numbers grew, but also as, one by one, he saw them turn to Christ for salvation. It was at that time that he wrote, "I have just begun to realize the true worth of souls and the secret of living near to Christ". He was then twenty-two years of age. The year 1860 was the year of his ordination and at the ceremony Dr. Walter Clarke addressed to him words which he never forgot. He bade him remember that he was "from that hour a minister; first, of the Word of God; second, of the Lord Jesus Christ; third, of the Holy Spirit; fourth, of the Church of God; and fifth, of the souls of men".

Arthur's first charge was of the souls of the First Congregational Church, Binghamton, New York. There, with his new bride, he set up home and resolved from the outset to put Christ first in everything. In the pulpit he preached the truth of God without fear or favour. He sought out the souls of men and women and pointed many to the Saviour. Similar features marked his ministry in the four pastorates that followed – at Waterford; at Fort St. in Detroit; at Second Church, Indianapolis, and at Bethany Hall, Philadelphia.

Arthur, in his ministry, delighted to tell out the gospel in its fullness and was convinced that its message was for the "whosoever". The stateliness or otherwise of the building in which he preached mattered little to him; in fact he preferred a simple commodious hall to an ornate church. One of his most fruitful ministries was in Whitney's Opera House in Detroit after the Fort St. Church had been destroyed by fire. In the sixteen months in the Opera House he saw more souls saved than in the previous sixteen years of his ministry. He longed to reach the masses and was convinced that a simple building where the people could assemble without embarrassment was in keeping with the message that he proclaimed.

As the years went by Arthur's horizons widened. From viewing the masses in the big cities, he caught a vision of the whole world. He longed and prayed that all would hear the simple gospel message. As a young man he had consecrated his all to God and was prepared to go overseas as a missionary if the Lord should send him. However, he felt that God's will for him was a ministry in the homeland and through his influence scores of young men and women went to the mission fields of the world. Indeed, of his own family of seven children, three of them dedicated their lives to God in overseas missionary work.

Arthur T. Pierson was an outstanding Bible teacher, greatly sought after throughout North America, the British Isles and beyond. His grasp of Biblical truth was comprehensive, his presentation skilled and masterly and through his ministry many were lifted onto a higher spiritual plane. His written ministry too, was richly blessed of God. Over fifty volumes have come from his pen and most of these have been preserved for us. Among the better known are; *Many Infallible Proofs*, pertaining to the Word of God and the Person of Christ; *The New Acts of the Apostles*, a publication of his Duff lectures; his lectures on the Bible at Exeter Hall, London, published in three volumes— *God's Living Oracles, The Bible and Spiritual Criticism, The Bible and Spiritual Life*; and *Knowing the Scriptures*, which is a gathering together of the fruits of fifty years of personal Bible study.

Arthur, in his ministry, was brought into close contact with other outstanding Christians and some of these left a deep and lasting impression upon him. Many days were spent at Northfield in the company of D. L. Moody. As a young man he had listened with rapt attention to C. H. Spurgeon and caught something of the fire of his passion for souls and then later, for a period of two years, surrounding and following Spurgeon's illness and death in 1892, he filled the pulpit in the Metropolitan Tabernacle. When Arthur was in Detroit, Major D. W. Whittle and Philipp Bliss came to the city for a gospel campaign and for one month stayed in the Pierson home. Their presence there was a benediction for they carried the presence of God with them.

During those days Arthur sat at their feet as a learner. He wrote for them a hymn, "With harps and with vials there stands a great throng" and was deeply impressed when he saw Mr. Bliss withdraw for a season of prayer before composing its music.

But the person who made the greatest impact on Arthur's life was George Muller of Bristol. From their very first encounter in 1878, when they travelled together by train across America, they were irresistibly drawn to each other. Arthur was then forty years of age. Muller was thirty-two years his senior but came into Arthur's life at a very crucial time and for the twenty years that followed they remembered each other daily in prayer. Only those who have studied the prayer life of George Muller can estimate the fruit of that prayer covenant. Besides, Muller opened up to Arthur a complete new teaching of the Bible, for until the time of their first meeting Arthur had been a post-millennialist but Muller's opening up of the truth of the Lord's return brought a new inspiration into his life.

Arthur was a man of deep conviction. When he was sixty years of age and at the height of his public ministry he obeyed the Lord in the ordinance of baptism by immersion. This was at no small cost to his individual and church relationships but he commented, "Whatever discord it might create in human relations, it has brought constant harmony with God, consistency with the gospel teaching and liberty to preach a full gospel message.—Had I this action to take again, I would only do it more promptly".

In the closing years of his ministry Arthur was linked with no human organization, "belonging to nobody but the Lord". He travelled widely in his Master's service. Throughout North America he ministered the Word of God with accompanying blessing. He crossed the Atlantic no fewer than twenty-six times, visiting Ireland, Scotland, England, France and Italy and wherever he went bringing challenge and blessing to large audiences in almost every meeting.

At the age of seventy-four, Arthur visited the Far East. He longed to see the work of God there at first hand. He visited Japan but when in Korea he was overtaken by ill health. This deterred him from continuing his itinerary and from Korea he returned to his Brooklyn home from which, on the early morning of the 3rd June 1911, he passed into the presence of his Lord. He had fought a good fight; he had finished his course and had finished it triumphantly.

Arthur T. Pierson, throughout life, was an ardent soul winner and for his gospel work he wrote a simple hymn,

The gospel of Thy grace my stubborn heart has won;
For God so loved the world, He gave His only Son,
That "Whosoever will believe shall everlasting life receive!"

The serpent "lifted up" could life and healing give,
So Jesus on the cross bids me to look and live;
For "Whosoever will believe shall everlasting life receive!"

"The soul that sinneth dies", my awful doom I heard;
I was for ever lost, but for Thy gracious word,
That "Whosoever will believe shall everlasting life receive!"

"Not to condemn the world", the Man of Sorrows came;
But that the world might have salvation through His name;
For "Whosoever will believe shall everlasting life receive!"

"Lord, help my unbelief!" Give me the peace of faith,
To rest with child-like trust on what Thy gospel saith,
That "Whosoever will believe shall everlasting life receive!"

This hymn befits its author. A.T. Pierson's singular aim in life was the proclamation of the gospel. He longed that all might know **"that whosoever will believe shall everlasting life receive!"**

And today, each time this hymn is sung, A. T. Pierson still continues to declare the same glorious theme that he proclaimed through life, **"that whosoever will believe shall everlasting life receive!"**

What a message it is! – ringing out from the Cross of Christ, echoing down the centuries of time and reaching to the hearts of needy sinners – **"that whosoever will believe shall everlasting life receive!"**

This message is the core of the gospel. It comes from the Lord Himself. In it there is provision for all, without limitation and without distinction, for **"whosoever will believe shall everlasting life receive!"**

These are words of simplicity; these are words of clarity; these are words of promise.
"WHOSOEVER WILL BELIEVE SHALL EVERLASTING LIFE RECEIVE!"
Through them storm-tossed souls find safe anchorage. Through them weary souls find rest.

"Praise the Lord, and leave tomorrow"

William Gibson Sloan (1838-1914)

William Gibson Sloan

Praise the Lord, and leave tomorrow
  In thy loving Father's hands;
Burden not thyself with sorrow,
  For secure the promise stands.
    He is faithful!
Leave thy troubles in His hands.

Trust today, and leave tomorrow,
  Each day has enough of care;
Therefore whatsoe'er thy burden,

PRAISE THE LORD, AND LEAVE TOMORROW

God will give thee strength to bear,
He is faithful!
Cast on Him thine every care.

Pray today, and let tomorrow
Bring with it whate'er it may;
Hear thy loving Father promise
Strength according to thy day.
He is faithful!
Trust Him, therefore, come what may.

Watch today, and leave tomorrow,
For tomorrow may not come;
For today thy loving Saviour,
May appear to take thee home.
He is faithful!
Look for Him, the coming One.

Work today, and leave tomorrow;
All around there's urgent need;
All around there's sin and sorrow;
Broadcast, daily sow thy seed.
God is faithful!
He shall bless thy work indeed.

Thus by trusting, watching, praying,
Each day, as the time rolls on,
We shall find the promised blessing,
Daily strength till Jesus come.
He is faithful!
He will come to take us home.

This hymn epitomizes the life of its author, William G. Sloan, the pioneer missionary from mainland Scotland to the Faroe Islands. Every "today" of his life, he lived for God; every "tomorrow" of his life, he left with God. The hymn, besides, exhorts us to follow the same path.

William Gibson Sloan was born on the 4th September 1838 into a simple cottage home at Bridgend, Dalry, Ayrshire, Scotland. He was the fourth son and fifth member of the family of eight children of Nathaniel and Elizabeth Sloan. His parents were simple cottage weavers. Theirs was a very simple lifestyle. William's mother died when he was just eight.

The Sloan family were members of the Church of Scotland and William was baptized there as an infant. When he was eighteen, lasting impressions of eternal things were made upon his heart through the death of his younger brother. William was at Matthew's bedside when he died and as he looked upon his lifeless form he was caused to face the searching question within, "If I had died instead of Matthew, where would I be?"

At the age of twenty William went as a storeman to the Calder Iron Works. This meant leaving home. In the Calder district at that time there was a great movement of the Spirit of God (1859-1861) and William came under its influence. Ever since his brother's death he had carried a burden upon his heart. He sought salvation, and one day in the back kitchen of a store at Longriggend he recalled the words of Psalm 103. "Bless the LORD, O my soul—Who forgiveth all thine iniquities—As far as the east is from the west, so far hath He removed our transgressions from us." And as he repeated these words of Scripture they shone like shafts of light into his darkened soul, bringing assurance of salvation and inward peace. William was then twenty-four years of age.

Following conversion, William had a sincere desire to please the Lord. In his place of employment, he was required to sell alcoholic beverages. He felt he could not do this with a clear conscience and he thereupon resigned his job without prospect of other employment. He involved himself in the work of the Lord and started to preach the gospel in his home county of Ayrshire. There he came into contact with Samuel Dodds, the Free Church missionary who had come from Ulster. Samuel was three years his senior and was handicapped by blindness resulting from an attack of measles in childhood. Samuel and William had kindred hearts and together they prayed and read the Scriptures.

William had contact with the Religious Tract and Book Society of Scotland, a work of the Church of Scotland, and this group encouraged him to go to the Shetland Islands as a colporteur. He set sail for Shetland on 16th January 1863, departing from Leith and arriving at Lerwick. His entire luggage consisted of a few personal belongings and a quantity of Bibles, books and pamphlets. This marked the beginning of a new life, among the crofters and fishermen of the North.

William secured lodgings in Lerwick and set about his work, calling at homes, selling literature, bearing witness for the Lord and praying with families for their loved ones at sea. At the crofter's homes he was generally welcomed and received much kindness. On the whole he found a hunger for the Word of God.

William spent about two and a half years in Shetland. During this time he continued to study the Scriptures; therein he discovered the truth of believer's baptism and was baptized by immersion. Then, in the early part of 1864, he identified himself with a small company of believers to "break bread". After that he renounced his membership of the Church of Scotland and wrote accordingly to the Tract Society with which he was employed. Thus, step by step, William moved on with God; he knew that God was leading.

In Shetland, William encountered a group of fishermen who were not natives of that part. They greatly interested him and on enquiry he learned that they had come from a group of islands in the far North called the Faroe Islands. They spoke another language. William enquired much about these folk and the land from which they had come and whether there was any gospel witness among them. On learning that there was none William's heart was deeply burdened. He longed to reach them with the gospel and on the 28th May 1865 as he sat in his Lerwick lodging, he resolved to go to Faroe. "I feel urged and willing to go and work there in God's Name and strength, and I am convinced that my work will not be useless for the Lord. I feel weak when I think of myself, but strong in the Lord and His mighty power". And he concluded, "May the Lord, who never makes a mistake, guide me with His Spirit. May the grace of the Father, Son and Holy Ghost be with my spirit in this my solemn undertaking. Therefore, with the Lord's help, I decide to go to Faroe Islands to preach Jesus. Amen".

William set sail in a fishing smack to his new field of labour equipped with some Danish Bibles, a Danish dictionary and grammar, and a few personal belongings. He carried on his person a letter of introduction from a Shetland businessman to the registrar in Torshavn, the capital town of Faroe. When the fishing smack anchored in inclement weather outside the mouth of Torshavn harbour William transferred to shore in a rowing boat. Naturally speaking, the prospect was daunting. He had come to a new people of an entirely new culture and of a new language. Nevertheless, he was conscious that God was with him. He found lodgings in the seaman's hostel and made his way to the registrar's office with his letter of introduction. From there he was directed to the Governor of the islands to obtain permission to sell the Danish Bibles. Permission, however, was denied. He, thereupon, sought out the bookbinder of the town, H. N. Jacobsen, and was kindly received by him. Mr. Jacobsen offered him a room in his home and a place at his table. William acknowledged the Divine leading and praised God for providing so wonderfully. Mr. Jacobsen was to be a great help to him in his study of the Danish language and William in return would learn and contribute a little in the bookbinding trade.

On Lord's days, William went to the Lutheran Church. There he found the services to be totally dead, merely a ritual. Then, when the services were over, the people spent the remainder of the Lord's days in drunkenness, dancing and card playing. William's heart was impressed by the greatness of the spiritual need. He visited around the town of Torshavn and adjacent villages, speaking to the people in broken Danish and seeking to convey the simple truths of the gospel in word and in song.

William spent only seven weeks in the Faroes on this first visit. By arrangement with the Tract Society he must get back to Shetland but, before leaving, he resolved that he would return again and also that he would preach the gospel to them before departure. This he did in the open air, speaking to them in broken Danish.

William then severed his links with the Tract Society and returned south to mainland Scotland, desirous that God would confirm to him his future path. God did so and, over the next ten years, William made frequent visits to the Faroe Islands, each visit usually lasting several months. William moved among the villages and hamlets there, visiting the homes, holding Bible studies, preaching and singing the simple gospel both indoor and in the open air and visiting the sick.

In the year 1875, William moved permanently to the Faroe Islands. There he laboured tirelessly and as a consequence souls were saved. In 1879 a little hall, "Ebenezer", was erected in Torshavn. In the following year the first baptism took place and because of opposition it was arranged for five o'clock in the morning. As the result of William's consistent godly witness and acts of kindness, opposition was slowly broken down, men and women were saved and little testimonies were established throughout the islands. In the work others came to help and together they worked harmoniously. William was a true yoke-fellow, setting an example to his younger brethren in patience, courtesy, kindness and prayerfulness.

William also paid short visits to Iceland and there engaged in similar work, visiting and preaching the simple gospel and God attended his labours with blessing in salvation. All the while he kept up contact with the Orkney and Shetland Islands and in the latter, in 1887, he saw a movement of God at Selivoe when some forty people professed faith in Christ. These new converts were baptized by immersion and a New Testament assembly was planted.

In 1881 William married a native Faroese girl, Elsebeth Isaksen, one of the early converts and a real trophy of Divine grace. Elsebeth proved in every way a real "help meet". She was Faroese by birth and understood the Faroese people, their ways and their language. After their marriage, William and his bride made their home in a small attic over the hall in Torshavn. God blessed William and Elsebeth with a family of six children, three boys and three girls. Their youngest boy, Andrew, later stepped into the work of the Lord in Faroe shortly after his father's death.

On Friday, 4th September 1914, the labours of William G. Sloan in the Faroe Islands came to a close. He was active in the work right to the end. It was his seventy-sixth birthday. Two days earlier, he had spoken to the saints in Torshavn of the Lord's return and on the day before he died he was found at the harbour in Torshavn distributing tracts among the fishermen. On the morning of his passing he witnessed to his attending doctor, a Jew, of his personal faith in Christ. He then called for Andrew, his son, and gave to him the calendar reading for that day, "Trust in the Lord with all thine heart and lean not unto thine own understanding. In all thy ways acknowledge Him and He shall direct thy paths" (Prov.3:5,6). William exhorted Andrew to follow that Divine precept through life. He then commended the family to the Lord in prayer, took leave of them and went to be with his Saviour. His body was laid to rest in the land of his labours, the funeral attendance being the largest ever witnessed in the capital town of Torshavn.

And still today, William G. Sloan lives on in Faroe; his every memory is fragrant.
But wherein lay the secret of his life, so wholly lived for God?
The secret! – Every "today" he lived for God; every "tomorrow" he left with God.

"We praise Thee, O God, for the Son of Thy love"

William Paton Mackay (1839-1885).

William Paton Mackay

    William Paton Mackay, a native of Montrose in the North East of Scotland, was born on 13th May 1839. As a young man he studied at Edinburgh University and graduated from there both in Arts and in Medicine. Notwithstanding, William gave his life to the proclamation of the gospel. He was an ardent soul winner. Conversion's experience had wrought a mighty change in his life, "the somewhat wild, daring and reckless medical student was changed into an earnest, go ahead and fearless evangelist". He longed to tell others of the Saviour and in this regard was much encouraged by such noteworthies as Sir James Young Simpson, Professor of Midwifery at Edinburgh, Duncan

Matheson, the eminent Scottish evangelist and Richard Weaver, the converted collier so marvellously used of God throughout Britain.

Professor Sir James Young Simpson himself was a great soul winner. Though he is remembered today as the discoverer of the anaesthetic properties of chloroform, he was also a man greatly used of God in the conversion of "many a student, many a patient and many others in all positions in society". William P. Mackay had been recently converted under the ministry of Dr. H. M. Williamson and, as a young medical student, came under his astute eye. Professor Simpson perceived him as a potential soul winner and greatly encouraged him to exercise his energies in that direction.

Duncan Matheson and his mission work throughout Scotland are legendary. With a heart on fire for God Matheson carried the glorious gospel to his fellow men. He frequented the feeing-markets of Scotland and young Mackay, at that time still a student, joined him in his evangelistic work. It was good training ground. At the markets they met with strong opposition but their trust was in God and prayer was their great recourse in times of difficulty. On occasions, when kneeling together in public on the outskirts of a crowd, they experienced the jeers and the spittle of their taunters. Matheson was wont to say, "Keep the Word at them". Matheson laboured unceasingly. "Rest!" said he, "No, I can't. Eternity! Eternity!" Years later, on reflecting on their experiences together, William wrote, "The life of Duncan Matheson may well stir us all up to live more in light of eternity, working to please but One, working to gather souls to that glorious One, and build them up in the knowledge of Him who is the Light of eternity".

William had a close and enriching association with Richard Weaver and often deputized for him in his preaching engagements. He spent time at the Weaver home at Fallisbroome near Macclesfield. Indeed, William and his young bride spent part of their honeymoon there and many subsequent visits were paid to that home.

William's life work, however, was centred in the city of Hull. From his going there as a young man right to the close of his life he saw the hand of God with him in a most remarkable way. His ministry there commenced in December 1868. Earlier that year, having received a call to the Presbyterian Church in Prospect Street, he visited Hull on three consecutive Lord's days. Those early visits were memorable. When he first arrived he found a very small company meeting in the Royal Institution but on his final visit, "The service was marked with great power and a solemn impression remained on the large audience. When he retired from the platform, for a considerable time none rose from their seats. It was a foretaste of greater blessing yet to come".

Just prior to William's going to Hull the company meeting in the Royal Institution had acquired a more spacious church accommodation at the corner of Prospect Street and Baker Street. Their newly acquired property had been originally built by Andrew Jukes B.A. at the time when he dissociated from the Church of England but, when his health broke down and he could no longer preach, the building was sold. It proved a most suitable meeting place, with accommodation for a thousand people. This was the centre for William P. Mackay's ministry for the next sixteen years up until the time of his death, and the birthplace of many souls.

William P. Mackay arrived in Hull as a young man of twenty-nine. He had a double-barrelled qualification from Edinburgh University, but more importantly, he had a heart on fire for God. He was a man of great energy and tremendous capacity for work, a man of great ability who had the gift of mastering any subject to which he devoted his attention. Above all, he was a man who had "power with God and with men". Soon the church was filled to capacity with eager listeners, and spiritual blessing attended his ministry. Within four years of his going, membership increased tenfold and many were converted to God. In his church report of 1872 William stated, "We believe that unless the Church of God is aggressive as well as pure, evangelistic as well as evangelical, it is not fulfilling its mission on earth, and is in danger of disappearing as an influence for God, by contentment with mere solvent respectability".

The work at Hull grew and extended well beyond the church building in Prospect Street. "A striking sight could have been seen every Lord's day evening, when a band of men, whose hearts the Lord had touched, assembled outside the church after the quarter-to-six prayer meeting, divided into four bands to preach the gospel in the open-air, and thus evangelized nearly every square, terrace and row in the older and poorer portion of Hull". Tract distribution accompanied the preaching of the Word. Lodging houses were visited with the gospel. Sunday schools were commenced and these grew to six in number with over sixty teachers and a total attendance of over a thousand children. Outreach works sprang up in other districts of the city and surrounding towns. "God was in the midst of His people".

Soon wider demands were made on William's gift and time. Other nonconformist churches in Hull sought his services and he became a well-known figure on their platforms. He was much in demand for conference and evangelistic work with necessary long journeys throughout England, Scotland, Ireland, Sweden and America. But, whenever possible, he endeavoured to be with his own flock on the Lord's day.

William built a little villa in Oban in Western Scotland and there he spent his annual holiday. Even on holiday he kept busy in the gospel. Many flocked to Oban on the Lord's days "to hear Mackay preach" and the Free Church on those occasions was always crowded. During his last vacation there, he went on a boat trip from Oban to Thurso, aboard the steamer, "Clansman". The steamer called at Portree, Isle of Skye, and he with others went ashore. When returning in the darkness, he missed his footing on the gangway and fell between the pier and the steamer, striking his head on the hull of the vessel. When rescued from the water, he was unconscious. He was taken to a nearby hotel where he rallied for two days, but passed away in the early morning of Saturday 22nd August 1885. On the day of his funeral, businesses were suspended, shops were closed, and the streets were lined as he was borne to his grave.

The faithful pastor, the loving husband and father, the earnest worker had been called home at the early age of forty-six. The loss was great. One tribute expressed it as follows, "Thus came to a close, alas! humanly speaking, too soon, the life of one who was instrumental in bringing many sinners to the feet of our Lord, and in building up His people in clear Scriptural truth". William, but a short time before his death, had written an article for the "British Evangelist", of which he was the editor. He entitled it, "Change your money" and therein he exhorted and urged believers to make proper use of their talent of wealth. "Dear fellow-servant, get so accustomed to serve your Lord Jesus Christ, and Him alone, that your entrance into glory will not be unnatural, and thus an abundant entrance will be yours". Thus it was fulfilled for himself, and so soon.

William Paton Mackay, in his preaching, extolled the great doctrines of the gospel. "The poor sinner has not to come and steal a pardon while justice slept, but mercy handed a pardon on the point of the sword of justice". He declared the truth of God without apology. Once, when in Chicago city in America, he said to his large audience, "If ever I utter the words 'I think', when speaking to the people, I hope they will go to sleep, and remain asleep until I have done with thinking. We are not to give men our thoughts, but God's words". On his heart and lips eternity was indelibly engraved and the hope of the Lord's return was to him a vivid reality. He regarded the grave, not as "man's long, last home", rather, " 'tis but a lodging place, held from week to week, till Christ shall come".

William Paton Mackay was also a student of the Word and a writer. As a student, he availed himself of every possible help. His own Bible was quite a curiosity. He called it, "En-hakkore", after the water yielding jawbone wherewith Samson slew a thousand men (Judges 15:19). As a writer he kept busy with his pen and several volumes were the outcome. During the early years of his ministry at Hull he published *Grace and Truth*, a volume which he had taken ten years to produce, writing and rewriting it with much prayer and proving by the Word. "Every page abounds in graphic illustrations of the power of the gospel to save the lost". It reached an immense circulation throughout Europe and was translated into many languages. Almost a quarter of a million copies were printed and sold and it was accompanied by great blessing. Then there followed from his pen, *The Seeking Saviour, Abundant Grace, Notes on the Shorter Catechism* and *The Books of the Bible*, as well as a large number of gospel booklets.

William P. Mackay also wrote quite a number of hymns. Some seventeen of them appeared in William Reid's Praise Book in 1872. Several of these are still in use and have proved quite popular,

"Come, let us reason, saith the Lord"
"No works of law have we to boast"
"The Lord is risen; now death's dark judgment flood"
"When we reach our peaceful dwelling"
"With Christ we died to sin"
"Worthy, worthy is the Lamb"
"We praise Thee, O God, for the Son of The love"

This last hymn, **"We praise Thee, O God, for the Son of Thy love",** was written in 1863, in William's early Christian experience. At a public meeting, he was leading in prayer and his soul was so filled with gratitude to God that while speaking to God, yet unconscious of any poetic effort, he used the words, "We praise Thee, O God, for the Son of Thy love". The phrase lingered in his mind, and he afterwards adopted it as the first line of his now popular hymn,

WE PRAISE THEE, O GOD, FOR THE SON OF THY LOVE

We praise Thee, O God, for the Son of Thy love,
For Jesus who died, and is now gone above.

Hallelujah, Thine the glory!
Hallelujah, Amen!
Hallelujah, Thine the glory!
Revive us again!

We praise Thee, O God, for Thy Spirit of light,
Who has shown us our Saviour, illumined our night.

All glory and praise to the Lamb that was slain,
Who has borne all our sins, and has cleansed every stain.

All glory and praise to the God of all grace
Who has bought us and sought us, and guided our ways.

Revive us again, fill each heart with Thy love,
May each soul be rekindled with love from above.

Revive us again, rouse the dead from their tomb!
May they come now to Jesus, while yet there is room.

This hymn is addressed to God. It is a hymn for the sanctuary. It begins with **praise to God for His gifts** and closes with **prayer to God for revival.** Such exercises arise within the heart. They proceed from a heart fired by devotion. Divine Love kindled a flame in the heart of W. P. Mackay and he kept it burning brightly right to the close. And from that life there was ever "something going up to God" and "something going out to others".

"The fire shall ever be burning upon the altar; it shall never go out".
(Lev. 6:13)

"He dies! He dies! The lowly Man of Sorrows"

Charles Russell Hurditch (1839-1908)

Clapton Hall
(Spiritual home of Charles Russell Hurditch)

He dies! He dies! The lowly Man of sorrows,
On whom were laid our many griefs and woes;
Our sins He bore, beneath God's awful billows,
And He has triumphed over all our foes.

> I am He that liveth, that liveth, and was dead;
> I am He that liveth, that liveth, and was dead;
> And behold ... I am alive ... for evermore ...
> Behold ... I am alive ... for evermore,
> I am He that liveth, that liveth, and was dead;
> And behold ... I am alive ... for evermore.

> *He lives! He lives! What glorious consolation!*
> *Exalted at His Father's own right hand;*
> *He pleads for us, and by His intercession*
> *Enables all His saints by grace to stand.*
>
> *He comes! He comes! O blest anticipation!*
> *In keeping with His true and faithful word;*
> *To call us to our heavenly consummation –*
> *Caught up, to be "for ever with the Lord".*

The lines of this soul-stirring and triumphant hymn were written by Charles Russell Hurditch, a young Devonian who came to London during the 1858-62 Revival and there, in the capital city, over the next half-century, threw all his energies into the work of God, and with much attendant blessing. His youngest daughter, Grace, in her autobiography, "Peculiar People", writing under the pseudonym of "Septima", has thrown interesting sidelights on her father's personal and home life.

Charles Russell Hurditch was born in Exeter in the county of Devon on 20th December 1839. He was converted to God in his fifteenth year and thereafter became an ardent soul-winner. On his eighteenth birthday he recorded his aspirations, "My eighteenth birthday – filled with an inexpressible thirst after God, I long to do something for Him. Oh! that I may be a flame of fire burning with love and zeal for His honour and glory". And there, in his native county of Devon, as a young man still in his teens, he set out on his life's mission of bearing the glad tidings of the gospel to his fellow countrymen and women.

At the age of twenty Charles Russell Hurditch went to London and there he found the city astir with spiritual revival. Clergymen and laymen were conducting services daily in churches, in halls and in market places. Thousands thronged to those gatherings, all eager to hear the Word of God. Men and women cried out as the Spirit of God convicted them of their utter sinfulness and need of salvation. The meetings often lasted three to four hours and many experienced personal salvation through faith in Christ. The revival, however, did not have the blessing of the Established Church and it sought to oppose, but interestingly, when the question of using unconsecrated buildings for Divine service came before Parliament, the Earl of Shaftesbury stated in the House, "It is not the locality that will desecrate the Word of God, but the Word of God that will consecrate the locality".

Young Russell threw all his energies into the revival movement. He was gifted as a public speaker and many suggested to him that he should enter college for some training for his life's work. These suggestions, however, Russell declined. "I could not conscientiously enter upon a course of man's training for God's ministry. My soul burns to be set apart for the work of an evangelist".

The year 1864 brought changes. Mr. Henry Hull, a prominent Christian worker in the city of London and secretary of the Young Men's Christian Association (YMCA) at Stafford's Rooms, Edgeware Road, died unexpectedly and his passing left vacant the secretaryship of the YMCA. Russell was requested to take on the responsibility and accepted. This gave him a base for his work in the city, yet leaving him free to continue as an evangelist. God greatly blessed his efforts and many spiritual children were the result.

Russell married on the 11th May 1865. His bride, Mary Holmes, was the daughter of a stationer in the city. In his first communication to Mary by letter he laid bare his heart, "I desire to live only for Christ and I believe this is your desire". Thus it proved to be and throughout life she proved to be a true helpmeet for him in every way. Both were fervent soul winners and, while Russell took the public place, Mary was a great support in the work. She was "a sweet shy woman". "She might have aspired to social eminence; instead she accepted a humbler position and elevated it by her contented and gracious spirit— entirely free from vulgar ambition, pride and selfishness, she had learned the spirit of Christ to be meek and lowly in heart, and thus had found rest".

A short time after marriage Russell identified with the assembly of believers meeting at Clapton Hall and thereupon he resigned as secretary of the YMCA. He and Mary embarked upon a life of faith. They raised a family of seven children, while at the same time carrying on a vast organization of gospel and philanthropic work. They found a spiritual home in the assembly at Clapton Hall and gave themselves wholeheartedly to the upbuilding of the testimony there. From an early beginning in an "Iron Room" with eleven members the assembly grew to over four hundred within twelve years, reaching a peak of over seven hundred by the year 1888. Those were blessed days at Clapton Hall as God gave the increase, and the saints were wisely guided and refreshed under the leadership and ministry of such as Denham Smith, Shuldham Henry, John G. McVicker and Russell himself.

Russell was an enthusiast, a man of immense energy who also had the gift of inspiring others. Halls were built, halls were purchased and halls were rented for the preaching of the gospel. Russell encouraged the young men to go out by twos or threes into the villages and towns of the Home Counties with the gospel tent or gospel caravan.

Russell's commitment and workload were phenomenal, both in oral and in written ministries. From his daughter's record we learn, "He published in succession five magazines, changing their character and style according to the needs of the day. Thirteen million gospel papers and tracts, of which he was the editor, had been issued from his office in sixteen years. He compiled two hymn books—(and was himself the composer of thirty of the hymns)—which reached a circulation of over half a million. Then there were his constant preaching tours throughout England, Ireland, Scotland and Wales. 'Launch out into the deep' was one of my father's favourite mottoes". Added to all this was his work among the poor and the needy. There was gross poverty in the area where Russell lived, and daily his heart was touched by the plight of the people. He organized soup kitchens and coal and food tickets and tried to find employment for the men. The needs of the day were overwhelming. Russell and Mary did what they could.

Russell and Mary's life's objective had been to win souls for Christ and to care for the people of God, and together they devoted their lives to that purpose. They kept open house and many young men and women found love and hospitality there. Many also found the Saviour there. When the entire contents of a large home in the neighbourhood were willed to Russell, he purchased with the proceeds a property on the south coast of England and converted it into a "House of Rest" for Christian workers, whether from the homeland or overseas. Thus Russell and Mary gave themselves without stint to the work of God and the needs of others.

Then, in the early hours of 25th August 1908, the labours of Charles Russell Hurditch ceased, and he was called into the presence of his Lord whom he loved so dearly and had served so devotedly.

Charles Russell Hurditch left behind him a small legacy of hymns, numbering about thirty. Of them Dr. John Julian has written, "All Mr. Hurditch's hymns are characterized by great simplicity and earnestness". His better known compositions include,

"O Christ, Thou heavenly Lamb!" (*Divine Power desired*), written at the time of his going to London, "Arm of the Lord, awake! Exalt the Saviour slain" (*Home Missions*), written during the Revival years, "Arise, ye saints, arise and sing" (*God is light*), a companion hymn for

Howard Kingbury's "God is love", "Farewell for the present, farewell" (*Friends parting*), written and intended for such occasions, and "He dies! He dies! The lowly Man of sorrows" (*Good Friday*), which in its original commenced, "He dies! He dies! The Son of God most holy".

This last hymn, **"He dies! He dies! The lowly Man of sorrows"** is probably the best known and most popular of all Charles Russell Hurditch's compositions. The heart of Russell was filled and thrilled by the great foundation truths of the gospel that he preached — the death of the Saviour — **"He dies!"**, the resurrection of the Saviour — **"He lives!"** and the coming again of the Saviour — **"He comes!"**, each event so momentous and triumphant, and each with tremendous implications.

Charles Russell Hurditch, early in life, had caught a vision of the living Christ, had felt His touch and heard His voice, and the glory of that Patmos-like experience never left him. It completely transformed his life.

A living Saviour–who was dead! A living Saviour–alive for evermore!

> "And when I saw Him, I fell at His feet as dead.
> And He laid His right hand upon me,
> Saying unto me, "Fear not: I am the First and the Last: I am He that liveth, and was dead;
> and, behold, I am alive for evermore, Amen; and have the keys of hell and of death" (Rev.1: 17,18.).

Thus fortified, Charles Russell Hurditch, as a young man, stepped forth upon his life's work and never slacked till his work was done. The presence and the power of the living Saviour never failed.

"Let us sing of the love of the Lord"

Daniel Webster Whittle (1840-1901)

Daniel Webster Whittle

Daniel Webster Whittle, popularly known as Major Whittle, gained his title of "Major" as a young man in the United States Army. He became a well-known preacher of the gospel and in that sphere God used him greatly. Besides, he was a writer of hymns. His compositions were among the most popular in the stirring days of evangelical activity at the close of the nineteenth century and many of them are still sung today with fervour and appreciation.

Daniel Webster Whittle was born at Chicopee Falls, Massachusetts, U.S.A. on 22nd November 1840 and was named after the American statesman, Daniel Webster. He grew up in New England and in his teens gained employment as a cashier of the Wells Fargo Bank in Chicago. The advent of the American Civil War in 1861, however, effected a great change in Whittle's life. Hy. Pickering in his book, "Twice-born Men" has documented the events surrounding that change, as told by Whittle in his own words.

"When the Civil War broke out, I left my home in New England and came to Virginia as lieutenant of a company in a Massachusetts regiment. My dear mother was a devout Christian, and parted from me with many a tear, and followed me with many a prayer. She had placed a New Testament in a pocket of the haversack that she arranged for me.

"We had many engagements, and I saw many sad sights, and in one of the battles I was knocked out, and that night my arm was amputated above the elbow. As I grew better, having a desire for something to read, I felt in my haversack, which I had been allowed to keep, and found the little Testament my mother had placed there.

"I read right through the book — Matthew, Mark, Luke, to Revelation. Every part was interesting to me; and I found to my surprise that I could understand it in a way that I never had before. When I had finished Revelation, I began at Matthew, and read it through again. And so for days I continued reading, and with continued interest; and still no thought of becoming a Christian, I saw clearly from what I read the way of salvation through Christ.

"While in this state of mind, yet still with no purpose or plan to repent and accept the Saviour, I was awakened one midnight by the nurse, who said: "There is a boy in the other end of the ward, one of your men, who is dying. He has been begging me for the past hour to pray for him, or to get someone to pray for him, and I can't stand it. I am a wicked man, and can't pray, and I have come to get you".

"Why", said I, "I can't pray. I never prayed in my life. I am just as wicked as you are". "Can't pray!" said the nurse; "why, I thought sure from seeing you read the Testament that you were a praying man. And you are the only man in the ward that I have not heard curse. What shall I do? There is no one else to go to. I can't go back there alone. Won't you get up and come and see him at any rate?"

"Moved by his appeal, I rose from my cot, and went with him to the far corner of the room. A fair-haired boy of seventeen or eighteen lay there dying. There was a look of intense agony upon his face, as he fastened his eyes upon me and said: "Oh, pray for me! Pray for me! I am dying. I was a good boy at home in Maine. My mother and father are members of the Church, and I went to Sunday school and tried to be a good boy. But since I became a soldier I have learned to be wicked. I drank, and swore, and gambled, and went with bad men. And now I am dying, and I am not fit to die! Oh, ask God to forgive me! Pray for me. Ask Christ to save me!"

"As I stood there and heard these pleadings, God said to my soul by His Spirit, just as plainly as if He had spoken in audible tones, "You know the way of salvation. Get right down on your knees and accept Christ, and pray for the boy." I dropped upon my knees and held the boy's hand in mine, as in a few broken words I confessed my sins, and asked God for Christ's sake to forgive me. *I believed right there that He did forgive me,* and that I was Christ's child. I then prayed earnestly for the boy. He became quiet, and pressed my hand as I pleaded the promises. When I arose from my knees he was dead. A look of peace was upon his face, and I can but believe that God, who used him to bring me to the Saviour, used me to get his attention fixed upon Christ and to lead him to trust in His precious blood. I hope to meet him in heaven.

"Many years have passed since that night in the Richmond Hospital, and I am still trusting and confessing the Lord Jesus Christ".

Towards the close of the war Whittle was promoted to the rank of major and when the war was over he returned to Chicago and became treasurer of the Elgin Watch Company. In Chicago he met with D. L. Moody and they became fast friends. Moody encouraged him to enter full-time gospel work and in 1873 Major Whittle resigned from the Elgin Watch Company to become an evangelist. Of the circumstances of that decision while at work in Chicago he said, "I went into the vault and in the dead silence of the quietest of places I gave my life to my heavenly Father to use as He would".

In gospel work Major Whittle did the preaching but looked to others to take care of the singing. He formed partnerships with some of the most godly and finest musicians of the land. His first companion in the work was Philip P. Bliss. Bliss joined with Whittle in 1874 and for a period of two years the partnership of "Whittle and Bliss" was renowned around Chicago and beyond, and was greatly blessed by the Lord. Bliss from time to time stayed in Whittle's home at No. 43 South Street, Chicago and there he penned two of his most memorable compositions, "I am so glad that our Father in heaven" and "Hold the fort, for I am coming".

Major Whittle had a great love for children and wherever he went in his labours for the Lord he conducted meetings for children. He had the ability to set before children the truths of the gospel in a clear and simple manner, and often illustrated his message on blackboard or by simple chemical experiment.

Whittle's partnership with Philip P. Bliss, however, was short-lived. At the close of the year 1876 Bliss died tragically in the Pacific Express train disaster at Ashtabula, Ohio. Whittle, on receiving the news, rushed to the scene in hope of finding trace of Bliss's body or that of his wife, but in vain. Few had escaped the conflagration that followed the crash. It has been recorded that at the scene of the disaster he met with James McGranahan who had gone there on the same errand. Whittle had heard of McGranahan, of his gift as a musician and of his zeal for the work of the Lord. The Major challenged him to join him as a successor to the lamented Bliss. And thus commenced Whittle's second partnership, that of "Whittle and McGranahan", which lasted for more than a decade.

God greatly blessed the "Whittle and McGranahan" partnership and together they had the joy of seeing the birth of many souls, and also, the birth of many gospel songs. Whittle wrote the words and McGranahan set the compositions to music. This partnership came to a close about 1890, when McGranahan's health started to fail. Whittle then joined with George C. Stebbins and this third partnership, "Whittle and Stebbins", was again a happy and fruitful one. Together they moved widely throughout North America and the British Isles. Their visit to Ireland toward the close of the nineteenth century was most fruitful. It followed closely on Mr. Moody's visit to the city of Dublin. Together they proclaimed the glorious gospel in cities and towns throughout Ireland, their concluding meetings being in the city of Belfast.

Major Whittle's service for God came to a close on 4th March 1901. He was then just sixty years of age. From Northfield, Massachusetts, he went to be with his Lord whom he had served so faithfully for over twenty-five years. He is buried at Northfield, Massachusetts.

Major Whittle, besides being an active evangelist, was also a notable hymnwriter. He wrote under the pen name of "El Nathan", and is credited with the writing of some two hundred hymns. Some have judged his hymns as lacking literary merit but, notwithstanding, his compositions have been greatly used of the Lord. Mr. Moody was known to have remarked of them, "I think Major Whittle has written some of the best hymns of this century". Major Whittle's best-known and best-loved compositions include,

"Come sing, my soul, and praise the Lord"
"Dying with Jesus by death reckoned mine"
"I know not why God's wondrous grace"
"I looked to Jesus in my sin"
"Jesus is coming! Sing the glad word!"
"Let us sing of the love of the Lord"
"Once again the gospel message"
"Our Lord is now rejected"
"There shall be showers of blessing"
"They tell me the story of Jesus is old"
"Thou remainest, blest Redeemer"
"When God of old the way of life"

There is great diversity of subject matter in Whittle's hymns. But irrespective of his theme he never fails to infuse a warmth into his compositions. And in return his hymns are sung with great fervour.

Major Whittle, throughout life, had witnessed the transforming power of the gospel in the lives of men and women. Wherever he went he never shirked from making its message known. The story of the love of God never ceased to fill and thrill his soul and on this theme his hymn, **"The love that gave Jesus to die"**, is perhaps one of his sweetest compositions.

Let us sing of the love of the Lord;
As now to the Cross we draw nigh,
Let us sing to the praise of the God of all grace
For the love that gave Jesus to die!

O, the love that gave Jesus to die!
The love that gave Jesus to die!
Praise God, it is mine, this love so divine,
The love that gave Jesus to die.

O, how great was the love that was shown
To us – we can never tell why –

Not to angels, but men – let us praise Him again
For the love that gave Jesus to die!
Now this love unto all God commends,
Not one would His mercy pass by;
"Whosoever shall call", there is pardon for all
In the love that gave Jesus to die.

Who is He that can separate those
Whom God doth in love justify?
Whatsoever we need He includes in the deed,
In the love that gave Jesus to die!

The love that gave Jesus to die could be none other than Divine.
It flows out to all in their need, bringing to each all that they need.

"Before the throne of God above"

Charitie Lees Smith (1841-1923)

Charitie Lees Smith

Charitie Lees Smith was a daughter of rural Fermanagh in the North of Ireland, the fourth child of Rev. George Sidney and Charlotte Lees Smith. In the family there were seven children, five boys and two girls and Charitie was the younger of the two girls. She was born at Bloomfield in Co. Dublin on 21st June 1841. Her mother, Charlotte Lees, was the daughter of Thomas Orde Lees and granddaughter of Sir John Lees Bart. of Bloomfield and this family link with Bloomfield probably accounts for Charitie's birth there.

Charitie's father, Dr. George Sidney Smith was a very distinguished minister in the Church of Ireland. He had been born in Edinburgh in 1805 and had received most of his education at Trinity College, Dublin where he obtained B.A. degree in 1825, a Fellowship in 1831, M.A. degree in 1832 and B.D.& D.D. in 1840. He was appointed Professor of Biblical Greek in 1838 and was Donnellan Lecturer in 1850. Prior to the disestablishment of the Church in 1870, Trinity College held the right of appointment of ministers to certain parishes throughout Ireland and in 1838 George Sidney Smith was appointed to the living of Aghalurcher in Co. Fermanagh. His ministry there extended over a period of twenty-nine years (1838 - 1867) and throughout that period he retained the Chair in Biblical Greek at his parent College in Dublin.

But Dr. Smith was much more than a distinguished scholar. He was a man of true piety and the fruits of his ministry were evidenced in the homes and lives of his parishioners. Within three years of his going to Aghalurcher the small Sunday school there of forty children had grown to seven Sunday schools with a total attendance of eight hundred children. During his Aghalurcher ministry a great movement of the Spirit of God, the 1859 Revival, swept throughout the eastern counties of Ireland, from Co. Antrim to Co. Wicklow. Dr. Orr observed retrospectively that "the movement was generally approved among Presbyterians but only approved in part by the clergy of Establishment". The Presbyterian population of Co. Fermanagh at that time was only two per cent, and the movement did not extend to the county in any big way. Nevertheless the Smith home and the Aghalurcher parish were not entirely unaffected by it, for W. S. Burnside D.D., who followed Dr. Smith in the Aghalurcher parish, recorded of his predecessor's ministry, "the awakening of souls dead in sin to newness of life, the conversion of sinners, the reclamation of backsliders, the instruction of the ignorant, the comforting of the mourners and the edification of the congregation". Indeed, W. S. Burnside testified from first hand knowledge that "many careless sinners were awakened, enlightened, justified, sanctified, saved, who after a consistent life died in the full assurance of the hope of eternal glory". Such was the environment and spiritual climate surrounding Charitie's childhood.

It is noteworthy that Charitie's verse first appeared in leaflet form during the revival years. One of her first compositions, **"O for the robes of whiteness"** was dated 1860. It was entitled, "Heaven desired". It is the language of a soul in its first love to Christ.

Oh for the robes of whiteness!
  Oh, for the tearless eyes!
Oh, for the glorious brightness
  Of the unclouded skies!

Oh, for no more weeping,
  Within that land of love
The endless joy of keeping
  The bridal feast above!

Oh, for the bliss of flying,
  My risen Lord to meet!
Oh, for the rest of lying
  For ever at His feet!

Oh, for the hour of seeing
  My Saviour face to face!
The hope of ever being
  In that sweet meeting-place!

Jesus! Thou King of Glory,
  I soon shall dwell with Thee;
I soon shall sing the story
  Of Thy great love to me.

Meanwhile, my thoughts shall enter
  E'en now before Thy throne,
That all my love may centre
  In Thee, and Thee alone.

Charitie, in her first love, yearned for heaven. She longed to be with Christ. But the time was not yet; she was scarcely nineteen years of age.

Charitie realized that she must live on earth and became deeply exercised as to how her life on earth should be lived. In the following year (1861) she expressed her thoughts in verse, **"Lord, I desire to live as one who bears a blood-bought name"** and entitled it, "Holiness desired".

> Lord, I desire to live as one
>   Who bears a blood-bought name,
> As one who fears but grieving Thee,
>   And knows no other shame;
>
> As one by whom Thy walk below
>   Should never be forgot;
> As one who fain would keep apart
>   From all Thou lovest not.
>
> I want to live as one who knows
>   Thy fellowship of love;
> As one whose eyes can pierce beyond
>   The pearl-built gates above.
>
> As one who daily speaks to Thee,
>   And hears Thy voice divine
> With depth of tenderness declare
>   "Beloved! Thou art mine".

(A further two verses were added by Charitie in 1867)

But Charitie discovered that within her heart there was a propensity to sin. She could not attain to the standard expressed in her hymn, "Holiness desired". Then in the year 1863 she penned what was to become perhaps the sweetest of all her compositions, **"Before the throne of God above"**. She entitled it, "The Advocate".

> Before the throne of God above
> I have a strong, a perfect plea;
> A great High Priest, whose name is Love,
> Who ever lives and pleads for me.
>
> My name is graven on His hands,
> My name is written on His heart;
> I know that while in heaven He stands,
> No tongue can bid me thence depart.
>
> When Satan tempts me to despair,
> And tells me of the guilt within,

*Upward I look, and see Him there
Who made an end of all my sin.*

*Because the sinless Saviour died,
My sinful soul is counted free;
For God, the Just, is satisfied
To look on Him, and pardon me.*

*Behold Him there – the bleeding Lamb!
My perfect, spotless Righteousness,
The great, unchangeable, "I AM",
The King of glory and of grace!*

*One with Himself, I cannot die;
My soul is purchased by His blood;
My life is hid with Christ on high,
With Christ, my Saviour and my God.*

In this lovely meditation Charitie looks above, away from the defilement within and the defilement around. Within heaven's august sanctuary she sees her Lord. In His own right He is there, "the Lamb of God", "the great I AM", "the King of glory". In all the perfections of His person He is there. In all the merits of His atoning sacrifice He is there. And in all the capacity of His mediatorial offices He is there. But sweetest of all to Charitie's heart is the thought, **"He is there for me. His acceptance there is my acceptance there"**. I'm *"on His hands"*. I'm *"on His heart"*. Let Satan rage and accuse, if he will. There is nothing that can separate me from Him. I am accepted there in all the perfections of Christ for I am *"one with Him"*. Thus all accusing voices are silenced. Charitie's troubled heart is stilled, her faith fortified for the journey.

In the year 1867 Charitie's father, after twenty-nine years of unbroken and faithful service in Aghalurcher, moved to the parish of Drumragh in Co. Tyrone, as rector of St. Columba's Church in the town of Omagh. The rectory, at "Riverland Glebe" at Tattyreagh, some five miles from the town, then became the family home. Charitie continued to write her precious compositions and these she collected together, amended, and published in a small volume entitled, *Within the Veil*, by C. L. S. (1867). This was just two years prior to her marriage. In this respect she followed the example of her contemporary,

Fanny Humphreys (later Mrs. C. F. Alexander) who, living in the neighbouring town of Strabane had just two years before her marriage published her early verse as "Hymns for Little Children" in 1848. Charitie was married on 21st October 1869 in the city of Edinburgh. Her husband, Arthur E. Bancroft of the Royal Navy was from the city of Liverpool.

There is nothing on record of the middle years of Charitie's life but when we meet her again she is in the eventide of life and widowed for a second time. She bears the name of Charitie L. de Cheney (given in some records as Charitie L. de Chenez), and is living with the Smith family in Oakland, California. Among the younger members of the Smith family Charitie is affectionately known as "Aunt Cher". The Smiths had another home on the Pacific Coast at Moss Beach, some twenty-five miles south of San Francisco. They had named it, "Seal Cove" and there "Aunt Cher" spent much of her time. In her advanced years she is still writing verse and one of her most beautiful compositions, **"Redemption – Resurrection – Restoration"**, was written at "Seal Cove" when she was eighty years of age.

Away! Away! – to the home above!
Up-borne on the wings of Eternal Love!
The cage is broken! The bird is free,
And death is conquered, O Christ in Thee!
And I'll sing what the angels can never sing,
The song of redemption through Thee, my King!

No more the weakness of slow decay –
The labour and sorrow from day to day –
The failing heart, and trembling knees –
Forever! Forever! – released from these;
Done with mortality, done with strife;
And mortality swallowed up of life.

Yet lay the worn body away with care,
God's Holy Spirit has sojourned there!
Nor think He despiseth that helpless clay;
Nay, He'll guard it safely till that glad day
When the voice of Christ shall reclaim His own,
And present them faultless before the throne!

> *O Jesus, our Saviour, bring quickly the hour*
> *When body and spirit transformed by Thy power,*
> *With Thee in the glory triumphant shall reign,*
> *Delivered from weakness, corruption and pain!*
> *Redeemed by the wonderful, life-giving tide*
> *That flowed on the cross from Thy dear wounded side.*
>
> *Then mighty Restorer, what glory to see,*
> *This two-fold redemption accomplished in Thee!*

Thus at the close, as at the beginning, Charitie longed to be released from earth and to be with Christ. From the age of eighteen, when she first took up her pen, right till the age of eighty when she laid it down, her vision of things eternal never waned. Then, at the age of eighty-two, in the year 1923, Charitie's vision was realized. She passed away from her earthly home in Oakland, California to be with Christ. Her life-long longing was fulfilled, her yearning heart was satisfied.

"I'm waiting for Thee, Lord"

Hannah Kilham Burlingham (1842-1901)

Tombstone of Hannah Kilham Burlingham
(Bengeworth Cemetery, Evesham)

A row of flat tombstones in the secluded and neatly kept rear garden of the Friends Meeting House in Cowl Street, Evesham in Worcestershire arrests the attention of the visitor to that quiet retreat. All bear the name of "Burlingham". The two central slabs are inscribed "Henry Burlingham" and "Hannah Burlingham". Both died in their eighties, Henry in the first month of 1896 and Hannah five months previously. These were the parents of Hannah K. Burlingham.

The Burlinghams of Evesham were a well-known and highly respected family. They were Quakers. Henry's father, Richard, had come to Evesham in 1803. Richard was the son of John Burlingham, the august glove maker of Worcester who made gloves for King George III. In Evesham the Burlingham family ran an ironmongers' business at the bottom of Port Street. Their reputation has gone on record, as of "sober lives and solvent circumstances".

Hannah Kilham Burlingham (H.K.B.) was the eldest daughter and the second of nine children of Henry and Hannah Burlingham. She was born on 17th March 1842 and was named after her mother, Hannah Corbett, who had come from Manchester. At the time of Hannah's birth, her father purchased a large house on the outskirts of the town, in Port Street in the district of Bengeworth. This became the Burlingham family home and, remarkably, remained Hannah's home throughout life.

In the Burlingham home, godliness and piety, love and respect were daily in evidence and prayers for the children were the regular practice. Theirs was a happy household, but, when Hannah was still a girl, sorrow and bereavement entered the home and claimed three of the children. Later she wrote,

> *Three lilies, gathered by the Master's hand;*
> *Three treasures, given to Him who gave them erst.*

Hannah was endowed with remarkable poetic ability and even as a child was passionately fond of music. Quaker traditions, however, were somewhat restrictive and Hannah never learned to play any musical instrument. Still the regular practice of hymn singing in the home was much to Hannah's delight. She expressed her poetic ability early in life and, when still a schoolgirl, received a prize for her excellent poem on the school excursion.

Early in life Hannah got to know the Saviour and early in life she consecrated her life to Him, all her natural talents and all her time were given to Him. She dearly loved her Lord, His Word and His people and not long after she came of age she withdrew from the Society of Friends and identified herself with a company of like-minded believers in the town, gathered simply to the Name of the Lord Jesus.

In personal testimony Hannah was faithful, and especially with her young friends. She spoke to them often of the claims of the Saviour and exhorted them to trust Him early in life. She was well aware of the subtle dangers of procrastination.

> *When life's spring time has faded, its music died away,*
> *When thy hopes have given place to fears;*
> *When the clear sky is shaded, for summer will not stay,*
> *Oh! who shall wipe away thy tears?*

Hannah lived a life, wholly separated unto the Lord. She would not allow anything to come between her and the Saviour. The world with its alluring attractions had no place in her heart,

> *Dark, dark world! I would not stay*
> *Amid thy painted scenes of splendour;*
> *I hasten towards the golden day,*
> *Thy tinsel treasure I surrender,*
> *Dark, dark world!*

Hannah dearly loved nature. Rambles through the laneways, the fields and the woods were her great delight. She discerned in the world of nature around her the handiwork of God and appreciated that everything was in perfect accord with Scripture. To Hannah, the beauty of nature and the beauty of God's Word were one, the God of creation was the God of revelation. And as she rambled through the countryside, surveying the beauty of a landscape or contemplating the wonders of the flowers and the trees, she constantly drew from them valuable spiritual lessons.

Hannah's life span, however, was short, covering scarcely sixty years. She had lived at home with her parents up until their death (1895/96) and then, for the remaining five years, shared the family home with her younger sister, Sarah Anne. At the time of her parents' passing Hannah penned a poem, entitled, "In Memoriam".

> *Gone unto GOD.*
> *Gone to the Father, in His house to dwell;*
> *Gone through the shadowed vale that Jesus trod.*
> *Beloved, it is well!*

Then the experience of which she had written concerning her parents became her own, and on the 15th May 1901, after an acute illness of only three days, she went to be with her parents and with her Lord. Her body was laid to rest in the nearby little walled-in cemetery of Bengeworth, to await the resurrection morning.

Hannah K. Burlingham had lived a beautiful life, of love to her Lord and love to others. That love found its expression in acts of kindness and practical generosity and when she passed away her earthly estate amounted to just a few pounds. But she was rich in heavenly treasure! A personal and an intimate friend paid this tribute, "I never met any one who loved her Bible as she did. Though she was interested in current topics, they were wholly subservient to her one great interest. Her love for her Lord and Saviour was real and deep, and one felt, that with her, everything else must take a 'back place' ".

Hannah K. Burlingham was a true poet. Her natural talent, coupled with a deep spirituality and a mind saturated with the Word of God, resulted in compositions from her pen judged to be some of the finest in the English language. In both her translation works from the German and in her original verse, she has brought to us hymns and poems, rich in tenderness, beauty and scriptural worth.

Hannah appreciated that there was a rich treasure in German hymnody and at an early age she set herself to translate some of these works into English. These translations are a rich heritage to the English speaking world. Some forty-two of them are listed in Dr. John Julian's Dictionary of Hymnology and a brief glance at some of the opening lines as, "One Song of Songs – the sweetest", "What God doth is divinely done", "Up, Christian! Gird thee to the strife", "As truly as I live, God saith", "How beauteous shines the Morning Star!" and "'Tis spring, the time of singing", will convey something of the wide scope of the subject matter and the richness and fragrance of her renderings. Perhaps the best known today and most widely used of her translated hymns is, "O (Lord) Jesus, Friend unfailing", a rendering of Kuster's, "O Jesu, Freund der Seelen", written in 1829 and translated by Hannah in 1865.

Besides, Hannah's own personal compositions are rich and sweet. She commenced to write verse when only a girl and her best hymns were penned when she was in her twenties. In those early years she was a frequent contributor to the "British Herald", a magazine edited by William Reid, a Scottish clergyman and much of her verse has been reproduced in Reid's Praise Book (1872). "Her poems were the fruit of exercise", lessons learned in the school of God and taught by the experiences of life, its disappointments, its sorrows and bereavements, to which she was no stranger.

Most of Hannah's verse received publication a few months after her death in a precious little volume entitled, *"Wayside Songs"*. This contained one hundred and nine of her pieces and in its preface the editor writes, "It is to be regretted that the book was not brought out during the lifetime of the writer, and under her own supervision; but although often urged to publish in a collected form what she had written, her friends were unable to overcome her reluctance to do so".

Many of Hannah's compositions are in use today and are favourites with believers in assembly fellowship, as,

"Behold the Man upon the throne"
"Bright, bright home! Beyond the skies"
"God in mercy sent His Son"
"Heirs of salvation, chosen of God"
"I'm waiting for Thee, Lord"
"Jesus Christ, Thou King of glory"
"O God of matchless grace"
"O the love of Christ is boundless"
"On His Father's throne is seated"
"Praise the peerless Name of Jesus"
"The glory shines before me"
"The gospel is of God to magnify His Son"

The truth of the Lord's Return was one of Hannah's favourite themes. The anticipation of that event thrilled her heart. It was the moment for which she daily waited,

Come, Lord, Come! We wait for Thee,
We listen still for Thy returning;
Thy loveliness we long to see,
For Thee the lamp of hope is burning,
Come, Lord, Come!

And when she wrote of that subject, it was not with cold prospective, but with warmth and wistfulness and in expressions which touch the spirit and set the heart a longing.

I'm waiting for Thee, Lord,
Thy beauty to see, Lord,
I'm waiting for Thee, for Thy coming again.
Thou'rt gone over there, Lord,
A place to prepare, Lord,
Thy home I shall share at Thy coming again.

I'M WAITING FOR THEE, LORD

'Mid danger and fear, Lord,
I'm oft weary here, Lord;
The day must be near of Thy coming again.
'Tis all sunshine there, Lord,
No sighing nor care, Lord,
But glory so fair at Thy coming again.

Whilst Thou art away, Lord,
I stumble and stray, Lord;
O hasten the day of Thy coming again!
This is not my rest, Lord;
A pilgrim confest, Lord,
I wait to be blest at Thy coming again.

Our loved ones before, Lord,
Their troubles are o'er, Lord,
I'll meet them once more at Thy coming again.
The blood was the sign, Lord,
That marked them as Thine, Lord,
And brightly they'll shine at Thy coming again.

E'en now let my ways, Lord,
Be bright with Thy praise, Lord,
For brief are the days ere Thy coming again.
I'm waiting for Thee, Lord,
Thy beauty to see, Lord;
No triumph for me like Thy coming again!

The theme of this hymn is **the Lord's return**, its recurring refrain, *"Thy coming again"*. In each of the five stanzas Hannah speaks of "a night" and she speaks of "a morning". The first three lines of each stanza are "the night", the last three lines are "the morning". Concerning the night there is much of disquiet and of danger, but the morning is assured and is nearing. Well Hannah knows that when it breaks it will be "a morning without clouds". And in such rapt anticipation she breathes her inmost longing to her Beloved,
"I'm waiting for Thee, Lord".

"Not now, but in the coming years"

Maxwell Newton Cornelius (1842-1893)

Maxwell Newton Cornelius

Maxwell Cornelius sat by the bedside of his dying wife. Hers had been a trying and lingering illness through which he had attended faithfully and watched patiently. His mind was grappling with life's age-long and insoluble problem. Why? They had been so happy together! They had devotedly sought to serve the Lord together! Now life's precious bond was about to be severed. But why? Maxwell Cornelius, as he sat there, looked back over life.

He had been born on 30th July 1842, of farming stock at "Penns Woods" in Allegheny County in the western part of Pennsylvania. He grew up on the farm there and when he came of age left home to serve his apprenticeship as a carpenter and brick mason. Success had come his way and he set up his own business as a building contractor in the city of Pittsburgh. Then a serious accident occurred and this changed everything for him.

While erecting a house in the city of Pittsburgh his leg was severely crushed. The limb was so fractured and mangled that the attending physician advised amputation and gave him some days to prepare for the ordeal. In those days there was no anaesthesia and the patient remained conscious throughout the procedure. Such operations carried a high mortality, but there appeared to be no alternative. Maxwell recalled the day of the ordeal very clearly, of telling the physician that he was ready and of asking beforehand for his violin as he wished to play one more tune, perhaps his last. He clearly remembered tears in the physician's eyes as he played the melody. Surgery was carried out and he came through the operation safely, but subsequent handicap necessitated that he give up his business. In those circumstances Maxwell "sought the Lord" and gave himself to the Lord to be used of Him as He saw best. He felt called to the Christian ministry. But first he needed some education.

Maxwell attended Vermilion Institute, Ohio and from there proceeded to The Western Theological Seminary of the Presbyterian Church in Pittsburgh where he graduated in 1871. He was then in his twenty-ninth year. After a two-year pastorate at The Oakdale Presbyterian Church in Pennsylvania he proceeded to the Presbyterian Church in Altoona and there ministered for nine years (1876-1885). His early years at Altoona were times of blessing and happiness but after a period his wife's health started to fail and on that account he accepted a call to the "far west", to a young church in Pasadena, California where the climate was more pleasing. Pasadena, at that time, was regarded as a holiday resort for patients with chronic illness and many suffering from tuberculosis made recourse there.

In Pasadena, Maxwell gave himself whole-heartedly to the work of God. When he arrived in 1885 there was a small company of around a hundred attending the church, but soon, through his ministry, the congregation increased to about one thousand. As a consequence a larger church building was required and plans were drawn up accordingly. Everyone was enthusiastic and happy about the project and many pledged to help forward the work financially. But when work on the church was nearing completion a serious economic depression with resultant business failures overtook them and many who had made commitments could not meet them. Serious debt resulted. The congregation became despondent and Maxwell as minister was left to meet the financial obligations as best he could.

This financial burden had been a struggle for years but Maxwell was happy to recall that finally the debt had been cleared completely. Nevertheless, all the while his wife's health was deteriorating and her daily care was claiming more and more of his time. Life's pathway had not been easy and now, as he sat by his wife's bedside, great questions arose in his heart. What was the meaning of it all? What was its purpose? Why had what he most longed for always eluded him? Why the dark clouds instead of the sunshine? Why the song about to cease which had scarce begun? Why? Why? There seemed to be no answer. Everything was veiled in mystery. His faith in God began to stagger.

Maxwell decided to confide in a close Christian friend and share with him his perplexity. This he did and his friend replied, "Have faith in God — perhaps you will understand some day, if not now". He thought about the words of his friend's reply, "Not now! — Perhaps some day! — Sometime I'll understand". His faith steadied. He appreciated as never before that there was meaning to life. His thoughts took form and he jotted them down in verse.

A short time afterwards his wife passed away to be with Christ. Maxwell conducted the funeral proceedings personally and concluded the service by reading to the gathered friends the words of his lately composed poem.

Not now, but in the coming years –
It may be in the better land –
We'll read the meaning of our tears,
And there, some time, we'll understand.

We'll catch the broken threads again,
And finish what we here began;
Heaven will the mysteries explain,
And then, ah then, we'll understand.

We'll know why clouds instead of sun
Were over many a cherished plan;
Why song has ceased when scarce begun;
'Tis there, some time, we'll understand.

> *Why what we long for most of all*
> *Eludes so oft our eager hand,*
> *Why hopes are crushed and castles fall;*
> *Up there, some time, we'll understand.*
>
> *God knows the way, He holds the key,*
> *He guides us with unerring hand;*
> *Some time with tearless eyes we'll see;*
> *Yes, there, up there, we'll understand.*

A local newspaper published an account of Mrs. Cornelius' death together with details of the funeral service including the lines of Maxwell's poem. A copy of the columns later came into the hands of Major D. W. Whittle, the American evangelist. When he read the poem he was so impressed by the beauty of the verses that he cut them out and placed them in his Bible. Some months later he composed a further stanza.

> *Then trust in God through all thy days;*
> *Fear not! For He doth hold thy hand;*
> *Though dark thy way, still sing and praise;*
> *Some time, some time we'll understand.*

Major Whittle then passed on Maxwell Cornelius' poem together with the stanza of his own composition to his dear friend, James McGranahan of Pennsylvania. Mr. McGranahan set the whole to music, using the lines of Major Whittle as a chorus to the hymn, and giving to us the delightful tune that accompanies the hymn today.

In 1890 Maxwell Cornelius moved from Pasadena to serve the Lord at Howard Church, San Francisco. After a short ministry there he moved again to his last pastorate in the Eastern Presbyterian Church in America's capital city of Washington D.C. After a brief period of only two years (1891-1893) his health broke down. In his illness he was cared for in his home at No. 611 Maryland Avenue by devoted members of the family and friends and then, on 31st March 1893, he went to be with the Lord, at the early age of fifty years.

Maxwell Cornelius had known life's sorrows. The path of his earthly pilgrimage had been through a valley. Indeed, the valley had been deep and dark, like to those valleys in the very far north where the sun never penetrates in wintertime, utterly inhospitable and forbidding.

But the valley may be transformed by the Divine presence!

The valley of weeping (Baca) may become a well. (Psalm 84),
The valley of dry bones may vibrate again with new life. (Ezek. 37),
The valley of Achor (troubling) may prove to be a door of hope (Hosea 2),
The valley of the shadow may become a hallowed communion. (Psalm 23).

The valley of Maxwell Cornelius was transformed by that Presence and yielded up rich treasure. His heart, so sorely crushed, soared on high and burst into song. And Maxwell's valley song has become a precious legacy to succeeding generations.

The message of Maxwell's valley song is that of the Lord to Simon Peter, "What I do thou knowest not now; but thou shalt know hereafter" (John 13: 7).
Some time, up there — we'll read the meaning of our tears.
Some time, up there — we'll understand.
But we will have to wait!

It is said that Persian carpets are woven on great looms, the weavers working from the underside. From their perspective everything appears a muddle of tangled threads with numerous loose ends. So we weave life's pattern. What we see now often appears as only a tangled muddle. But there is a Divine Designer and He is weaving a pattern. He chooses the threads, the bright threads and the dark. One day the pattern will be complete, for the Divine Designer is the "Alpha and the Omega", and what He commences, that He completes. And one day life's canvas will be unrolled. Then all will be made plain.
Then we shall know, then we shall understand.

"Not now — but — **hereafter".**

"O Lamb of God, we lift our eyes"

Alexander Stewart (1843-1923)

Alexander Stewart

The name, Alexander Stewart, calls to mind two individuals, both outstanding Christian lawyers of the nineteenth century. One lived in the early part of the century, was linked with the town of Stafford and saw established there one of the early assemblies of God's people in that part of England. The other lived in the late nineteenth and early twentieth centuries and was linked with Glasgow and Prestwick in Scotland. It is this latter Alexander Stewart who is the subject of this present sketch.

Alexander Stewart was born in the city of Glasgow in the year 1843, the year of "The Disruption" within the Church of Scotland, when many with a genuine and personal faith in the Lord Jesus seceded from that Church to form the Free Church of Scotland. Alex's parents were members of the Church of Scotland and Alex had a religious upbringing. As a youth, however, Alex lived a godless life and never frequented any place of worship.

At the age of nineteen Alex had his first serious thoughts of spiritual and eternal matters. He was brought face to face with these realities one day after recovering from a giddy attack on one of Glasgow's streets. "Death!" he thought, "then Eternity!" He knew he was not prepared and in his soul trouble he sought salvation. His search continued for some nine months. He attended church and personally consulted his minister but was not helped. He accepted responsibility for a Sunday school class, yet all the while was in the dark as to the way of salvation.

Then one day the light of the glorious gospel shone into his dark heart. Let Alex himself tell of that experience. "I was lying on my bed one day in sore anxiety of soul when the Scripture came to me, 'It is finished', and immediately I entered into peace. I saw for the first time that I was eighteen hundred years on the other side of a finished work. I had been looking forward to something to be done by me, whereas I now saw that the work had been finished by another, the Lord Jesus Christ, on the Cross of Calvary".

Having entered into peace and the joy of salvation, Alex then joined the Established Church but after his first communion became so miserable that he left and did not frequent any religious meeting place for two years. Nevertheless, down deep in his heart there was a longing for a spiritual home, a place where he could fellowship with other believers, a place where his heart could rest. One Sunday morning he went to a meeting of Exclusive Brethren in Sauchiehall Street in Glasgow and there he was welcomed to partake of the Lord's supper. There he met with notable brethren, such as Dr. W. T. P. Wolston and Andrew Miller, men of spiritual calibre, men whose fellowship he greatly appreciated. But, as time went on, there was a growing conviction within Alex's heart as to the exclusivism of that fellowship. Human regulations were debarring him from fellowship with other genuine believers. His heart had not yet found a true spiritual home.

Alex had a fervent love for his Lord and a love for his fellow men. He longed to tell others of the Saviour whom he had found. Shortly after conversion he began proclaiming the glad tidings of the gospel in the open-air in the Cowcaddens district of Glasgow, helped by another young man, Murray McNeil Caird of Wigtownshire, who at that time was studying law in the city. Alex was gifted in the presentation of the gospel. One who knew him well described, "his rich commanding voice, gentlemanly bearing, marked ability joined with deep spirituality, securing for him at all times, whether outside or inside, a respectful and attentive hearing". God blessed those early gospel efforts and souls were saved. And right throughout life Alex never ceased to herald forth the gospel's glorious message. Indeed, as an old man of almost eighty years of age, his striking figure was often seen in open-air gospel testimony standing on the shore or at 'The Cross' in Prestwick, his hometown in retirement.

Some of Alex's early converts in the city of Glasgow, as a consequence of their study of the Scriptures, started to meet collectively each Lord's day to "break bread". Alex identified with them and there found a spiritual home. At first they met in Clarendon Hall in the city, then later moved to Union Hall. In that company Alex was an able leader and a gifted teacher of the Word of God.

Alex's spiritual gift as a teacher of the Word of God drew large audiences from all over the city of Glasgow. His ministry was weighty, scriptural and directed to the heart. When he discerned a spiritual need, he sought to meet that need with wholesome ministry. His messages were often "words in season". At a time when there was unease and much dispute about "appointment" of elders in the assemblies of God's people, Alex gave such an address at the Half-yearly Meeting in Glasgow on "The Shepherd Rule of the Lord Jesus" and the consequent obligations resting upon under-shepherds that there were afterwards fewer aspirants to that office. He stated that the Lord Jesus had led, had fed and given His life for the sheep and "because He laid down His life for us: we ought to lay down our lives for the brethren" (1 John 3: 16). He emphasized that it was not the recognition of the office that mattered, but the doing of the work. As a consequence of his address, no more was heard thereafter of the "appointment" of elders. In ministry, Alex often enjoyed the happy companionship of his Glasgow associate, John R. Caldwell, (editor of "The Witness" for almost forty years). Alex travelled widely in ministry throughout Scotland and England and for over fifty years was recognized by all as an acceptable and able conference speaker.

Alex, by profession, was a lawyer and conducted a busy practice in the city of Glasgow. He never married. He gave virtually all his material things and all his spare time to the work of the Lord. When he retired from his Glasgow law practice, he moved to Prestwick on the Ayrshire coast. He identified with the small assembly there and under his rich and upbuilding ministry the assembly flourished

The closing years of Alex's life were marked by indifferent health and toward the end he was confined to bed. Nevertheless he enjoyed much of the presence of the Lord, and approached death with complete composure. In parting with a friend who had come to visit him, he said, "If we never meet again, remember it has been mercy from first to last". To another he remarked, "I'm only a sinner, saved by grace". Alex passed away into the presence of the Lord whom he loved and served so faithfully on 27th April 1923, at eighty years of age, thus bringing to a close "sixty years of fragrant testimony" of "a man of sterling character".

Alex, besides his gifts as an evangelist and teacher of God's Word, had also the pen of a ready writer. He wrote many booklets, one of which entitled, *Salvation Truths* was much used in personal work and was greatly blessed of the Lord. He contributed articles to "The Witness" and wrote a few hymns. Two of his hymns are of special merit and appear in "The Believers Hymn Book". It is as author of these two hymns that Alex is remembered today and has a special place in the hearts of the Lord's people.

1. *Lord Jesus Christ, we seek Thy face,*
   Within the veil we bow the knee;
   O let Thy glory fill the place,
   And bless us while we wait on Thee.

   We thank Thee for the precious blood
   That purged our sins and brought us nigh,
   All cleansed and sanctified to God,
   Thy holy Name to magnify.

   Shut in with Thee, far, far above
   The restless world that wars below,
   We seek to learn and prove Thy love,
   Thy wisdom and Thy grace to know.

   The brow that once with thorns was bound,
   Thy hands, Thy side, we fain would see;
   Draw near, Lord Jesus, glory-crowned,
   And bless us while we wait on Thee.

2. *O Lamb of God, we lift out eyes*
   To Thee amidst the throne;
   Shine on us, bid Thy light arise,
   And make Thy glory known.

We know Thy work for ever done,
   Ourselves alive and free;
Graced with the Spirit of the Son,
   Made nigh to God in Thee.

Yet would we prove Thine instant grace,
   Thy present power would feel;
Lift on us now Thy glorious face,
   Thyself, O Lord, reveal.

From Thy high place of purest light,
   O Lamb, amidst the throne,
Shine forth upon our waiting sight,
   And make Thy glory known.

These two compositions of Alexander Stewart are companion hymns. Each hymn is a prayer. In each there is request for an experience of **"the glory of the Divine Presence"** in the midst of God's gathered people.

A vision of Divine glory was ever the quest of the people of God.
"Shew me Thy glory". (Moses) (Exod. 33:18)
"Shew us the Father". (Philip) (John 14: 8)
Visions of Divine glory were guarded in the old economy.
"No man shall see Me, and live" (Exod.33: 20)
"We shall surely die, because we have seen God" (Manoah)(Judg. 13:22)
The supreme vision of Divine glory was in the incarnation of the Son of God.
"The Word became flesh – we beheld His glory" (John 1:14)
"The only begotten Son – He hath declared Him" (John 1:18)
That vision of the Divine glory was glorious in its manifestation.
"His Son – The brightness of His glory" (Heb. 1:2,3)
"The glory of God in the face of Jesus Christ" (2 Cor. 4:6)
Visions of Divine glory prostrate the beholder in profoundest reverence.
"Moses made haste and bowed his head – and worshipped" (Exod. 34: 8)
"And when I saw Him, I fell at His feet" (John) (Rev. 1: 17).

These two hymns of Alexander Stewart are the language of uplifted hearts in the sanctuary.
They should be sung thoughtfully and sung prayerfully.

From Thy high place of purest light,
O Lamb, amidst the throne,
Shine forth upon our waiting sight,
And make Thy glory known.

"We love to sing of the Lord who died"

Thomas Donald William Muir (1855-1931)

Thomas Donald William Muir

T.D.W. Muir of Detroit was of Scottish descent. His father, James Proudfoot Muir had immigrated to Canada from Lanarkshire. His mother, Agnes McKinnon, had been born in Canada; her ancestors, though, were from the Isle of Skye. Thomas was born in the village of Ormstown in S. Quebec on the morning of 25th February 1855.

Shortly after Thomas' birth, his father, who had been in business in Ormstown, moved to the city of Montreal in the employment of the Grand Trunk Railway. The family followed and there Thomas spent his boyhood. The family belonged to the Presbyterian Church but sometimes, because of convenience, they went to a little Baptist Church nearby. In that little Baptist Church and while sitting under the ministry of a godly young man named Richmond, Thomas had his first thoughts of eternity and his need of salvation. When he reached fifteen years of age the family moved to Hamilton, Ontario, but some time before then Thomas' father had been converted, the outcome of a near-drowning accident in the St. Lawrence River.

In the year 1874 two gospel preachers, Donald Munro and John Smith (both Scottish immigrants), came to Hamilton at the invitation of a godly couple living there. They started to preach the gospel in a third floor room of a building in King Street. After preaching for some six weeks and seeing no apparent interest in the message, one of the evangelists packed his bag with intent of moving to another field. Just then, it pleased God to save three young men in one night, Thomas D.W. Muir, his brother, Kenneth, and an acquaintance, William L. Faulknor (who later carried the message of the gospel to Central Africa). But let Thomas tell of that experience in his own words.

"Behind the platform and tacked to the wall was a large printed bill in the shape of a question – *'Friend, thou art travelling to eternity, to an everlasting heaven or an endless hell, which?'* During the forty-five minutes we were in that hall, that question burned its way into my conscience, and I went home in deep trouble of soul. Two nights later I was back again, and faced the same question – this time to acknowledge that I was a sinner, and dying as I was would perish forever, but while John 3:36 was quoted from the platform, I looked away from self and sin, and found peace through faith in the Lord Jesus Christ, the Son of God, who on Calvary 'died for my sins according to the Scriptures, and was buried and rose again the third day, according to the Scriptures' (1 Cor. 15:3).

"Seated by my side was a young man with whom I was slightly acquainted, William L. Faulknor. Like myself, he had been invited to come and hear these men, and their plain, decisive way of preaching the gospel had opened his eyes to see that a religious profession that he had, was not Christ, and he was anxious to be saved. Turning to him, I asked, "Will, have you everlasting life?" "No," was his reply, "but I want it. Have you got it?" "Yes," I gladly answered, "I received Christ as my Saviour a few minutes ago, and I know I have everlasting life, for His Word has said it". A few minutes later dear William Faulknor also trusted Christ and went home rejoicing in the Lord. On the seat behind us sat my brother who, unknown to us, was also in soul anxiety. He too closed in with God's offer of salvation, and became a child of God through faith in Christ. These three cases of blessing that evening accounted for the unpacking of the valise (travelling bag) when the preachers got home that night".

Right from the day of conversion Thomas became a soul winner. He took two young women to the meetings in King Street and both were gloriously saved. Their father, however, a Mr. Sproul, was very antagonistic and forbade them to go back. Then Thomas very courageously stepped into the situation. He visited Mr. Sproul in his home, opened to him the Scriptures and through the words of John chapter 3 had the joy of leading him to Christ. The next evening found all the Sproul family at the gospel meeting and at that meeting Mrs. Sproul whispered to Thomas that she had trusted Christ the previous night while listening at the keyhole as he explained the way of salvation to her husband.

Thomas was baptized and then, at the age of twenty, and just eleven months after conversion, he stepped out into full time service for the Lord, to bring the message of the gospel to his fellow men and looking to God alone to provide for his needs. God honoured that step of faith and Thomas through life proved the absolute faithfulness of God. His first meetings were held in the second floor of a carpenter's shop in S. Ontario and then for some years Thomas laboured in the rural districts of that same province where he was much used of the Lord.

In the year 1881 Thomas went to Michigan State, U.S.A. for the first time. This proved to be a great milestone in his life. A sister living there, who had been saved in Canada, invited him to bring the gospel to her native town. His journey there from Hamilton was partly by train and partly by stagecoach. The late arrival of the train necessitated his stay overnight in a little country town. He invested almost all his means in renting a room in a nearby "hotel" and, after selecting a suitable spot for an open air meeting and covering the whole area with gospel tracts, he lay down to rest. When he awoke it was dark and there was no street illumination. He made his way to the previously selected spot, mounted a covered water tank and began to sing a gospel hymn. Through the darkness he could discern that there was quite an audience. Then, helped of God, he proclaimed the message of the gospel in all its fullness. He distributed more tracts and spoke to inquiring souls of the way of salvation. And though Satan bitterly opposed his lonely effort that night, God was pleased to work in the salvation of souls.

Next morning Thomas made his way to his destination in Michigan. There he faced further difficulties. There was no one to help and no place to preach except an old schoolhouse. In the schoolhouse there was no illumination and the nights were dark. Thomas procured some turnips, split them, scooped them out and used the hollowed out turnips as lightholders. But, more importantly, he had brought to the people in the old schoolhouse spiritual light, the light of the gospel, and as he proclaimed it nightly God was pleased to bless in salvation.

The city of Detroit on the shore of America's great waterway at that time was not the city that we know it today. Still it had a large populace and Thomas moved there with the message of the gospel. He made Detroit his home and thereafter would be known as "T.D.W. Muir of Detroit". In that city Thomas preached in the open air, in tent, vacated store or wherever he got opportunity. In the early days there was no one to help other than his beloved and devoted wife. Thomas erected his gospel tent in an Irish district of Detroit called Corktown and there he saw a remarkable work of grace and the establishment of the Central Gospel Hall testimony. Detroit remained the centre of Thomas' labours for the next fifty years and during his lifetime he saw seven other assemblies planted in the Detroit area.

Thomas also moved widely throughout Canada and the U.S.A, preaching the gospel and teaching the people of God. He was not an eloquent preacher but God was with him. His message to sinners was the simple gospel, the story of the Cross. When souls were saved, he taught them from God's Word the truths of believer's baptism and gathering simply to the Lord's Name. Thus Thomas laboured consistently and faithfully right up to the close of life.

Thomas' labours for God ended on 7th February 1931. After five weeks of painful illness in Detroit hospital, he entered into his rest. His funeral service was held three days later at Central Gospel Hall in the presence of many whom he had seen brought to Christ. It was an occasion of great mourning and with a feeling of tremendous loss, yet at the same time it was an occasion of joy, of triumph and of challenge. The fearless warrior was with his Lord. And as the company sang the words of the Christian's "Goodnight" ("Sleep on, beloved") and the words of Thomas' own hymn, "The Blessed Hope" ("O child of God, there is for thee a hope that shines amid the gloom"), hearts were comforted and stayed and directed onward to the coming again of the Lord.

The world had lost a faithful herald of the Cross, the assemblies in

Detroit and beyond had lost a devoted pastor and the church of God had lost a gifted teacher. T.D.W. Muir was a man greatly beloved, a true shepherd among the people of God; indeed, he moved as a father among them. The bigotry of partisan brethren meant little to him. He had a big heart and his sympathies extended to all in genuine need. In his bearing he portrayed the meekness and the gentleness of Christ. T.D.W. Muir was a wise counsellor with "rare judgment". He carried with him wherever he went a sense of the presence of God and often "without speaking a word or moving a finger, his very presence brought in order". Indeed, as was stated at his funeral service, "He was like a great mountain whose magnitude can only be realized in distance". And so it has been, for as the years have passed, more and more the people of God have appreciated the greatness of their loss in Mr. Muir's passing.

But first of all T.D.W. Muir was an evangelist. He loved the gospel. He proclaimed it faithfully and he proclaimed it fully. He proclaimed it by word and he proclaimed it by pen, and for his gospel work he composed some lovely gospel hymns.

One of his best known and sweetest is, **"We love to sing of the Lord who died",**

> *We love to sing of the Lord, who died,*
> *And His wondrous love proclaim;*
> *How there's life and peace through the Crucified,*
> *And salvation through His name.*
>
> *Salvation! Salvation!*
> *Vast, full and free;*
> *Through the precious blood*
> *Of the Son of God,*
> *Who was slain on Calvary.*
>
> *O the height and depth of His boundless love,*
> *And His mercy who can tell,*
> *When He came to the cross from the throne above,*
> *To save our souls from hell!*
>
> *Our sins and guilt were upon Him laid,*
> *He the wrath of God endured,*
> *By His precious blood an atonement made*
> *And our full discharge procured.*

> *Ascended now to God's right hand,*
> *A conqueror o'er the grave;*
> *He bids us tell through every land*
> *His mighty power to save.*

The message of salvation filled and flooded the heart of T.D.W. Muir, and throughout his more than fifty years of unremitting service he delighted to make it known. The message of salvation is the grandest and the sweetest message that has ever been told. It will never, never grow old, nor will it ever lose its power. Through its message the sinner's deepest need can be met, fully and forever.

> *Salvation! Salvation!*
> *Vast, full and free;*
> *Through the precious blood*
> *Of the Son of God,*
> *Who was slain on Calvary.*

"In loving kindness Jesus came"

Charles Hutchinson Gabriel (1856-1932)

Charles Hutchinson Gabriel

In the world of American hymnody, Charles Hutchinson Gabriel ranks as one of its foremost writers. In his generation he was termed "the king of hymn writers". He was both poet and musician, and a beautiful blend of these two talents is featured in his compositions. He infused into his verse a simplicity easy to be understood and a warmth that has scarcely ever been equalled. His hymns are as fresh today as when first written.

Charles Hutchinson Gabriel was born in a simple prairie shanty in the district of Wilton in the state of Ohio, U.S.A. His parents had gone there, with their three children, from the state of Virginia in

1850. They had purchased a quarter section of virgin land at six dollars an acre and built their simple home, a wooden structure plastered inside and out. There was scarcely a tree about them to afford any kind of shelter from the storms and snow of winter or shield them from the blazing heat of summer. Into that simple home Charles was born on 18th August 1856.

When Charles was about five a schoolhouse was erected three-quarters of a mile from their home, and in the winter months, when there was no work to be done on the farm, the children received a very elementary schooling. There Charles received his early education. He was a talented lad and very musical. He well remembered that when he was nine years of age he saw a musical instrument for the first time. And he could clearly recall when he first heard a melodeon. He had ridden ten miles to hear it. Its music enchanted him and he could not forget its strains as he worked day by day on the farm or when he lay down at night to sleep.

Charles' parents were believers in the Lord Jesus Christ and early in life Charles too came to know the Saviour. His father was very musical and the Gabriel home was often the gathering centre in that district of the prairies where the neighbours assembled in the evenings for a time of singing and fellowship. And on such occasions Charles' father was their leader.

Charles dearly loved music and at an early age started to write verse. He always had a great ambition to become a musician. He once told his mother of his great desire to write a famous song. And in reply his mother said, "I would rather you write a song that will help someone than see you President of the United States". However, Charles lacked training and the family was poor.

At the early age of seventeen Charles left home and started out in the world, alone and unaided, to seek the realization of his boyhood dreams. He had limitless energy and persevered in the face of many difficulties. And he succeeded. He was entirely a self-made man. For though he never received any tuition in music, he rose to the very top of his profession. And in his later years, none knew better than he did just how to put the finishing touches on a piece of music or the words of a hymn, or how best to bring them harmoniously together.

Charles personally was a man of simple tastes. He was warm and sympathetic in his disposition, a great lover of the common people and especially of children and was always a ready helper of those in need.

IN LOVING KINDNESS JESUS CAME

As a composer Charles worked tirelessly. He sometimes wrote under the pseudonyms of H.A. Henry or Charlotte G. Homer. He did most of his work at home and it was his rule to try and write something new each day. Much of his work was done through the hours of the night while the world around him slept. His fame as a successful composer became widely known and soon many demands were made upon his time. He was involved in the compilation of a large number of songbooks, including some thirty-five for gospel work and eight for Sunday school work. In his later years he was closely associated with the Homer Rodeheaver Publishing Company.

In early years Charles taught singing schools, sometimes among the coloured folk, sometimes among the cowboys, sometimes among the Indians and occasionally among the Japanese of San Francisco. For a period of three years he was music director for the Grace Methodist Episcopal Church in San Francisco and then, in 1892, he moved to the city of Chicago to be near to a music-publishing centre. In that city at that time there were many evangelists, both preachers and singers, as Moody, Sankey, Bliss, Whittle, Mc Granahan, Case, Excell and Stebbins. Charles came to know many of these men personally and indeed he became another in that long line of Chicago noteworthies. His eventide years were spent in Berkeley on the western coast of California and there he kept busy with his compositions right to the close of life. He died in Los Angeles, California on 15th September 1932 at the age of seventy-six and is interred in the chapel of the Pines.

David J. Beattie of Carlisle was an intimate acquaintance of Gabriel for the last twenty years of his life and in his "Romance of Sacred Song" says of him, "His soul was full of music and his heart throbs with love for the Master". Beattie also shares with us extracts from one of Gabriel's last letters and these give some insight into the life of this outstanding yet self-effacing man. "My sixty years of Gospel Song have been eventful and tolerant, interesting and tedious, hopeful and discouraging. Failure more often than success marks the path I have travelled. And now, since the years have led me up the eastern slope and over the mountain top of life, and I am hurrying down towards the silent sea that lies shimmering before me, I begin to realize that my work has not been so much a failure as I had concluded".

Nor indeed has it! Some of the most beautiful hymns in the English language stand as a memorial to his talent and dedication. Gabriel knew the essentials of a good hymn. He once stated, "First, the text must be systematically constructed, be spiritual and devotional; it should begin with an immediate declaration of subject, followed by an explication presented in a logical and intelligent manner. Gospel music is the language of the heart; the expression of hope, trust, longing, sorrow, joy, and even despair of the soul. It is the spontaneous overflow of happiness and a healing balm for the wounds of life; it is both sermon and song, praise and prayer, oblivion and remembrance". And such ingredients, delicately balanced, are amply exemplified in his personal compositions.

Gabriel composed sweet and fitting melodies for the words of many hymnwriters. A few are here listed, with the writer of the words indicated in brackets.

"Blessed Lily of the Valley" (Grace Elizabeth Cobb).
"I'm pressing on the upward way" (Johnson Oatman Jr.).
"I must needs go home by the way of the Cross" (Jessie Brown Pounds).
"I need Jesus" (George Webster).
"Only in Thee, O Saviour mine" (Thomas O. Chisholm).
"There are loved ones in the glory" (Ada R. Habershon).
"What a wonderful change in my life has been wrought!" (Rufus H. Mc Daniel).
"Why should I feel discouraged?" (Civilla D. Martin).

Furthermore, Gabriel wrote both the words and the music of many beautiful hymns. In these compositions his talents, as both poet and musician, are delightfully portrayed. Again, the following is but a small selection.

"God is calling the prodigal" ("Calling the prodigal").
"In loving kindness Jesus came" ("He lifted me").
"I stand all amazed at the love" ("Oh, it is wonderful!").
"I stand amazed in the presence" ("My Saviour's love").
"O sweet is the story of Jesus!" ("The wonderful story").
"Standing in the market places" ("Reapers are needed").
"There's a call comes ringing o'er the restless wave" ("Send the light").
"When all my labours and trials are o'er" ("O that will be glory!")

These hymns are a precious collection. Some are gospel hymns, some are missionary and some are devotional. Many themes engaged the heart of Charles H. Gabriel. But of them all there was none more precious to him nor more wonderful than that of the Saviour's love. The fact that the Saviour should love him personally moved him deeply. Its truth warmed and filled his heart and he poured forth his musings into verse.

> *I stand amazed in the presence*
> *Of Jesus the Nazarene,*
> *And wonder how He could love me,*
> *A sinner, condemned, unclean.*

Then again, in anticipation of a future with his Saviour that will never end, he wrote,

> *O, that will be – glory for me –*
> *Glory for me – glory for me –*
> *When by His grace I shall look on His face,*
> *That will be glory, be glory for me.*

This latter hymn, sometimes called "The Glory Song" was Gabriel's most popular composition. The beaming countenance and simple prayers of a humble believer in Christ, named Ed Cord, inspired its writing. Ed was the director of the St. Louis Sunshine Rescue Mission and so radiant was his face that he was nicknamed "Old Glory Face". And Ed's prayers invariably finished with the words, "and that will be glory for me!"

Then, in the year 1905, Gabriel wrote the words and the music of one of the sweetest and tenderest of all his compositions, **"In loving kindness Jesus came"**.

> *In loving kindness Jesus came,*
> *My soul in mercy to reclaim,*
> *And from the depths of sin and shame*
> *Through grace He lifted me.*

> *From sinking sand He lifted me;*
> *With tender hand He lifted me;*
> *From shades of night to plains of light,*
> *O, praise His name, He lifted me!*

> *He called me long before I heard,*

Before my sinful heart was stirred;
But when I took Him at His word,
Forgiven He lifted me.

His brow was pierced with many a thorn,
His hands by cruel nails were torn,
When from my guilt and grief, forlorn,
In love He lifted me.

Now on a higher plane I dwell,
And with my soul I know 'tis well;
Yet how or why, I cannot tell,
He should have lifted me.

"**He lifted me**". That is the title of Gabriel's hymn and that is its theme.

He lifted me! No one else but the Saviour **could** have done it!
He lifted me! No one else but the Saviour **would** have done it!
He lifted me! But why He **should** have done it Gabriel could not understand.

Yet how or why, I cannot tell,
He should have lifted me.

And on this note Gabriel takes his leave.

"Glory to Thee, Thou Son of God, most high"

Edward Christian Quine (1857-1942)

Edward Christian Quine

Edward Christian Quine, as his surname denotes, was a Manxman. The home of the Quines on the Isle of Man was Ballaharry Farm situated in the parish of Marown, almost in the centre of the Island. That holding had been handed down within the family for ten generations and had been held in the Quine name since 1729. Edward Christian Quine was born there on 3rd January 1857. He was the second son in the family of ten children of John Quine and Sarah Cain.

The Isle of Man always held a large part in Edward's heart. It was his beloved "Ellan Vannin". He had been born there. He grew up there. He spent his early years there. And then, after his adventures at sea, his years of business in the city of Liverpool and a short stay in Australia, he returned to the Island again at the age of fifty-five. There he spent a further thirty years and there he died. He is buried on the Island.

Edward, though brought up on a farm, always had a great fascination for the sea and for sailing ships. He maintained this interest right throughout life. In his late teens he went to sea and for some years enjoyed the thrills and challenges of round the world voyages in a sailing ship. Throughout life, seascapes and sailing ships were Edward's favourite subjects as an artist. As a writer, stories of the sea were his favourite theme. For many years, he contributed regularly to a seaman's magazine, "Sea Breezes", published by the Pacific Steam Navigation Company (P.S.N.C.) and therein, under the penname of "Captain Hawser", he recounted his personal youthful experiences at sea. Furthermore, in Marown Parish Churchyard where Edward's body rests, the carving of an anchor distinctively marks the Quine family tombstone.

When Edward returned from his round of adventures at sea, he settled in the city of Liverpool. There he engaged in business, first as a bread salesman, then as a master baker and from there he advanced to become agent for Frost's Flour Mills of Chester. During his time in Liverpool, Edward met his fiancée, Frances Jane Birkett. They were married in July 1879 and together set up home in the city. There they raised their family of three sons and one daughter.

Edward had come from a Methodist family. Early in life he had come to know the Lord Jesus as his personal Saviour. He became a diligent student of the Word of God and its truths directed his pathway through life. Through his reading of the Scriptures the Spirit of God guided him to a fellowship of like-minded believers, gathered to the Name of the Lord Jesus and meeting in Boaler Street Hall in Liverpool. There Edward found a spiritual home and there he actively participated in the exercises of that company as they met to remember the Lord Jesus and as they proclaimed the glorious message of the gospel to the people of the district. Thus Edward spent thirty years in the city of Liverpool, engaged in business and happy in the fellowship of the Boaler Street assembly believers.

Edward then emigrated to Australia. He set sail on 30th January 1912, aboard the "Everton Grange" in company with Mr. J. Halliday, a fellow believer from Boaler Street Hall. They were minded to explore the New World together, set up business in the building trade and then, when things became established, to send for their wives and families.

Edward, is his diary, has given us some interesting detail of their outward sea voyage in 1912. Besides recounting weather conditions and the storms encountered, he wrote of the happy times of fellowship with other believers aboard the "Everton Grange". With the captain's permission, meetings were conducted each Lord's day for the proclamation of the gospel. Edward was the regular speaker at these services and as many as forty-five children and two hundred and fifty adults attended. After eight weeks at sea, the "Everton Grange" dropped anchor in Melbourne, on Sunday 31st March 1912.

Business in the New World proceeded as they had planned. Contacts were made and orders were taken for building. Then, on 22nd May, when Edward had been less than two months in that new land, he received a cablegram from the Isle of Man, "Mortality – come home". It proved to be the death of his mother. His father was already deceased and his older brother had died some four years earlier without leaving a successor. Edward now assumed responsibility for the property at Ballaharry Farm. He immediately settled up affairs with Mr. Halliday and set sail for home. Leaving Melbourne on 19th June aboard the "Ballarat", he arrived in London on 12th August. He went directly to Liverpool to join his family and from there proceeded to the Isle of Man. The Island thereafter became his home.

Edward lived for a time in a rented cottage at Union Mills and then acquired a home at Woodbourne Square in the capital town of Douglas. After a few years, he then moved to "Falconia" in Princes Road and this became his home in Douglas for the remainder of his life. Edward's grandchildren, William E. Quine of Lancashire and May Bunting of Belfast, both recount spending some of their childhood years in Douglas with their grandfather during World War 1. May went to school there and one of her duties, as a young girl of nine or ten, was to go daily to the Post Office, copy out the headline war news and bring it home to grandfather.

The remaining thirty years of Edward's life were spent in "retirement". His chief ambition during these years was the spiritual upbuilding of the saints of God and the spread of the gospel on the Island. Initially he could find there no company of believers meeting simply after the New Testament pattern, though there had been an assembly at an earlier date. He thereupon gathered some believers together, taught them simple New Testament church truths and an assembly was re-established.

Edward was an active evangelist, a gifted teacher of the Word of God and a spiritual guide among the people of God. He was a regular figure for many years at open-air gospel meetings held on the Promenade and other venues in the seaside town of Douglas. As a teacher of the word of God, he spent most of his time helping believers on the Island, though in his latter years he was in demand as a conference speaker on mainland Britain. Dispensational truths and truths concerning the Person of the Lord Jesus were Edward's favourite themes. At New Year time, and for many years, he gathered together a group of believers from the north of the Island in one of the large guesthouses on the Mooragh Promenade in Ramsey. There, in a large room and around an open fire he opened up to them the precious truths of Holy Scripture. Oftimes he was the only one present with ability to teach, but his gift was such that he could hold the rapt attention of his audience for several hours at a stretch.

Thus Edward Quine occupied himself in the things of the Lord right to the close of life. He passed away peacefully at his home, "Falconia", on the 11th January 1942, at the ripe age of eighty-five years. After a service in the home, conducted by John Casement, his body was laid to rest in the family burial plot in Marown Parish Churchyard, near to the village of Crosby.

With the passing of Edward C. Quine, the Isle of Man lost an able teacher, a spiritual leader and a wise guide. As a teacher he had sought to impart to others the precious truths that he personally had gleaned from the Word of God. Very little of his teachings remain today, save his contributions to "The Witness" magazine, a few pamphlets and a few hymns.

Three of Edward Christian Quine's hymns remain. These were originally circulated in printed leaflet form. They were entitled – "Calvary", the "Coming of the Lord" and "Home, sweet Home". The best known of these is that entitled, "Calvary", and commencing, **Glory to Thee, Thou Son of God most High!** This is the hymn by which Edward Christian Quine is remembered today. It has found its way into a few hymnbooks and is often sung by saints met together at the Lord's supper.

> *Glory to Thee, Thou Son of God most High!*
>   *All praise to Thee!*
> *Glory to Thee, enthroned above the sky!*
>   *Who died for me!*
> *High on Thy throne, Thine ear, Lord Jesus, bend,*
> *As grateful hearts now to Thyself ascend!*

GLORY TO THEE, THOU SON OF GOD, MOST HIGH

Deep were Thy sorrows, Lord, when heaven frowned –
   Gethsemane!
Bloodlike Thy sweat, Lord, falling to the ground
   So heavily!
Dark was the night, but heaven was darker still!
O, Christ my God! – is this the Father's will?

Thorns wreathed Thy brow when hanging on the tree!
   Man's cruelty!
Why lavish love like this, O Lord, on me?
   Thou lovest me!
Would that my soul could understand its length –
Its breadth, depth, height, and everlasting strength!

Thy precious blood was freely shed for me
   On Calvary!
To save me from a lost eternity!
   Glory to Thee!
Nor death, nor hell, nor things below – above,
Can sever me from Thy eternal love!

Like shoreless seas, Thy love can know no bound!
   Thou lovest me!
Deep, vast, immense, unfathomed, Lord – profound,
   Lord, I love Thee!
And when above, my crown is at Thy feet,
I'll praise Thee still for Calvary's mercy seat!

In this hymn Edward Christian Quine tells the story of the Cross with deepest reverence. Almost every line is punctuated by an exclamation mark and these invite us to pause and to ponder. In the closing stanza we arrive at an arresting climax, "Calvary's mercy seat".

"Calvary's mercy seat"

Here the imagery of the tabernacle is fitting and most suggestive.
A dark place! No natural light ever penetrated the holy of holies with its earthly mercy seat. In like manner Calvary was a dark, dark experience for the Saviour.
A lonely place! On the Day of Atonement the high priest went alone into that awesome earthly sanctuary. So Calvary was a lonely, lonely

experience for the Saviour.

A *"meeting place"!* As the blood-sprinkled mercy seat was the meeting place for God and man in the old economy, so Calvary today is the meeting place of a holy God and the guilty sinner.

"Calvary's mercy seat"!
We are privileged to ponder it now. We do so, with unshod feet and with adoring heart.
Then above, its immensity and profundity will occupy our hearts eternally.

"I Cannot tell why He, whom angels worship"

William Young Fullerton (1857-1932)

William Young Fullerton

William Young Fullerton was Irish by birth. As a teenager he moved to mainland Britain and there spent the rest of his life. His deep missionary interest and Irish roots were the well springs from which has come his lovely hymn, set to the famous traditional Irish melody, "Londonderry Air". The hymn is entitled **"The Saviour of the World"**.

> I cannot tell why He whom angels worship
> Should set His love upon the sons of men,
> Or, why, as Shepherd, He should seek the wand'rers,
> To bring them back, they know not how or when:

But this I know, that He was born of Mary,
When Bethl'hem's manger was His only home,
And that He lived at Nazareth and laboured,
And so the Saviour, Saviour of the world, is come.

I cannot tell how silently He suffered,
As with His peace He graced this place of tears,
Or why His heart upon the Cross was broken,
The crown of pain to three and thirty years:
But this I know, He heals the broken-hearted,
And stays our sin, and calms our lurking fear,
And lifts the burden from the heavy-laden,
For yet the Saviour, Saviour of the world is here.

I cannot tell how He will win the nations,
How He will claim His earthly heritage,
How satisfy the needs and aspirations
Of East and West, of sinner and of sage:
But this I know, all flesh shall see His glory,
And He shall reap the harvest He has sown,
And some glad day His sun shall shine in splendour
When He the Saviour, Saviour of the world, is known.

I cannot tell how all the lands shall worship,
When, at His bidding, ev'ry storm is stilled,
Or who can say how great the jubilation
When all the hearts of men with love are filled:
But this I know, the skies will thrill with gladness,
And myriad myriad human voices sing,
And earth to heav'n, and heav'n to earth, will answer,
At last the Saviour, Saviour of the world, is King!

William was born on 8th March 1857 into a home adjoining on Shaftesbury Square in the city of Belfast. He was the only boy in the family. There were several sisters. Perhaps William's earliest childhood memory was the tragic death of his father, resulting from a crushing between two stacks of swaying timber. William was then only three and that event left a lasting impression on him. William's mother, widowed at this early age, faced life bravely. With a courageous heart and an unwavering faith, she shouldered the responsibilities of the home and of the family business (a brickyard coupled with an agency for Bangor Blue slates).

Sundays regularly found the Fullerton family at the old Presbyterian Church in the centre of the city. There William and the family sat under the ministry of Dr. John Morgan. Then, when William was about thirteen, there was a change of minister. Their new minister, Dr. H. M. Williamson, unlike his predecessor, was a true evangelist, and his presentation of the gospel was such that William longed to be Christ's. Though only a youth, his heart deceived him into thinking that salvation could be attained through human effort. He tried, but in vain, and after weeks of struggling to better himself by more reading of the Bible, more prayer, repentance and at times weeping, he finally found salvation in trusting the Saviour. On that unforgettable Sunday in July 1870 as he sat in the old Sunday school, the new minister, in his first address to the children, said, "All you have to do to be saved is to take God's gift and say 'Thank You' ". For William, this shed new light. Hitherto he had been trying to get God to accept his gift but on that Sunday afternoon he accepted God's gift, and that simple act of faith brought rest to his troubled heart.

William, by nature, was a shy person, but in his own timid way he sought to bear witness for his Saviour. One of his first experiences was a simple cottage meeting in the very poor home of one of his Sunday school pupils and in those surroundings he had the joy of leading his first soul to Christ.

The visit to Belfast in 1874 of D. L. Moody and Ira D. Sankey was a great milestone in William's life. He sought to help in the meetings as best he could and God used him. But there was something deeper, something personal, a challenge from God as to his own path in life. "There is but one thing to do, one thing to live for", he concluded. Then one morning, as Mr. Moody spoke of the use God can make of the weak and despised things of this world and as Mr. Sankey sang, "Here am I, send me",

> *Let none hear you idly saying,*
> *"There is nothing I can do!"*
> *While the souls of men are dying*
> *And the Master calls to you,*

William felt that the souls of men and the Master's call were making a double claim upon his life. The supreme task of his life henceforth would be that of soul winning. He was then seventeen years of age. William had received his education at the local Model School and when school days finished he served a five-year apprenticeship in the linen trade. Business took him on a visit to London and the following year he went there to live. On his first Sunday in London he went to the Metropolitan Tabernacle to hear C. H. Spurgeon. This was another great milestone in William's life. Spurgeon was to have a great influence on him and they two became fast and lifelong friends. The young Presbyterian soon threw in his lot with the Baptists. Later in life he would write his mentor's biography.

Right from his early days in London William engaged increasingly in the work of the Lord, preaching the glorious gospel at street corners and in lodging houses and conducting missions in and around the city. He studied at Pastor's College. Spurgeon was then at his best and William picked up and stowed in his mind some of Spurgeon's treasured gems, as, "the best preacher is the man who charges his gun with all he knows, and then, before he fires, puts himself in".

In 1879, after finishing at Pastor's College, William went forth as an evangelist, in conjunction with J. Manton Smith. Over a fifteen-year period they two visited almost every town of any size in mainland Britain. Their first mission was in Bacup in the Rossendale Valley of Lancashire. Their task there seemed daunting and they were much cast upon God. Years afterwards William learned that after his first meeting, on 22nd April 1879, the believers in Bacup offered his comrade, Manton Smith, a ten-pound note if he would send him back to London. But before the week was out there were many brought to Christ and among them the son of the man who was foremost in wishing him to leave.

In 1884 William married Miss Rust of Leicester. Leicester then became his base for the remainder of his evangelistic years. Then in 1894 a call came to succeed F. B. Meyer as pastor at Melbourne Hall in Leicester. This he clearly felt to be God's will. He accepted the call and for the next eighteen years carried on a powerful and very fruitful ministry there. Throughout those years the tide of blessing flowed and looking back there were many cherished and fragrant memories.

William had a special exercise and care for the young. The children's work in Leicester grew till there were four Sunday schools with two thousand, five hundred scholars and around two hundred teachers. He was a great believer in the faith of a child, sometimes baptizing and receiving into the fellowship those as young as nine years of age. From Melbourne Hall outreach works extended to the poorer parts of the city. In the Crown Street area a simple mission hall was the centre where many drunkards, gamblers and gaolbirds were won for Christ. William had faith in the power of Christ to save and he knew no greater joy than to see lives transformed by the power of the gospel. He was a great believer that great sinners made great saints.

In the midst of his Leicester ministry William spent a winter in Algeria. Then in 1907 he went on a visit to China, with C. E. Wilson as his travelling companion. An outline of their journeyings is related in *New China: A Story of Modern Travel*. Oftimes difficulties seemed insurmountable and deprivations almost intolerable. Rising at 4 a.m. to begin their journey before sunrise, they rested at nights in filthy Chinese inns or occasionally in opium dens. On one occasion they plodded on steadily for three weeks to reach their destination, but their coming was a tremendous boost to the isolated workers in that part of Inland China and was attended with great blessing.

In 1912 William was appointed Home Secretary of the Baptist Missionary Society. His tour of Inland China, and his visits to Japan, Ceylon, N. Africa and Palestine had equipped him for that work. In those lands he had witnessed at first hand what isolated workers and native believers suffered for the Name of Christ – deprivations, loneliness, dangers and martyrdom. He could easily relate to practical missionary problems. As secretary he travelled widely and carried with him the presence of Christ wherever he went. His vision was big and during those years there grew within him a glow of expectation of the final triumph of Christ.

Then came his sixtieth year, and this was another milestone. On his sixtieth birthday he published his autobiography, *At the Sixtieth Milestone*, and in the same year was appointed President of the Baptist Union. His responsibilities were ever increasing and his influence ever widening. Now he was much on demand at evangelical conventions. But at heart and to the end William was a lover of the souls of men.

William's closing years were marked by uncertain health but he maintained a spiritual glow right to the close. He remained active in the work of the Lord till one week before his death. The close came in the early hours of 17th August 1932. Bidding adieu to scenes of earth, he took his leave to receive the gracious welcome and the commendation of the Saviour, whom he loved and served, and to whose feet he had led so many. A memorial service was held at Bloomsbury and afterwards burial took place at Mortlake.

William Young Fullerton had regarded life as one glorious pilgrimage. Towards its close he wrote, "He who planned the journey grants His own presence day by day. – The road I have travelled has been varied and most pleasant: if I have known the sorrows I have also known the joys of life; if there have been many failures, there has been much restoring grace; if there have been stretches where the flints have cut the unshod feet, there have also been sweeps where the sward has been strewn with flowers; if sometimes the mists have made it difficult to find the way, oftener the blue skies have been overhead. And my Guide is King of the Country that I am passing through".

William Young Fullerton was truly a great servant of Christ – an ardent evangelist, a devoted pastor, a great advocate of missionary enterprise and, in addition, no mean writer. With a deft and skilful touch, he wielded the pen of a ready writer. His store of knowledge was great but he did not parade it. In the last twenty years of his life many devotional and expository works came from his hand. Besides his autobiography, he penned *the biographies of the Spurgeons (C. H. Spurgeon and his son, Thomas Spurgeon)* and also that of *F. B. Meyer*, his predecessor at Melbourne Hall. His books included *"Life's Dusty Way"*, *"Souls of Men"*, *"Christ in Africa"*, *"Practice of Christ's Presence"*, *"The Legacy of Bunyan"*, *"The Christ of the Congo River"* and *"The Christly Life"*.

But William is best remembered for his hymn, **"I cannot tell why He whom angels worship"**. This hymn was born out of a warm missionary heart. When William wrote it in 1929 some advised him not to repeat the word *"Saviour"* in the last line of each stanza but substitute instead some qualifying adjective. But he would have none of it. It must remain *"Saviour, Saviour"*. He must emphasize the Saviour as *"the Saviour, Saviour of the world"*, for he believed it with all his heart.

The format of William's hymn is a balance in each stanza of **the incomprehensibles** and **the certainties.**

The things beyond his understanding form the first half of each verse and are prefixed, *"I cannot tell"*.

The things of which he was confident conclude each verse and are prefixed, *"but this I know"*.

The message throughout is of the Saviour.

The first two stanzas look back to the Saviour's first coming and to **what He has done.** Of the fact that the Saviour had come, William had no doubt. The reason "why" baffled him.

The last two stanzas look onward to the Saviour's return and to **what He will yet do.** The manner of its fulfilment puzzled William, but of the Saviour's final triumph he had no doubt.

"There are loved ones in the glory"

Ada Ruth Habershon (1861-1918)

Ada Ruth Habershon

    Standing unique upon the canvas of Holy Scripture is the figure of Deborah, a wise counsellor, a woman of vision, a mother in Israel, a fearless leader of the people of God. She led the people to victory and gave to them a song. In like manner the figure of Ada Ruth Habershon stands upon the page of testimony for Christ at the close of the nineteenth century. She too was a woman of faith whose trust was in God alone. She too stood undaunted in the face of the enemy; the people of God resorted to her and she led them fearlessly. She too gave them a song, indeed, she gave them a thousand and more, truly a remarkable woman.

Ada Ruth Habershon was born at St. Marylebone on 8th January 1861, the youngest daughter of Dr. S.O. Habershon of London. She had two brothers and two sisters. Her youngest brother died when only a baby. Her parents knew the Lord personally and daily lived to serve Him. Both were zealous for the work of the Lord, uncompromising in their witness for Christ and great soul winners. Her father was a pioneer of the Medical Prayer Union, in which he took a lifelong interest. He witnessed daily to his patients in hospital and each new medical student received from him a personal copy of the book of Proverbs and an invitation to Bible readings in the Habershon home.

Dr. and Mrs. Habershon kept an open home — for medical students, for servants of the Lord and, indeed, for all the people of God. The topic of conversation in the home was usually of the Lord, of His word and of His work. Ada could recall visits to the home of some notable servants of Christ. She remembered especially that of Dr. Robert Moffat of Africa and of herself, as his "wee lassie", sitting happily on his knee and completely captivated by his lion stories.

Early in life Ada got to know the Saviour. Let her, herself, tell of her experience,

> *The Shepherd found me in His boundless grace*
> *Before I even knew that I was lost;*
> *My tiny footsteps scarcely had begun*
> *To tread the path of danger ere I saw*
> *The Shepherd close beside me.*
>   *'Twas enough!*
> *No sense of danger made me seek His arms,*
> *I did but catch a glimpse of His dear face,*
> *Then gladly let Him lift me to His breast.*
> *And only after that, when I was safe,*
> *And felt His arms encircling me with love,*
> *Did He Himself point out the road beneath,*
> *And make me see the precipice below.*
> *I saw His love before I saw my need,*
> *I knew my safety long before I knew*
> *The awful death from which He rescued me;*
> *I only know He found me – I am His.*

As a child Ada was outgoing, vivacious and winsome. She went to boarding school in Dover and then, after several happy years there, returned to London to continue her studies at the South Kensington School of Art. Ada, like her parents, was also a soul winner and had the privilege of leading several of her school companions to Christ. During her teenage years she attended the Metropolitan Tabernacle and there she got to know Mr. Spurgeon. She greatly valued his friendship and ministry and in turn introduced to him several of her revered friends from Ireland, as Denham Smith, F. C. Bland and Richard J. Mahony.

When Ada was seventeen, she became a member of the assembly, meeting at St. George's Hall, Langham Place, a testimony which had been planted there in 1875 by her father and Denham Smith. Ada had an insatiable hunger for the Word of God and she delighted to hear its truths expounded by such visiting teachers as Shuldham Henry, John G. McVicker, F. C. Bland, Dr. Robert McKilliam and Richard J. Mahony. Denham Smith had a special place in her life. He was then living in London and became a familiar figure in the Habershon home. Ada and he shared deeply in the things of God. Denham Smith had a lovely tenor singing voice; he was a composer of hymns and tunes and many evenings they spent together around the piano. Ada helped him to compile his new hymnbook, *The New Times of Refreshing*. Besides, she wrote for him many notes for his lectures and books and also assisted in the compilation of his prophetic chart.

In 1883 Ada began regular attendance at the "Gray's Yard Ragged Church and Schools", a work in which her parents had had a deep interest since its inception in 1870. There she sought to win the "down and outs" for Christ and God greatly blessed that work. When attendances increased and conditions in the overcrowded, poorly ventilated old building became almost intolerable, new premises were sought. In that regard, Ada, together with her father, after much exercise and prayer, raised almost ten thousand pounds for the purchasing of a new facility in Duke Street, Manchester Square, and there the work continued.

In the year 1884 D. L. Moody and Ira D. Sankey came to London for their second mission. Ada threw all her energies into that work. She had a good singing voice and on several occasions accompanied Mr. Sankey. Indeed, she had many talents; all these she laid at her Master's feet – her voice, her intellect, her pen, all were exclusively for Him.

Bereavement and sorrow marked the year 1889 for Ada. First, she lost her true and treasured friend, Denham Smith. Then, five weeks later, her mother died. This was followed in another four months by the death of her father. Such losses brought big changes. Ada, together with her unmarried sister, moved house, from the family home in Brook Street to a more suitable residence in Devonshire Street. She had now more time at her disposal but she gave it all to the Lord and kept busy. There was work among the young women, ladies' Bible studies, mothers meetings, work at the hospital, work at the women's branch of the Prophecy Investigation Society, besides visiting the poor and needy. And such spare time as she could find, she devoted to Bible study.

In 1895 Ada visited the U.S.A. at the request of Mr. Moody. After an intensive four months there, she returned home exhausted. Her health had been overtaxed and changes were now necessary. There must henceforth be less physical activity and she would devote more time to study and writing. The last 20 years of Ada's life were packed full and much has come from her pen.

Her **booklets** were timely and valuable. When she perceived a need, she wrote to meet that need. *"Keep to the Old Paths"* was published when some were abandoning the great foundation truths of the faith; *"The New Theology and its Origin"* appeared when doctrinal errors were rife; *"The Strong Man Spoiled"* when the tongues movement worked havoc, and *"Satan's Devices"* in an effort to deliver some from the snares of the evil one. In all these Ada was fearless in her defence of the truth of God. Besides, she wrote *"The Dispensational Series"* in her latter years. Its first issue was entitled "The Dispensations" and its last issue "Israel's Exodus, Past and Future". This latter issue made a great impact and was written at the time of the Balfour Declaration, with its promise to find a national home for the Jewish people in the land of Palestine.

Her **gospel tracts** were greatly used of God and circulated widely. The one entitled, "A Remedy for those who are Nervous of Air Raids and other Alarms" reached a circulation of fifty to sixty thousand and proved a great help and blessing during the World War I years. Some of her tracts were translated into other languages

Her **poems** were greatly appreciated and brought much cheer and comfort to tried and lonely saints. That entitled, "I am a prayer" is worthy of special mention. It appeared in pamphlet form and was based on Psa.109:4, "but I ... prayer". This poem shed a meaningful light on the exercise of prayer – the soul's presentation and attitude at the throne of grace bespeaking the need, the Lord Himself the rich supply.

I've found the reason why Thou canst bestow,
Exceedingly abundant, far above
What I can ask or think! It is
Because Thou art the answer – I the prayer

Ada **books** were varied in their content. Some nine major works were published during her lifetime.

The Priests and Levites: A Type of the Church, The Study of the Types, Outline Studies of the Tabernacle, The Study of the Parables, The Study of the Miracles, Exploring the New Testament Fields, The New Testament Names and Titles of the Lord of Glory, Hidden Pictures, and *The Bible and the British Museum.* (This last work had a preface by Sir Robert Anderson KCB, LLD. and copies were presented to King Edward VII, King George V, the King of Italy and the Director of the British Museum). But perhaps Ada's greatest literary work of all, *The Illuminated New Testament,* she left unfinished. (Ada was very unexpectedly called home from her labours to her reward on 1st February 1918).

Ada Ruth Habershon's contribution to the work of the Lord was vast. Right from childhood her talents and time had been entirely for the Lord. She had been greatly privileged – in her natural endowments, in her home life, and in her circle of friends. Her closest friends were some of God's choicest servants, men and women in the forefront of the work of the Lord. She had contact with evangelists, as Spurgeon and Moody, and this gave impetus to her work as a soul winner. She had contact with Bible teachers, as Denham Smith and others, and their influence stimulated a life-long study of the Word of God. She had contact with hymnwriters and composers, as Denham Smith, Ira D. Sankey and George C. Stebbins in early life. But perhaps the greatest influence of all was Charles M. Alexander.

During the Torrey and Alexander mission in London in 1905, Ada composed a fitting closing verse to "The Glory Song". Mr. Alexander requested that she write more and in the following twelve months she gave to him some two hundred new hymns. In all she wrote about one thousand hymns for Mr. Alexander and some twenty-six of these appear in Alexander's Hymns No.3. Of these, Ada was the sole author of twenty-two and the joint author of four. However, there are only a few of her hymns which are sung today, as "He will hold me fast", "Oh, what a change!", "The Pilot Song", "Just the case for Him", "Bearing His Cross", "Will the Circle be Unbroken?" and "Longings".

In her hymnwriting Ada looked entirely to the Lord. For each hymn she desired the right text of Scripture as the theme, right thoughts on the text, the right words to express her thoughts and the right metre and chorus. Above all, she prayed that God would use the hymn for His glory. Some days the Lord gave Ada more than a dozen new hymns but of all the hymns that she wrote, **"Will the circle be unbroken?"** is perhaps the best known.

> *There are loved ones in the glory*
> *Whose dear forms you often miss;*
> *When you close your earthly story*
> *Will you join them in their bliss?*
>
> *Will the circle be unbroken*
>   *By-and-by, by-and-by,*
>   *In a better home awaiting*
>   *In the sky, in the sky?*
>
> *One by one their seats were emptied,*
> *One by one they went away;*
> *Here the circle has been broken,*
> *Will it be complete one day?*

Ada Ruth Habershon had had the privilege of being raised in a Christian home and early in life being united to Christ. Yet she felt deeply for others. What an eternal tragedy it would be for someone, brought up in similar circumstances, to miss Christ and salvation and heaven!

It was to this end that Ada wrote this hymn, so full of pathos. She desired to awaken memories within such privileged hearts. For, was it not when memories of family and home were awakened within the prodigal's heart that he made his resolve, "I will arise and go"? And what a welcome and bounteous provision awaited his fulfilling that resolve!

"He giveth more grace when the burdens grow greater"

Annie Johnson Flint (1866-1932)

Annie Johnson Flint

The winds and storms of adversity blew hard upon the life of Annie Johnson Flint. Her buoyant spirit and simple trust in God remained undaunted, and from her crucible of suffering she gave to this world some of the most inspiring and comforting verse in the English language. Rowland V. Bingham has left on record something of Annie's triumphant life-story.

Annie was born on Christmas Eve in the year 1866 in the little town of Vineland, New Jersey, U.S.A. Her parents, Eldon and Jean Johnson, were of British descent. Annie's mother died at the early age of twenty-three, leaving behind a newborn baby as a sister and companion for Annie who was then just three. Father placed the two little ones in the care of a widow, but the arrangement proved unsatisfactory. The widow already had two children of her own and had not the resources to care for extra children. Then after two years, a Mr. and Mrs. Flint adopted the two little girls and gave to them the surname of Flint. (At the time of their adoption their own father, Eldon Johnson, was suffering from an incurable illness to which he soon afterwards succumbed).

The home, into which the two girls had come, was a good home. Annie and her sister were shown love and care and were given a good start in life. In the home life was simple. There was always ample food to eat and clothes to wear, but any extravagance or waste was deplored. Discipline, morals and spiritual values received high priority in the daily routine. The Flint home was situated on a farm and Annie, as a child, delighted in the freedom of the countryside and in the beauty of God's creation.

Moreover, the home to which Annie and her sister had come was a Christian home. Mr. and Mrs. Flint were Baptists. When Annie was eight years of age, the family moved from the farm into the town of Vineland. At that time Methodist Revival Meetings were being conducted in Vineland and in those meetings Annie got to know the Saviour. Though only eight years of age she simply yet confidently put her trust in the Lord Jesus for salvation.

When Annie was fourteen, the family moved again, this time to Camden town in the State of New Jersey. There Annie continued her schooling. As a schoolgirl she was described as "a pretty dark-eyed girl, with a clear olive complexion and long black curls. She was kindhearted, merry and vivacious – a general favourite with the boys and girls at school". She was fond of reading and had a special flare for poetry. At school Annie had a specially close friend with kindred talents. "Every Saturday afternoon we met, a select literary society of two, to read our favourite poets and then we attempted verse ourselves".

Thus Annie grew up among her young friends in Camden. She was cheerful and outgoing in her nature and always looked on the brighter side of life. She made friends easily, was generous in disposition and had a tender sympathy for the needs of others. On the other hand she had her shortcomings and in early life manifested outbursts of temper and bouts of impatience and sulking.

When Annie finished high school she embarked on a one-year course of teacher training and then returned to her old school as teacher of a primary class. But soon the winds of adversity started to blow and in her second year of teaching she developed a severe arthritis, which, in spite of all the medical care available at that time, pursued a progressive and debilitating course. It was with difficulty that she was able to finish three years of teaching. She then had to give up work and there followed three years of increasing disability. Just at that time she suffered the loss of both adoptive parents, within a few months of each other.

Once again the girls were left alone. They had very little money in the bank and faced great difficulties. Aunt Susie, an old family friend, then came to the rescue. She organized treatment for Annie in the Sanatorium at Clifton Springs and this arrangement promised some hope. However, Annie's arthritis proved unremitting and at the close of the period of treatment the doctors pronounced a grave prognosis. "Annie was going to be a helpless invalid".

Annie's path proved difficult. However, she was a very resourceful person and set herself to make use of her poetic talent. With twisted fingers and swollen joints she plied her pen. She started by designing hand-lettered cards and gift books, incorporating into them some of her own verse. She then composed Christmas carols and with help from two card publishers found an outlet for her work. Many found help from her poems and encouraged her to keep going. Annie's work then found wider circulation through magazines and ultimately her verse was compiled into little brochures. Her first collection, *"By the Way, Travelogues of Cheer"* appeared in 1919 and brought blessing to many hearts. Annie was thus encouraged and through the early years of her disability was enabled to produce further collections of poems. All the while she carried on her own correspondence and maintained her independence.

But then the time came when Annie had to face new problems. She could no longer carry on her own correspondence and had to dictate her letters to others. Financial needs mounted up and there was no state aid. Annie's independence was under threat and she could not easily let it go. She persistently resisted all offers of help and especially anything that might be termed charitable help. Then one day matters came to a head. A lady friend presented her with a monetary gift. Annie, as aforetime, showed her resentment. Then the lady said, "You know Jesus Christ said, 'It is more blessed to give than to receive', but how can there be any givers to whom the blessing can come unless there are those who are willing to receive? It takes two halves to make a whole". Then she asked Annie that if their roles were reversed and she had the means, would she not like to give? Annie appreciated the reasoning, conceded, and then gladly accepted the gift.

Annie now required periods of respite care in the Sanatorium. These were times of pressure, yet it was in times like these that she penned her best verse. One of her most precious and most helpful little poems was born when she was a patient in Clifton Springs. A little lady had called, bringing with her all her personal troubles and poured them into Annie's ear. Then a letter followed her visit, containing more tales of woe. She told Annie she didn't see why God had allowed such hard things to come into her life. Annie replied by letter and put her reply into verse. She entitled it, **"What God hath promised"**.

> *God hath not promised skies always blue,*
> *Flower-strewn pathways all our lives through;*
> *God hath not promised sun without rain,*
> *Joy without sorrow, peace without pain.*
>
> *But God hath promised strength for the day,*
> *Rest for the labour, light for the way,*
> *Grace for the trials, help from above,*
> *Unfailing sympathy, undying love.*

Then there were, besides, visits from well meaning, but untaught, Christian friends who told Annie that bodily healing was included in the Atonement and that illness was not God's will. Such false reasoning initially proved disturbing but Annie always listened patiently, and then, after the visitors had gone, resorted to the Scriptures and to prayer. She concluded that some of God's choicest saints were those who had experienced life's greatest trials.

She prayed often, as did Paul, that her affliction might be removed from her, yet was always happy to rest in the Divine promise, "My grace is sufficient for thee: for My strength is made perfect in weakness". Then she would add, again in the words of Paul, "Most gladly therefore will I rather glory in my infirmities, that the power of Christ may rest upon us" (II Cor. 12: 9).

The closing years of life for Annie brought no relief from suffering.

For over forty years she had not had a single day free from pain and for thirty-seven years she had not been able to walk. Yet Annie did not parade her affliction. She rested on the purpose of a sovereign God and upon all the promises He had given. And what multitudes of promises she found in her Bible! all underwritten by an omnipotent, unerring and faithful God. She rejoiced in the preciousness of the scripture, "For all the promises of God in Him are yea, and in Him Amen" (11Cor. 1:20). For Annie this scripture settled all her questionings and fears. Then she went on to pen her own little commentary on this precious verse.

"Is God–?" "Hath God–?" "Doth God–?"
Man's "Why?" and "How?"
In ceaseless iteration storm the sky.
"I am"; "I will"; "I do"; sure Word of God,
Yea and Amen, Christ answereth each cry;
To all our anguished questionings and doubts
Eternal affirmation and reply.

The close came on Thursday, 8th September 1932. Her doctor had called in the morning, but was summoned again in the evening. Appreciating that she might not rally, he asked if she had anything special to say before he would give her an injection. "I have nothing to say. It's all right". These, her last words, epitomized Annie's lifelong acquiescence in the will of God. Then, peacefully and triumphantly, she bid adieu to this world and passed into the other, to be with her Saviour.

Face to face – and that forever;
Face to face, where naught can sever;
I shall see Him in His beauty, face to face;
I have caught faint glimpses here,
Seen through many a falling tear,
But – what glory when I see Him face to face!

It has been said of Annie Johnson Flint, "Out of the crucible of suffering she ministered comfort to others". She was an apt pupil in the school of God, never rebellious. She had learned in the midst of life's trials the secret of taking **one day at a time**.

> One day at a time, with its failures and fears,
> With its hurts and mistakes, with its weakness and tears,
> With its portion of pain and its burden of care;
> One day at a time we must meet and must bear.
>
> One day at a time, and the day is His day;
> He hath numbered its hours, though they haste or delay.
> His grace is sufficient; we walk not alone;
> As the day, so the strength that He giveth His own.

But one of Annie's most precious little compositions are the lines, **"He giveth more grace when the burdens grow greater"**. Its lines have been set to music and have been of comfort to many a tried and suffering saint.

> He giveth more grace when the burdens grow greater,
> He sendeth more strength when the labours increase,
> To added affliction He addeth His mercy,
> To multiplied trials His multiplied peace.
>
> His love has no limit, His grace has no measure,
> His power no boundary known unto men,
> For out of His infinite riches in Jesus
> He giveth and giveth and giveth again.
>
> When we have exhausted our store of endurance,
> When strength has declined ere the day is half done,
> When we reach the end of our hoarded resources,
> Our Father's full giving is only begun.

In these lines Annie Johnson Flint would have us to know that, though the pathway of life be ever so trying, there is always Divine supply for every step of the journey, and bountifully supplied when needed most.

"Jesus, Lord, I need Thy presence"

George Goodman (1866-1942)

George Goodman

"It all depends who gets me", the small boy replied when asked what he was going to do when he grew up. And when pressed for further explanation, he added, "If Jesus gets me I shall be a missionary; if the devil gets me I shall be a burglar". The Lord got George Goodman when he was a young schoolboy and he became a missionary to boys and girls in Britain. Furthermore, George was a lawyer by profession. He had an incisive mind with ability of simple lucid expression and the profoundest truths he could frame in the simplest language. George Goodman dedicated these abilities entirely to the Lord and became "a very prince of expository teachers" among the people of God.

George was born into a large family in North London, the fifth member of a family of fourteen, seven boys and seven girls. Two of the girls died in infancy and his eldest brother at the age of eighteen. The Goodman home was a happy home. George was the life and soul of the family and especially of its younger members. He was a born leader and greatly gifted. His literary ability was first manifest when the family had mumps and was confined to house. He then launched a family magazine and this appeared weekly for several years. He rode a "penny farthing" bicycle and later a very early model of motorcycle, without clutch or gears, necessitating "a run start" and mounting while in motion. On this bike he delighted to take his younger brothers and sisters and thus became their hero. And when the family went on holiday to Switzerland, George, with his boundless energy and enthusiasm, was their leader as they explored the Alps together.

George's father had come from the village of Cranfield in Bedfordshire. He was of Puritan stock and had been converted as a young man through the influence of a young lady who later became his wife. When the family moved to Clapham Common in London they identified with a Congregational Church. George vividly recalled Sunday mornings and evenings there, the long file of Goodmans filling to capacity the two pews reserved for them.

George went to boarding school in Windsor. One day his mother received a letter from him, a letter that she afterwards treasured and preserved. The letter told of George's conversion. One of the masters at Windsor had accompanied him to Windsor Great Park and there, under an old oak tree, had pointed him to the Saviour. George was then but a young teenager. Nevertheless, from that day forward, he sought to live only for the One who had saved him.

George became a lawyer. He completed his education in Germany and then joined a firm of solicitors in Queen Victoria Street in London. On his first morning to join the firm he asked the Lord, "O Lord, help them find out I'm a Christian" and before the morning was through his prayer was answered. In consequence, George was respected by all in the firm for his Christian conviction and courage.

George's conversion gave him a concern for the conversion and spiritual welfare of others. Having been saved early in life himself, he took a special interest in the salvation of the young. When he was a student, and while holidaying with the family at Herne Bay in Kent, he was introduced to the work of Children's Special Service Mission (C.S.S.M.) and there, on the beach, George commenced his ministry among children. He had the rare gift, of first winning children to himself, and then of introducing them to the Saviour. In a unique way he could convey profound truth in simple language such as a child could understand. Children's work became his life-long interest and God greatly blessed that ministry. For twelve years he was writer of Scripture Union notes and his lucid and pithy comments on Holy Scripture had wide circulation and were greatly blessed. Besides, he was instrumental in founding the Caravan Mission to Village Children.

George was a man of deep conviction. Early in his Christian experience he was desirous to know the New Testament pattern of local church fellowship. God showed it to him. George obeyed and this led to his meeting with like-minded saints at Clapton Hall where he found a spiritual home. Shortly afterwards he published a booklet, *God's Principles of Gathering,* a small volume outlining the principles of gathering to the Lord's Name. This publication contained precious principles, applicable to every generation.

George's greatest gift was as a teacher of God's word. In early years, when his day's work in the City had finished, he travelled widely over the south of England bringing the Word of Life to both old and young. Then, just after World War I, he terminated his professional work and went into full time service for the Lord, commended by the company of believers at Clapton Hall. In the work of the Lord he kept busy. His days were spent studying and writing, his evenings, preaching and teaching. He visited the Continent and was there involved in establishing assemblies in Poland. In Eastern Europe he observed a large Jewish population and these weighed heavily upon his heart. He sought to reach them with the gospel and this he did through "The Hebrew Christian Testimony to Israel", of which he was a member of the advisory council.

For many years George made his home in Tunbridge Wells in Kent. He was regarded there as "a very great man of God and a wonderful Bible teacher". For many years he conducted a Bible class for young men, many of whom later became pillars in the assemblies of God's people. George spent his closing years in Eastbourne, making his home at St. John's Road. During World War 11 his home was bombed. This had a detrimental effect on his health and for a time he went to live with his daughter. His final illness was a great trial, physically, mentally and spiritually, and his departure to be with Christ (1942) was indeed a sweet release. It was "far better".

George Goodman left behind him a sweet memory, a great example and a rich legacy. His legacy provided preachers, teachers, missionaries and Sunday school teachers with a vast store of reliable exposition of Holy Scripture. George's writings were pithy and edifying, packed with illustrations and proverbial sayings. They sparkled with life. Vital lessons were driven home and Bible themes were made crystal clear. Many of these publications are now out of print, but the cream of his writings, addresses and private notes were later collected and collated into one volume by Percy O. Ruoff, *The Spiritual Legacy of George Goodman*. In this volume there is a short appreciation of George by his younger brother, Montague.

A few samples of George's choice crisp sayings are worthy of mention,

Of prayer,—"Prayer is not to get the will of man done in heaven, but the will of God done on earth".
Of praying,—"A runaway knock at heaven's door is of little value. Knock until the door is opened".
Of Tychicus,
"beloved brother – faithful minister – fellowservant in the Lord".
Of satisfaction,—"The worldling is satisfied with the world;
The believer is satisfied with Christ;
The backslider's lot is ever bitter".
Of disobedience,—"Disobedience is in fact a form of idolatry, for in it the heart worships the great god, 'self-will' ".
Of justification,—"Justified = Just –as – if – I'd – died".
Of the law of the Spirit of life and the law of sin and death (Rom.8).—
He illustrated it thus,

A father and his son were walking together in the garden in the springtime. "What is gravitation, father?" asked the boy. "Gravitation, my son, is a law or principle of nature by which everything is attracted or drawn down to earth, e.g. a stone, an apple". "Oh, but father", objects the child, "look at those beautiful tulips. They all go upwards. They are not drawn down". "True, my boy, but that is because there is another law at work. The law of life, which is stronger than the law of gravitation, has made them free from it as long as they live. See, if I destroy the life by cutting one off, it falls at once to the ground".
George Goodman wrote quite a number of hymns and poems. Some

eighty-three of these he collected in a book and a few have found their way into various hymnbooks — eight are in *Golden Bells*, two in *The Believers Hymn Book*. Much of his verse was written for children. He judged the teaching of texts of Scripture set to music as very valuable. His rendering of Rom. 5: 8 is very beautiful,

> God commends His love,
> Greater could not be;
> While I was a sinner
> Jesus died for me.

Quite apart from his book collection, a further two pieces of his own composition were found in his Bible at the close of life. These were the product of his final illness. They were lines born in anguish, and full of pathos. He entitled one, "The Bruised Reed — The Smoking Flax" and the other, "The Footprints".

> He led me to the way of pain,
>   A barren and a starless place,
> (I didn't know His eyes were wet,
>   He would not let me see His face).
> He left me like a frightened child,
>   Unshielded in a night of storm.
> (How should I dream He was so near?
>   The rain-swept darkness hid His form).
> But when the clouds were driving back
>   And dawn was breaking into day,
> I knew Whose feet had walked with mine,
>   I saw the footprints all the way.

His two hymns found in *The Believers Hymn Book* are, "The bread and wine are spread upon the board", termed "a hymn of worship at the Breaking of Bread", and **"Jesus, Lord, I need Thy presence"**.

> Jesus, Lord, I need Thy presence
>   As I journey on my way,
> For without Thee I am lonely,
>   And my feet are apt to stray;
> But if Thou wilt walk with me
>   Life shall calm and holy be.

JESUS, LORD, I NEED THY PRESENCE

Jesus, Lord, I need Thy wisdom,
For perplexing problems press,
And without Thee I am foolish,
Nor can bear the strain and stress;
But if Thou wilt counsel me
I shall true and upright be.

Jesus, Lord, I need Thy power,
For temptations come and go,
And without Thee I am helpless,
With no strength to meet the foe;
But if Thou wilt strengthen me
Life will all-triumphant be.

Jesus, Lord, I need Thy guidance,
Fire by night, and cloud by day,
For without them I am sightless,
Groping for the proper way;
But if Thou dost lead me on
I will follow Thee alone.

Jesus, Lord, Thy love so tender
Is my greatest need of all,
For without Thee pride and anger
From unguarded lips will fall;
But if Thou Thy love impart
I shall have a gracious heart.

George Goodman was conscious of the greatness of his need
on the journey of life.
Notwithstanding, he was confident that every need
was cancelled in Christ.

"There's a Shepherd who died for the sheep"

Hawthorne Bailie (1884-1964)

Hawthorne Bailie

The life of Hawthorne Bailie may be summarized in a word – Christlikeness. Those privileged to sit under his ministry will not readily forget the characteristic tremor in his hand and lip, the trembling in his voice or the radiance in his face as he ministered the things of God in the power of the Holy Ghost sent down from heaven. Those privileged to know him personally felt that to be in his presence was to be in the company of one who walked closely with God. Transparency and holiness were the hallmarks of his life.

The Lord was very real in the inner experience of Hawthorne Bailie, closer than breathing, nearer than hands or feet. Once when asked by a group of young Christians how he knew that the Lord was risen from the dead, he spontaneously replied, "I was speaking with Him just this morning". When he prayed, all were conscious of the fact that he was speaking to One with whom he was intimately acquainted. And when he rose to speak, he came to the desk as one stepping from "the secret place of the most High", his mind and heart saturated with the Divine presence and his face radiant with its glory.

Hawthorne Bailie was born into a godly home at Drumaness, Co. Down, N. Ireland on 19th December 1884. He was the second youngest in the fairly large family of William and Elizabeth Bailie. His younger brother died tragically in childhood. Hawthorne's father and uncle were millwrights in that part of Co. Down, making great water wheels, which were widely used at that time in the flax and linen industry. Then, with the introduction of newer technology, the use of waterpower gradually declined and millwrights were no longer needed. Consequently the Bailies sought employment in other branches of the industry and this necessitated moving to the city of Belfast.

Hawthorne's parents, Mr. and Mrs. Bailie senior, were believers in the Lord Jesus and on moving to Belfast made their spiritual home with the assembly of Christians meeting at Mourne Street. Hawthorne grew up in the city and like other young men sought to taste the delights of this world. He was a keen and very able footballer and played for Portadown. Indeed, so skilled was he in the game, that he was approached to sign on as a professional. Just at that particular time God intervened in his life in wondrous grace. The death of an older sister who had been a great influence on him caused him to think deeply of eternal matters. The workings of the Spirit of God within his heart led to a great crisis and one night, kneeling at his bedside, he accepted Jesus Christ as his personal Saviour and Lord of his life. Hawthorne Bailie was saved for eternity.

Hawthorne Bailie's experience of salvation was somewhat akin to that of Robert Murray Mc Cheyne.

...I came
To drink at the fountain, life-giving and free;
"Jehovah Tsidkenu" is all things to me.

Dr. Thomas Chalmers once coined the phrase, "The expulsive power of a new affection", and such was the experience of Hawthorne Bailie, of the new life that he had found in Christ. The thrills of football were eclipsed and completely dislodged by the joys of God's salvation. The Lord's word and the Lord's work were now Hawthorne's delight and the Lord's will his only ambition. He was soon baptized and joined himself to the company of believers meeting at Mourne Street. There he made his spiritual home and soon became busy in the work of the Lord. But this new life in Christ had serious implications! Hawthorne discovered that he was no longer his own. He belonged to Christ. How could he ever repay the debt of love that he owed to his Saviour and Lord? Another great crisis followed, and Hawthorne, then a young man of scarcely thirty years of age, placed his life and all that he had upon the altar for God, and in full fellowship with his brethren at Mourne Street stepped out into full time service for the Lord.

Hawthorne's first sphere of service was in a home in Carryduff, Co. Down where he joined Mr. Joe Stewart in the preaching of the gospel. God was pleased to bless there and many found the Saviour. Following this he moved to Cumbria in the North of England in gospel tent work, again accompanied by his close friend and fellow-worker, Joe Stewart. Those were days of testing, days when both men were much cast upon God. In those days they proved the faithfulness of God. Mr. Joe Stewart was unique in his way. One evening, when walking together prior to the gospel meeting, Mr. Stewart enquired of Hawthorne as to the subject matter of his exercise for the meeting. When Hawthorne disclosed the outline of his message, Mr. Stewart responded in his own inimitable way, "Now I've got a few wee birds in my pocket I'm going to let loose" and at the beginning of the meeting proceeded to preach Hawthorne's message.

Hawthorne Bailie, was by nature a shy man. His warmth of personality, however, made him beloved by all. He was interested in people and in every detail of their lives. With a sympathetic heart he could come near to those who were in trouble. He had as much time for and felt as much at home with the simplest believer in Christ as he did with the most profound theologian and as he moved among the saints in a kindly and courteous manner they all knew that he loved them. Throughout life he was never known to have spoken a derogatory word about any fellowbeliever. He was a great encourager of younger believers and made them to feel the importance of the little they were seeking to do for Christ.

Hawthorne Bailie, after the death of his parents, lived with his sister in East Belfast. Then, when she married, he lived for a time on his own. In 1932, he married Agnes Jean Anderson, a farmer's daughter of Craigavad, Co. Down and together they set up home in Clonlee

Drive in East Belfast. Jean proved a true helpmeet in the work of the Lord. They had one son, John, and his arrival in 1934 brought them much joy. Their standard of life was simple. Mr. Bailie never learned to drive and never owned a motorcar. Throughout all his years in the service of the Lord he usually travelled by public transport; indeed, he found that travelling thus gave opportunity for meditation as he went to his meeting.

In his own home Hawthorne Bailie was dearly loved. He had a wonderful sense of humour and was a very practical man, versatile in the skills of painting, plastering, carpentry or whatever. Indeed, his own brother once said of him that "he had a head like a hen; he could pick up anything". Notwithstanding, he spent much time each day alone with his Bible and with his Lord. He was a diligent student of the Word of God and for many years answered the questions in the "Questions and Answers" section of the Believer's Magazine. He compiled a very helpful little booklet, *Who are they? The Brethren*, and designed a simple yet very instructive chart on prophecy for his teaching ministry.

In Bible study Hawthorne Bailie aimed for much more than a mental understanding and mere head knowledge of the Scriptures. He desired above all else that the truths of God be written upon his heart. His times of study were saturated with prayer and the Spirit of God was pleased to write upon his heart many great truths, glorious truths concerning his Lord and practical truths of everyday Christian living. His own personal life was beyond reproach, transparent before God, and he was deeply exercised that the lives of his fellowbelievers should be likewise to the glory of God. He believed that God had set the standard high and this high standard applied to every detail of Christian living. Thus he ministered to the saints from his heart, of punctuality at work, truthfulness in conversation and transparency in every transaction.

In ministry Hawthorne Bailie spoke with absolute sincerity. His burden was to let fellowbelievers see that there was something worth living for, higher than the things of this world. The challenge of such ministry reached many hearts and they in turn went home to ponder before God their pathway in life. As he spoke of the service of the Levites, giving of their best years to the service of God, young men left the meeting with resolve to consecrate their lives to God. But in his public ministry Hawthorne Bailie was not bound. He was ever sensitive to the leading of the Spirit of God. On a memorable occasion at the Belfast Easter Conference, when the tenor of the ministry was somewhat heavy, he rose from his chair and gave a simple clear gospel message resulting in the conversion of a seeking soul in the audience. On another occasion on an Easter Monday afternoon, when the Conference was in session in Belfast, the writer encountered him walking alone some distance from the Conference centre. He had slipped quietly out of the company to hold communion with his Lord. And in the evening meeting, when he rose to speak, the effect was evident to all.

The ministry of Hawthorne Bailie was, in the main, a ministry of Christ. He appreciated that there were troubled and burdened hearts in every audience and such could be helped and comforted if he could but point them to their Great High Priest, Jesus, the Son of God, occupied for them in the heavenly sanctuary. The work of the Lord Jesus as Advocate he was wont to illustrate from a court room scene, telling of the man in the dock who, on feeling that his own defense advocate was not doing his job too well, rose to speak in his own defense, whereupon the judge addressed him, "Man, sit down; there is another here in this court today to speak on your behalf". Mr. Bailie would then point the saints to their Advocate in that highest of all courts, the very throne room of heaven, engaged there on behalf of His people.

Among the assemblies of the Lord's people Hawthorne Bailie was highly esteemed. He was a man of "balance" in all matters and scrupulously avoided anything that in any way might mar the unity of the saints of God, valued by his Lord as "precious". Extremes of fellowship caused him pain and were totally abhorrent to him. His heart embraced all the people of God.

Thus Hawthorne Bailie lived his life, a full life span of almost fourscore years. Toward the close he experienced much bodily weakness, but was devotedly cared for by his wife, Jean, in their home at No.14 Barnett's Road in East Belfast. Then from his earthly home he passed away to be with Christ on 12th May 1964 and was laid to rest, midst much sorrow and sense of loss, in the family burying plot in Dundonald Cemetery.

Hawthorne Bailie had an unforgettable life and ministry. Throughout, it was marked by godliness. Its secret lay in a great truth expressed in both Testaments, "He that dwelleth in the secret place of the most High shall abide under the shadow of the Almighty" (Psalm 91:1) and "But we all, with open (unveiled) face beholding as in a glass the glory of the Lord, are changed into the same image from glory to glory, even as by the Spirit of the Lord" (2 Cor. 3:18). "The secret place of the most High" was Hawthorne Bailie's dwelling place. There he made his home. There he "beheld the glory of the Lord" and a transformation was effected in his life which was evident to all. He carried its fragrance with him wherever he went and the memory of it lingers still amongst assembly believers in the North of Ireland.

Hawthorne Bailie has left for us, besides, a dearly loved little hymn, **"There's a Shepherd who died for the sheep"**. Its words are fragrant. He composed them in early life for use in gospel work and their acceptance and the fact that God was pleased to use them brought him much joy. Though he wrote other pieces, this one hymn is his only verse that has survived.

> *There's a Shepherd who died for the sheep;*
> *'Tis Jesus, the blest Son of God;*
> *And all who believe in His name*
> *Are saved through the sin-cleansing blood.*
>
> *I believe ... Jesus saves,*
> *And His blood washes whiter than snow,*
> *I believe ... Jesus saves,*
> *And His blood washes whiter than snow.*
>
> *There's a Saviour who died for the lost;*
> *Who suffered what tongue cannot tell;*
> *Yet love led Him on to the Cross,*
> *To save them from sin and from hell.*
>
> *There's a King who is coming to reign,*
> *Whose throne is on righteousness built,*
> *And all who salvation obtain*
> *Shall reign through the blood that was spilt.*

In this little hymn Hawthorne Bailie strikes at the core of the gospel with warmth, simplicity and clarity.

The focus is on the Saviour throughout, giving brief yet delightful glimpses of His saving ministry.

The repetitive sweet refrain is personal, the glad expression of the heart that is linked with Christ.

> *I believe ... Jesus saves,*
> *And His blood washes whiter than snow.*

Selected Bibliography

Allchin, A.M. *Ann Griffiths: The Furnace and the Fountain.* University of Wales Press, Cardiff 1987.
Andrews, John S. *Frances Bevan: Translator of German Hymns.* Evangelical Quarterly –34 No.4 (Oct. 1962), 35 No.1 (Jan. 1963).
Bailey, Albert E. *The Gospel in Hymns.* Scribners, New York 1950.
Beaton, D. *The Rev. John Morison.* King's College, London 1913.
Beaton, D. *Ecclesiastical History of Caithness and Annals of Caithness Parishes.* William Rae, Wick 1909.
Beattie David J. *The Romance of Sacred Song.* Marshall, Morgan and Scott Ltd., London and Edinburgh 1931.
Beattie David J. *Stories and Sketches of our Hymns and their Writers.* John Ritchie Ltd., Kilmarnock, Scotland 1934.
Bevan, Frances. *Hymns of Ter Steegen and Others.* Bible Truth Publishers, Addison, Illinois 1894.
Blanchard, Kathleen. *Stories of Popular Hymns.* Zondervan Publishing House, Grand Rapids, Michigan 1939.
Blanchard, Kathleen. *Stories of Favourite Hymns.* Zondervan Publishing House, Grand Rapids, Michigan 1940.
Boggs, Robert A. *Alexander Carson of Tobermore.* Baptist Union of Ireland, Belfast 1969.
Bonner, Carey. *Some Baptist Hymnists.* The Baptist Union Publishing Dept., London 1937.
Broome, J. R. *Life and Hymns of John Cennick.* Gospel Standard Trust Publications, Hertfordshire 1988.
Brown, Raymond. *Four Spiritual Giants.* Kingsway Publications, Eastbourne 1997.
B., J. R. *Hymns of Anne Steele.* Gospel Standard Baptist Trust 1967.
Carson, M. L. *A Few Hymns and Poems.* Standard School Stores, Armagh 1913.
Clark, M. Guthrie. *Sing Them Again.* Henry E. Walter Ltd., London 1955.
Clark, William. *Sing with Understanding.* Hughes and Coleman Ltd., London 1952.
Cooper, J. H. *Extracts from the Journals of John Cennick: Moravian Evangelist.* Moravian History Magazine, Glengormley, Co. Antrim 1996.
Cornwall, E. E. *Songs of Pilgrimage and Glory.* Central Bible Truth Depot, London.
Dallimore, Arnold A. *George Whitefield.* The Banner of Truth Trust,

Edinburgh 1970/80.
Duffield, Samuel Willoughby. *English Hymns*. Funk and Wagnalls Company, New York 1894.
Duncan, Canon. *Popular Hymns, their Authors and Teaching*. Skeffington and Son, London 1910.
Emurian, Ernest K. *Forty Stories of Famous Gospel Songs*. Baker Book House, Grand Rapids, Michigan 1959.
Evans. *Memoir of the Rev. J. H. Evans by his son*. J. Nisbet, London 1851.
Fawcett. *An Account of the Life and Writings of the late John Fawcett*. London 1818.
Flint, Annie Johnson. *Poems of Inspiration and Hope, and the Triumphant Story of Annie Johnson Flint*. Bible Memory Association, St. Louis, USA.
Forsaith, Peter S. *John Fletcher*. Foundery Press, Peterborough 1994.
Fromow, George H. *Teachers of the Faith and the Future. B.W. Newton and S. P. Tregelles*. The Sovereign Grace Advent Testimony, London 1969.
Fullerton, W. Y. *At the Sixtieth Milestone*. Marshall Brothers Ltd., London 1917.
Gadsby, John. *Memoirs of Hymnwriters and Compilers*. John Gadsby, London 1882.
Govan, H. E. *The Life of Gerhard Tersteegen*. James Nisbet and Co. Ltd., London 1898.
Guinness, Michele. *The Guinness Legend*. Hodder and Stoughton, London 1990.
Habershon, E. M. *Ada R. Habershon: A Gatherer of Fresh Spoil*. Morgan and Scott Ltd., London 1918.
Hatfield, Edwin F. *The Poets of the Church*. Anson, Randolph and Company, New York 1884.
Hood, E. Paxton. *Thomas Binney: His Mind-life and Opinions*. James Clarke and Co., London 1874.
Houghton, Elsie. *Christian Hymn-Writers*. Evangelical Press of Wales 1982.
Houghton, S. M. *Sketches of Church History*. The Banner of Truth Trust, Edinburgh 1980.
Houston, Anne L. *Lest We Forget: The Parish of Canisbay*. North of Scotland Newspapers, Wick 1996.
Hutchinson, James G. *Sowers, Reapers, Builders*. Gospel Tract Publications, Glasgow 1984.
Jones, Francis Arthur. *Famous Hymns and their Authors*. Hodder and Stoughton, London 1902.
Jones, William. *The Works of Samuel Stennett (Vol.1) with account of his life and writings*. Thomas Tegg, Cheapside, London 1824.
Julian, John. *A Dictionary of Hymnology. Vol.1, Vol.2. (Reprint of 1925 edition)*, Dover Publications Inc., New York 1957.

Keeler, W. T. *The Romantic Origin of Some Favourite Hymns*. Letchworth Printers Ltd. 1947.
Kelling, Fred. *Fisherman of Faroe*. Leirkerid Publications, Faroe Islands 1993.
Kent, John. *Original Gospel Hymns*. John Bennett, London 1833.
Knapp, Christopher. *Who Wrote Our Hymns (Reprint of 1925 edition)*. Bible Truth Publishers, Illinois.
Langhorne, H. E. *Some Favourite Hymns*. Skeffington and Son Ltd., London.
Lewis, H. Elvet. *Sweet Singers of Wales*. The Religious Tract Society 1889.
Light, Alfred W. *Bunhill Fields*. Farncombe & Sons Ltd., London 1913.
Long, Edwin M. *Illustrated History of Hymns and their Authors*. P. W. Ziegler and Co., Philadelphia, U.S.A. 1876.
Mable, Norman. *Popular Hymns and their Writers*. Independent Press Ltd., London 1945.
Mackay, W. P. *Abundant Grace*. Pickering and Inglis, London, Glasgow and Edinburgh.
Maclean, J. Kennedy. *Dr. Pierson and His Message*. Marshall Brothers Ltd., London and Edinburgh.
Macpherson, J. *Duncan Matheson – The Scottish Evangelist*. Morgan and Scott, London.
Martin, Hugh. *They Wrote Our Hymns*. S. C. M. Press Ltd., London 1961.
Miller, Josiah. *Singers and Songs of the Church*. Longmans, Green, and Co. 1869.
Morrison, Duncan. *The Great Hymns of the Church*. Simpkin, Marshall, Hamilton, Kent & Co.Ltd., London 1890.
Muir, T.D.W. *Our Record (Memorial Number – March 1931)*. Detroit, Michigan.
Nuelsen, John L. *John Wesley and the German Hymn*. A. S. Holbrook, Calverley, Yorkshire 1972.
Osbeck, Kenneth W. *Singing with Understanding*. Kregel Publications, Grand Rapids, Michigan 1979.
Parr, Robert and Sewter, Baron. *Broughton in Hampshire*. B. A. S. Printers Ltd., Hampshire 1990.
Pickering, Hy. *Chief Men among the Brethren*. Pickering & Inglis, London 1918.
Pickering, Hy. *Twice-Born Men*. Pickering & Inglis, London.
Pierson, D. L. *Arthur T. Pierson*. Fleming H. Revell Company, London and Edinburgh 1912.
Prospect Street Church and Presbyterianism in Hull. Thirty Year's Work (1868-1898). The Presbyterian Church of England.
Reynolds, William J. *Songs of Glory*. Baker Books, Grand Rapids, Michigan 1990.

Roach, Adrian. *The Little Flock Hymn Book, Its History and Hymn Writers.* Present Truth Publishers, Morganville, N. J. 1974.
Roberts, Imogen. *Sing Them for Me Ruth.* Heath Christian Trust, Cardiff 1989.
Ruoff, Percy O. *The Spiritual Legacy of George Goodman.* Pickering & Inglis Ltd., London 1949.
Ryle, John Charles. *The Christian Leaders of England.* Chas. J. Thynne & Jarvis, London 1868.
Scheffbuch, Beate and Winrich. *Den Kummer sich vom Herzen singen. (Band 1 and Band 2).* Stuttgart 1997.
Sheppard, W. J. Limmer. *Great Hymns and their Stories.* Lutterworth Press, London 1923.
Smith, Jane Stuart and Carlson, Betty. *Great Christian Hymn Writers.* Crossway Books, Wheaton, Illinois 1997.
Stead W. T. *Hymns that have Helped.* Doubleday, Page and Company, New York 1904.
Steele, Anne. *Hymns, Psalms and Poems.* Daniel Sedgwick, London 1863.
Stephenson, H. W. *Sarah Flower Adams.* Lindsey Press, London 1922.
Stoughton, John. *A Memorial of the late Rev. Thomas Binney.* Hodder and Stoughton, London 1874.
Stowell, Hugh. *Sermons by the Rev. H. Stowell.* William Tegg, London 1869.
Sutherland, Allan. *Famous Hymns of the World.* Frederick A. Stokes Company, New York 1905.
Taylor, William. *Twelve Favourite Hymns.* Alexander Gardner, Paisley 1907.
Temple, Arthur. *Hymns we Love.* Lutterworth Press, London 1954.
Terry, Lindsay. *Stories behind Popular Songs and Hymns.* Baker Book House, Grand Rapids, Michigan 1990.
Thomson, Ronald W. *Who's Who of Hymn Writers.* Epworth Press, London 1967.
Wainsgate, History of the Baptist Church (1750-1950). Dixon and Stell Ltd., Near Keightley, Yorks.
Waudby, Fred C. *Immortal Music.* Victory Press, London 1932.
Whittle, D. W. *Memoir of P. P. Bliss.* F. E. Longley, London 1877.
Whittle, Tyler. *Solid Joys and Lasting Treasure.* Ross Anderson Publications, Bolton 1985.
Williams, R. R. *The Hymns of Ann Griffiths.* The Brython Press, Liverpool 1947.
Winkworth, Catherine. *Christian Singers of Germany.* Macmillan & Co. 1869.
Wood, Arthur Skeffington. *Thomas Haweis 1734-1820.* S. P. C. K., London 1957.

Index of Authors

	Page
Adams, Sarah Flower	144
Auber, Harriet	109
Bailie, Hawthorne	306
Berridge, John	41
Bevan, Emma Frances	191
Binney, Thomas	133
Burlingham, Hannah Kilham	246
Carson, Margaret Ledlie	197
Cennick, John	53
Cornelius, Maxwell Newton	252
Davies, Samuel	59
Evans, James Harrington	121
Fawcett, John	84
Flint, Annie Johnson	294
Fullerton, William Young	281
Gabriel, Charles Hutchinson	269
Goodman, George	300
Griffiths, Ann	114
Guinness, Henry Grattan	203
Habershon, Ada Ruth	288
Haweis, Thomas	77
Homburg, Ernst Christoph	17
How, William Walsham	174
Hurditch, Charles Russell	228
Kent, John	103
Lowry, Robert	180

	Page
Luther, Martin	10
Mackay, William Paton	222
Malan, Henri Abraham César	127
Morison, John	91
Muir, Thomas Donald William	263
Neander, Joachim	22
Olivers, Thomas	65
Pierson, Arthur Tappan	210
Quine, Edward Christian	275
Rothe, Johann Andreas	28
Ryland, John	97
Sloan, William Gibson	216
Smith, Charitie Lees	239
Steele, Anne	47
Stennett, Samuel	71
Stewart, Alexander	257
Stowell, Hugh	138
Tersteegen, Gerhard	34
Tregelles, Samuel Prideaux	156
Walker, Mary Jane	162
Warner, Anna Bartlett	168
Whitfield, Frederick	186
Whittle, Daniel Webster	233
Wigram, George Vicessimus	150

Index of Hymns (First Lines)

(Title hymns in bold type)

                                                               Page

A mighty Fortress is our God 10
All the way my Saviour leads me 181
And did the Holy and the Just? 47
Arise, ye saints, arise and sing 231
Arm of the Lord, awake! Exalt the 231
As sinners saved, we gladly praise 125
As truly as I live, God saith 249

Before the throne of God above 239
Behold the Lamb of God 77
Behold the Man upon the throne 250
Blessed Lily of the Valley 272
Blest be the tie that binds 84
Brethren, let us join to bless 53
Bright, bright home! Beyond the skies 250

Change is our portion here 125
Christians, go and tell of Jesus 182
"Come, let us reason", saith the Lord 226
Come, let us to the Lord our God 94
Come sing, my soul, and praise the Lord 237
Come, ye that love the Lord, and let 181
Come, ye that love the Lord and listen 73
Crowned with thorns upon the tree 204

Dying with Jesus by death reckoned mine 237

Eternal Light! Eternal Light! 133

Faint not, Christian, though the road 121
Farewell for the present, farewell 232
Father of mercies, in Thy Word 51
For all the saints, who from their labours rest 178
From every stormy wind that blows 142

Glory to Thee, Thou Son of God, most High 275
God commends His love 304
God in mercy sent His Son 250
God is calling the prodigal 272

	Page
God is here! Let us adore	38
Great God of wonders!	59
Hark! how the blood-bought hosts above	105
He dies! He dies! The lowly Man of Sorrows	228
He giveth more grace when the burdens grow greater	294
He sendeth sun, He sendeth shower	146
Heirs of salvation, chosen of God	250
Hold the fort, for I am coming	235
Holy Saviour! We adore Thee	156
How beauteous shines the Morning Star!	249
How sweet, my Saviour, to repose	127
I am so glad that our Father in heaven	235
I cannot tell why He, whom angels worship	281
I journey through a desert drear and wild	164
I know not why God's wondrous grace	237
I looked to Jesus in my sin	237
I must needs go home by the way of the cross	272
I need Jesus; my need I now confess	272
I need Thee every hour	182
I need Thee, precious Saviour	190
I saw the cross of Jesus	190
I stand all amazed at the love	272
I stand amazed in the presence	272
I'm pressing on the upward way	272
I'm waiting for Thee, Lord	246
In loving kindness Jesus came	269
In the heart of London city	164
It is a thing most wonderful	174
It is not death to die	130
Jesus Christ, Thou King of glory	250
Jesus, I will trust Thee, trust Thee with my soul	164
Jesus is coming! Sing the glad word	237
Jesus is our Shepherd	138
Jesus, Lord, I need Thy presence	300
Jesus loves me! This I know	168
Jesus, O Name divinely sweet!	75
Jesus, O Name of power divine	190
Jesus, our comfort and life	19
Jesus! Source of life eternal	19
Let us sing of the love of the Lord	233
Lo! He comes with clouds descending	57
Lord, I desire to live as one	241
Lord Jesus Christ, we seek Thy face	260

INDEX OF HYMNS (FIRST LINES)

Page

Lord Jesus, Friend unfailing 249
Lord Jesus, who didst once appear 41
Lord, teach a little child to pray 101
Low in the grave He lay 180

Majestic sweetness sits enthroned 71
Marvel not that Christ in glory 194
'Midst the darkness, storm and sorrow 191
My chains are snapt 197

Nearer, my God, to Thee 144
No works of law have we to boast 226
Not now, but in the coming years 252
Now I have found the ground wherein 28

O blessèd God!, how kind 103
O blessed Saviour, is Thy love? 72
O child of God, there is for thee 266
O Christ, Thou heavenly Lamb 231
O for the robes of whiteness! 240
O God of matchless grace 250
O Jesus, Thou art standing 178
O Lamb of God, we lift our eyes 257
O Lord, I would delight in Thee 97
O spotless Lamb of God, in Thee 164
O sweet is the story of Jesus! 272
O the love of Christ is boundless 250
O Word of God incarnate 179
On His Father's throne is seated 250
On Jordan's stormy banks I stand 75
Once again the gospel message 237
One day at a time 299
One more day's work for Jesus 182
One song of songs – the sweetest 249
Only in Thee, O Saviour mine 272
Our blest Redeemer, ere He breathed 109
Our Lord is now rejected 237

Praise the Lord, and leave tomorrow 216
Praise the peerless Name of Jesus 250
Praise to the Lord, the Almighty, the King of creation 22
Praise ye Jehovah! Come with songs before Him 183

Saviour, Thy dying love 181
Shall we gather at the river? 182
Sovereign grace! O'er sin abounding 106
Standing in the market places 272

	Page
Standing there amidst the myrtle	114
The bread and wine are spread upon the board	304
The glory shines before me	250
The God of Abraham praise	65
The gospel is of God to magnify His Son	250
The gospel of Thy grace	210
The Lord is my faithful Shepherd	19
The Lord is risen; now death's dark judgement flood	226
The wanderer no more will roam	162
There are loved ones in the glory	288
There is a Name I love to hear	186
There shall be showers of blessing	237
There's a call comes ringing o'er the restless wave	272
There's a Shepherd who died for the sheep	306
They tell me the story of Jesus is old	237
Thou hidden love of God	34
Thou Life of my life, blessed Jesus	17
Thou remainest, blest Redeemer	237
'Tis spring, the time of singing	249
To Christ, the Lord, let every tongue	75
'Twas on that night, when doomed to know	91
Up, Christian! Gird thee to the strife	249
We give Thee but Thine own	178
We love to sing of the Lord who died	263
We praise Thee, O God, for the Son of Thy love	222
We thank Thee, Lord, for weary days	194
We would see Jesus	171
Weeping will not save thee	182
What a wonderful change in my life	272
What can wash away my stain?	183
What God doth is divinely done	249
What raised the wondrous thought?	150
When all my labours and trials are o'er	272
When God of old the way of life	237
When we reach our peaceful dwelling	226
While we look within Thy word	183
Why should I feel discouraged?	272
With Christ we died to sin	226
With harps and with vials	214
Worthy of homage and of praise	153
Worthy, worthy is the Lamb!	226